Shakespeare in the Theatre: Sir William Davenant and the Duke's Company

SERIES EDITORS

Peter Holland, Farah Karim-Cooper and Stephen Purcell

Published titles

Patrice Chéreau, Dominique Goy-Blanquet
The American Shakespeare Center, Paul Menzer
Mark Rylance at the Globe, Stephen Purcell
The National Theatre, 1963–1975: Olivier and Hall,
Robert Shaughnessy
Nicholas Hytner, Abigail Rokison-Woodall
Peter Sellars, Ayanna Thompson
Trevor Nunn, Russell Jackson
Cheek by Jowl, Peter Kirwan
Peter Hall, Stuart Hampton-Reeves
Yukio Ninagawa, Conor Hanratty
The King's Men, Lucy Munro

Forthcoming

Sarah Siddons and John Philip Kemble, Fiona Ritchie
Phyllida Lloyd, Elizabeth Schafer

Shakespeare in the Theatre: Sir William Davenant and the Duke's Company

Amanda Eubanks Winkler and Richard Schoch

THE ARDEN SHAKESPEARE
LONDON • NEW YORK • OXFORD • NEW DELHI • SYDNEY

THE ARDEN SHAKESPEARE
Bloomsbury Publishing Plc
50 Bedford Square, London, WC1B 3DP, UK
1385 Broadway, New York, NY 10018, USA
29 Earlsfort Terrace, Dublin 2, Ireland

BLOOMSBURY, THE ARDEN SHAKESPEARE and the Arden Shakespeare
logo are trademarks of Bloomsbury Publishing Plc

First published in Great Britain 2022

Copyright © Amanda Eubanks Winkler and Richard Schoch, 2022

Amanda Eubanks Winkler and Richard Schoch have asserted their right
under the Copyright, Designs and Patents Act, 1988, to be identified as the
authors of this work.

For legal purposes the Acknowledgements on p. viii constitute an extension
of this copyright page.

Cover design: Ben Anslow
Cover image © Folger Shakespeare Library

This work is published open access subject to a Creative Commons
Attribution-NonCommercial-NoDerivatives 3.0 licence (CC BY-NC-ND 3.0,
https://creativecommons.org/licenses/by-nc-nd/3.0/). You may re-use, distribute,
and reproduce this work in any medium for non-commercial purposes,
provided you give attribution to the copyright holder and the publisher
and provide a link to the Creative Commons licence.

Bloomsbury Publishing Plc does not have any control over, or responsibility for,
any third-party websites referred to or in this book. All internet addresses given in
this book were correct at the time of going to press. The author and publisher
regret any inconvenience caused if addresses have changed or sites have
ceased to exist, but can accept no responsibility for any such changes.

A catalogue record for this book is available from the British Library.

Library of Congress Cataloging-in-Publication Data

Names: Eubanks Winkler, Amanda author. | Schoch, Richard W., author.
Title: Sir William Davenant and the Duke's Company / Amanda Eubanks Winkler
and Richard Schoch.
Description: London ; New York : The Arden Shakespeare, 2022. | Series: Shakespeare
in the theatre | Includes bibliographical references and index.
Identifiers: LCCN 2021031793 (print) | LCCN 2021031794 (ebook) |
ISBN 9781350130579 (hardback) | ISBN 9781350130593 (ebook) |
ISBN 9781350130586 (epub)
Subjects: LCSH: Shakespeare, William, 1564–1616–Stage history–1625–1800. |
D'Avenant, William, 1606–1668–Criticism and interpretation. | Duke's Company
(Theatre company) | English drama–Restoration, 1660–1700–History and criticism.
Classification: LCC PR3097 .W56 2022 (print) | LCC PR3097 (ebook) |
DDC 792.9/5—dc23
LC record available at https://lccn.loc.gov/2021031793
LC ebook record available at https://lccn.loc.gov/2021031794

ISBN: HB: 978-1-3501-3057-9
        ePDF: 978-1-3501-3059-3
        eBook: 978-1-3501-3058-6

Series: Shakespeare in the Theatre

Typeset by RefineCatch Limited, Bungay, Suffolk

To find out more about our authors and books visit www.bloomsbury.com
and sign up for our newsletters.

CONTENTS

List of Illustrations vi
Series Preface vii
Acknowledgements viii
Notes on the Text ix
List of Abbreviations x

Preface 1

1   Davenant Before the Duke's Company 5

2   Reopening the Theatres in 1660 21

3   New Performance Spaces 45

4   Davenant's Repertoire 67

5   Acting Restoration Shakespeare 95

6   Case Studies: *Macbeth* and *The Tempest* 119

7   Davenant's Legacy 143

Notes 163
Bibliography 197
Index 209

ILLUSTRATIONS

1 Sir William Davenant (1606–1668) by William
Faithorne, after John Greenhill, published 1672. 8

2 William Dolle, engraving of scenes at Dorset
Garden Theatre, in Elkanah Settle's *The Empress
of Morocco* (1673). 57

3 Opening stage direction, *The Tempest* (1674). 63

4 Thomas Betterton as Hamlet, ink and
watercolour drawing, undated. 78

5 [Sir William Davenant], *The tragedy of Hamlet
Prince of Denmark. As it is now acted at his
Highness the Duke of York's Theatre*, 1676,
Act 3, Scene 3. 82

6 Sir William Davenant, adaptation of *Macbeth*,
1674, title page. 84

7 Henry Harris as Cardinal Wolsey in
Shakespeare's *Henry VIII*, print by Henry
Edward Dawe, 1820. 115

8 Locke, 'Let's have a dance' reconstruction,
opening. Edited by Amanda Eubanks Winkler. 122

9 Banister, 'Go thy way' from *The Ariels Songs*
(1674/5). 128

10 Reggio, 'Arise, ye subterranean winds'. 132

SERIES PREFACE

Each volume in the *Shakespeare in the Theatre* series focuses on a director or theatre company who has made a significant contribution to Shakespeare production, identifying the artistic and political/social contexts of their work.

The series introduces readers to the work of significant theatre directors and companies whose Shakespeare productions have been transformative in our understanding of his plays in performance. Each volume examines a single figure or company, considering their key productions, rehearsal approaches and their work with other artists (actors, designers, composers). A particular feature of each book is its exploration of the contexts within which these theatre artists have made their Shakespeare productions work. Thus, the series not only considers the ways in which directors and companies produce Shakespeare, but also reflects upon their other theatre activities and the broader artistic, cultural and socio-political milieu within which their Shakespeare performances and productions have been created. The key to the series' originality, then, is its consideration of Shakespeare production in a range of artistic and broader contexts; in this sense, it de-centres Shakespeare from within Shakespeare studies, pointing to the range of people, artistic practices and cultural phenomena that combine to make meaning in the theatre.

Series Editors:
Peter Holland, Farah Karim-Cooper and Stephen Purcell

ACKNOWLEDGEMENTS

We warmly thank the Arts and Humanities Research Council in the United Kingdom for generously funding our research project 'Performing Restoration Shakespeare'. Although our work on that project was largely practice-based, it deepened our understanding of Sir William Davenant's adaptations of Shakespeare and thus helped to prepare us to write this book. Richard wishes to thank the Folger Shakespeare Library for awarding him a 2019 short-term fellowship to work on this book. He is also grateful to Queen's University Belfast for granting him a semester's study leave, which gave him the luxury of uninterrupted time for research and writing. Amanda thanks the Folger Shakespeare Library as well for their substantial support over the years. The College of Arts and Sciences at Syracuse University has also provided sustenance for her research, in the form of funding and teaching relief. Finally, we thank Mark Dudgeon, our editor at Arden Shakespeare, and the editors for the Arden series *Shakespeare in the Theatre* – Peter Holland, Farah Karim-Cooper, Bridget Escolme, and Stephen Purcell – who demonstrated their shared commitment to the history of Shakespeare in performance by commissioning this book.

© 2021 by Amanda Eubanks Winkler and Richard Schoch. This work is licensed under the Creative Commons Attribution Non-Commercial No Derivatives licence. Funded by Queen's University Belfast.

NOTES ON THE TEXT

Texts transcribed from early modern sources retain early modern spellings, capitalization, and punctuation with this exception: block capitals used in early modern titles have been eliminated.

ABBREVIATIONS AND LIBRARY SIGLA

GMO · *Grove Music Online* (www.oxfordmusiconline.com)

Lbl · The British Library, London

Lam · Royal Academy of Music, London

Lna · The National Archives, London

The London Stage · Van Lennep, William, E.L. Avery, and A.H. Scouten, eds. *The London Stage, 1660-1800: A Calendar of Plays, Entertainments & Afterpieces*. Part 1. Carbondale: Southern Illinois University Press, 1960.

NHub · Yale University, Beinecke Rare Book and Manuscript Library

ODNB · *Oxford Dictionary of National Biography* (www.oxforddnb.com)

Pepys · *The Diary of Samuel Pepys*. Edited by Robert Latham and William A. Armstrong. 10 Volumes. Berkeley: University of California Press, 1970–1983.

Preface

Today, we take for granted Shakespeare's prominent place in the global theatrical repertoire. From the Royal Shakespeare Company in Stratford-upon-Avon to the Shakespeare Festival in Stratford, Ontario, and from The Market Theatre in Johannesburg to the Beijing People's Art Theatre, Shakespeare's plays are a valued worldwide commodity. It's fact of life. A law of nature. It's just how things are.

Except that's not true. Actually, almost the opposite is true. Shakespeare's popularity in the playhouse repertoire declined after his death in 1616. Nor did the publication in 1623 of the First Folio – expensive, heavy, good for a private library but useless in a theatre – do much to revive his posthumous fortunes in the theatrical marketplace. By 1642, when the Puritans closed the theatres, only a few professional companies were still active. For the next eighteen years, theatre was more or less suppressed in London. When Charles II restored the theatre upon the restoration of the Stuart monarchy in 1660, Shakespeare was far from the most desirable of the pre-Civil War dramatists. Particularly when compared to John Fletcher's popular tragicomedies, Shakespeare's plays felt old-fashioned, poetically bloated, and bogged down by minor characters and confusing sub-plots. The Restoration threw a lifeline to Elizabethan and Jacobean dramatists – with almost no new plays to perform in 1660, it was the old ones or nothing – but rescuing Shakespeare wasn't anyone's goal.

2   SIR WILLIAM DAVENANT AND THE DUKE'S COMPANY

Indeed, Restoration theatre could easily have flourished without Shakespeare.

Yet Shakespeare gained a new lease on life in the Restoration. It was a time when much in London's theatrical world was changing. At last, women played women's roles. Theatres moved totally indoors and were built with proscenium arches. Massive stage spectacles were preferred over bare platform stages. Music and dance were fully integrated into the productions. And Shakespeare's plays – unlike those of his contemporaries – were strongly rewritten: King Lear survived, the witches in *Macbeth* sang and danced, and Miranda in *The Tempest* gained a sister. The first generation to stage Shakespeare after Shakespeare's lifetime changed absolutely everything. There was no other way forward.

Shakespeare's survival on the Restoration stage depended primarily on the effort, talent, and vision of one person: Sir William Davenant (1606–1668). Founder of the Duke's Company – one of the two acting companies formally licensed by Charles II in 1660 – Davenant was a consummate theatrical entrepreneur. His influence on how Shakespeare was adapted and performed in the Restoration was profound and lasting, not least because Davenant controlled every aspect of theatrical production: deciding the repertoire, writing his own Shakespeare adaptations, casting actors in roles, running rehearsals, training actors, and equipping his theatre with movable scenery to produce lavish visual effects. It's no exaggeration to say that in the eight years he spent leading the Duke's Company, Davenant didn't just rewrite Shakespeare – he rehabilitated Shakespeare. Were it not for Davenant, Shakespeare's plays might not have become central to the English theatrical repertoire.

This book is about how Sir William Davenant and the Duke's Company performed Shakespeare in the Restoration. It's neither a biography of Davenant nor an account of purely individual achievement. Rather, this book seeks to understand an influential movement in Shakespeare's theatrical afterlife, a movement exemplified by Davenant and the Duke's Company and one that influenced productions of Shakespeare for the next two hundred

PREFACE 3

and fifty years. Restoration versions of Shakespeare have long been criticized for being distorted or degraded versions of Shakespeare's texts, thereby missing entirely their theatrical and performative dimensions. In consequence, these Restoration plays are not studied for their own intrinsic theatrical value but only as textual evidence predictably confirming Shakespeare's unsurpassed dramatic genius. We strongly dissent from that narrow view. Accordingly, a principal historiographical aim of this volume is to rebalance scholarship by interrogating how Restoration Shakespeare operated as a complex theatrical – indeed, intermedial – experience and not merely as a dramatic text, let alone a dramatic text presumed inferior to its precursor. Overturning the persistent text-based emphasis in scholarship, this book is the first to examine Restoration Shakespeare from a performance perspective. Moreover, in recognition of how music and theatre were integrated in Davenant's major Shakespeare adaptations, this book is jointly authored by a historical musicologist (Eubanks Winkler) and a theatre historian (Schoch).

In the pages ahead we explore the antecedents of Davenant's approach to Restoration Shakespeare, the cultural and legal context of Restoration theatre, the new theatre spaces in which the Duke's Company performed, Shakespeare's place in the Duke's Company's repertoire, acting Restoration Shakespeare, and close analysis of Davenant's adaptations of *Macbeth* and *The Tempest*. By way of conclusion, we consider the lasting legacy of Davenant's approach to Shakespeare. In a way that few stage artists have ever done, Sir William Davenant honoured the theatrical past, invented the theatrical present, and shaped the theatrical future.

1

Davenant Before the Duke's Company

Contrary to the stories and rumours that he helped to put in circulation, Sir William Davenant was almost certainly *not* Shakespeare's son. But part of him longed to be. In his *Brief Lives*, the gossipy Restoration biographer John Aubrey recalled a conversation between Davenant and the poet Samuel Butler:

> Mr. William Shakespeare was wont to go into Warwickshire once a yeare, and did commonly in his journey lie at this house [the Crown] in Oxon: where he was exceedingly respected ... Now Sir William would sometimes, when he was pleasant over a glasse of wine with his most intimate friends e.g. Sam: Butler (author of Hudibras) etc: say that it seemed to him that he writt with the very spirit that Shakespeare, and was seemed contentended [*sic*] enough to be thought his Son: he would tell them the story as above, (in which way his mother had a very light report, whereby she was called a whore).[1]

Whether or not Davenant shared DNA with the Bard, he took up the mantle of Shakespeare, revering the author of *Macbeth* and *The Tempest* even as he adapted those and other Shakespeare plays to suit the growing audience interest in music and spectacle, interests cultivated in the elaborate

6 SIR WILLIAM DAVENANT AND THE DUKE'S COMPANY

masques that flourished at the Jacobean and Caroline courts.
This chapter will consider how Davenant's artistic proclivities
drew upon the legacy of Shakespeare and other pre-Civil War
playwrights, even as he pushed forward into new terrain,
bringing the aesthetics of the court masque and opera into the
public theatres. These earliest theatrical experiments anticipate
the approaches that Davenant later deployed in his adaptations
of Shakespeare for the Duke's Company.

Early life

Davenant was the son of John, a wine merchant and owner of
a tavern near Oxford, and Jane, praised by Aubrey as a woman
'of a very good witt'.[2] Shakespeare stayed at John Davenant's
tavern when he visited Stratford-upon-Avon, but there is no
evidence that he embarked on an affair with Jane, although
Shakespeare must have been a friend of the family. Wine taverns,
unlike inns, did not rent rooms and the playwright apparently
stayed there as a family guest. Contemporary accounts indicate
that Shakespeare served as Davenant's godfather when he was
baptized at St. Martin's, Carfax on 3 March 1606.[3]

Davenant's education was somewhat irregular. Unlike his
more academically inclined brothers, he did not attend the
Merchant Taylor school in London; instead, he was educated
nearer to home by the Oxford-based schoolmaster Edward
Sylvester and later by Daniel Hough, a fellow of Lincoln
College.[4] Upon his father's death in 1622, Davenant was sent to
London to be apprenticed to a merchant, but there is no evidence
he took up the post. Instead, flush with cash, Davenant sought
out a tailor, John Urswick (to whom he was constantly indebted),
and purchased an expensive wardrobe. Davenant understood
that in order to be successful, he needed to look the part.

Upon his arrival in London, the adolescent but ambitious
Davenant began a rigorous campaign of social climbing. He
started as a page in the household of Frances Howard, Duchess
of Richmond. A few years later he joined the household of

DAVENANT BEFORE THE DUKE'S COMPANY 7

Fulke Greville, Lord Brooke, a statesman and patron of poets. It was through Greville that Davenant met Endymion Porter, a well-connected courtier and patron of the arts, who became a friend and financial supporter. Through proximity to wealth, Davenant began moving in exalted circles, eventually, after Greville's death, lodging at the Middle Temple at the Inns of Court, although he was not formally admitted there. Davenant's ability to ingratiate himself with rich and powerful patrons would be an asset in a theatrical career that coincided with political upheaval and civil war.

Davenant's playwriting career began in the last years of the 1620s and he quickly established himself with the King's Men, the company in which Shakespeare had been sharer, playwright, and actor. His first play, the bloody tragedy *The Cruel Brother* (1627), bears the influence of Webster, Shakespeare, and particularly Fletcher's *The Bloody Brother*. In these derivative early plays, Davenant learned his craft through the age-old practice of *imitatio* – copying and embroidering upon a model.

Although Davenant had been savvy in his choice of dedicatees and his commendatory poems were by well-connected people, his next play, *Albovine* (1629), is a bit tone deaf, for it makes explicit reference to Charles I's transfer of affection to his wife, Queen Henrietta Maria, after the assassination of his favourite, the Duke of Buckingham. Davenant also chose a questionable dedicatee: James I's disgraced favourite Robert Carr, Earl of Somerset.[5] Perhaps because of the topical allusions, the play was published in quarto but never was performed. Despite the minor setback, the King's Men performed two other plays by Davenant in 1629: *The Colonel* and *The Just Italian*, showing that his miscalculation with *Albovine* did not have any lasting effects.

In 1630, Davenant's burgeoning theatrical career was derailed by syphilis, a disease that would deform his nose and seriously compromise his health. The queen's physician, Dr Thomas Cademan, apparently cured the playwright, and the physician's widow, Anne, later became Davenant's second wife. Davenant's second wife died in 1655, and later that same year he brought his third and final wife back from France, Henrietta Maria du Tremblay (later Lady Davenant). She would prove to be an able business partner to her husband after the Restoration.[6]

Davenant alluded to his travails with the pox in the comedy *The Wits* (1634), also performed by the King's Men. More importantly, *The Wits* is a substantial improvement over Davenant's previous efforts, as he drew upon the liveliness of contemporary city comedies, a popular early modern dramatic genre. He also used an older play as a model, in this case Thomas Middleton and William Rowley's *Wit at Several Weapons* (c. 1613). While neither *The Wits* nor *The Cruel Brother* is an adaptation in the formal sense, these early works nonetheless demonstrate Davenant's interest in using pre-existing materials to stoke the fires of his dramatic imagination.

FIGURE 1 *Sir William Davenant (1606–1668) by William Faithorne, after John Greenhill, published 1672. NPG D30156 © National Portrait Gallery, London.*

Davenant and the Caroline court masque

These early plays also bear the marks of another influence that would shape his later Shakespeare adaptations: court culture. After the misstep of *Albovine*, Davenant shrewdly cultivated courtly patronage, more strategically choosing powerful dedicatees and including commendatory verses by cavalier poets in his printed quartos. In the 1630s, Davenant's deeper involvement with court culture was becoming increasingly evident. The King's Men performed his romantic comedy *Love and Honour* (1634), but it actually found greater favour at court with Queen Henrietta Maria, consort of Charles I.[7] The preoccupations of the queen also shaped Davenant's *The Platonic Lovers* (1635), for it reflects her Neoplatonic interests.

Davenant's successful cultivation of patronage at court eventually gave him the opportunity to write court masques, a genre that blended spectacle, dance, singing, and spoken text. Playwright Ben Jonson and designer Inigo Jones had developed the genre at the court of James I, but by the 1630s their collaboration had reached its end, as each man struggled with the other for artistic primacy. After the dissolution of their partnership in 1631, several different poets were tried: Aurelian Townshend, James Shirley, and Davenant's friend Thomas Carew. But in 1635 the queen invited Davenant to write his first court masque, *The Temple of Love*. Apparently, he worked well with Jones, for he wrote all subsequent Caroline court masques, including *Salmacida Spolia* (1640), the final masque performed before the Civil War.

Davenant's work on court masques taught him valuable skills that informed his adaptations of Shakespeare in the 1660s. First, Davenant needed to align his aesthetic with the tastes of his elite audience, a skill that would serve him well in the 1660s, when the two public theatres were frequented by the king and his retinue.[8] Second, the masque genre required him to consider the ways in which dialogue, spectacle, music, and dance worked

10 SIR WILLIAM DAVENANT AND THE DUKE'S COMPANY

together to create meaning, a dramaturgical mode to which he would repeatedly return. Third, on a practical level, the creation of court masques was a collaborative enterprise: Davenant had to work well with others. He was a junior collaborator to the designer Jones – Davenant's job was to pen the lyrics and prose descriptions, while Jones was responsible for choosing the subject matter and the visual elements of the masque. Indeed, the young poet seems to have been stimulated by his work with Jones and the various composers and choreographers who contributed to the court masque, for he sought out similar collaborations for the rest of his life.[9]

In short, the court masque served as a training ground for Davenant, teaching him skills he would put to greater use in the 1660s. *Luminalia* (1638) is an excellent case study for exploring how the young Davenant honed his craft, for it combines visual splendour, music, and dance to great effect. The desire to marry the arts in a happy synthesis is set out in the preface, and it is this aesthetic that later influenced many of Davenant's Shakespeare adaptations:

> [T]he Queene commanded *Inigo Iones* Surveyor of her Majesties works to make a new subject of a Masque for her selfe, that with high and hearty invention, might give occasion for variety in Scenes, strange aparitions, Songs, Musick and dancing of several kinds; from whence doth result the true pleasure peculiar to our English Masques, which by strangers and travellers of judgement, are held to be as noble and ingenious, as those of any other nations.[10]

Davenant may have worked on *Luminalia* with Nicholas Lanier, Master of the King's Musick and a composer known for his experiments with recitative, a style imported from Italian opera that sought to imitate speech in song.[11] No music from the production survives, but it is tempting to speculate that Davenant's later interest in opera was sparked during this period. Indeed, *Luminalia* bears some resemblance to Davenant's later operatic experiments, including his

DAVENANT BEFORE THE DUKE'S COMPANY 11

Shakespearean ones. In addition to solo songs, the masque features musical dialogues between characters that culminate in choral singing, a structural feature found in Davenant's later works.

From his experience on *Luminalia*, Davenant may have also learned important lessons about how music enhances the power of spectacle. Instrumental music accompanied stunning lighting effects and covered the noise of wondrous machines as they ascended and descended. Most remarkably, dancers performed on machines:

> the upper part of the heaven opened, and a bright and transparent cloud came forth farre into the Scene, upon which were many *Zephryi* ... These to the Violins began a sprightly dance, first with single passages, and then joyning hands in rounds several ways. Which Apparition for the newnesse of the Invention, greatnesse of the Machine, and difficult of Engining, was much admir'd, being a thing not before attempted in the Aire.[12]

Davenant honed one final skill during his tenure writing court masques: diplomacy. His ability to negotiate politically fraught situations would serve him well in the 1650s and beyond. *Salmacida Spolia* (1640), the final masque presented before the outbreak of civil war, is a case in point. By 1640, Davenant was tightly bound to the court – he had been the primary writer of court masques for five years and in 1637 succeeded Ben Jonson as Poet Laureate.[13] Davenant naturally was a supporter of the king, but even the most devoted sycophant must have acknowledged the deteriorating political situation. It is not surprising that Davenant found it impossible to please everyone in *Salmacida Spolia*, although he tried mightily. The masque simultaneously argues that the overflowing fractiousness of Caroline society could be controlled, even as it shores up the very thing that caused the problem: the king's claim that he possessed the divine right to rule absolutely.

12 SIR WILLIAM DAVENANT AND THE DUKE'S COMPANY

Davenant's strategy worked with his royal employers – Charles and Henrietta Maria apparently were pleased with the masque – but a contemporary witness reported a less positive response among the audience.[14] Perhaps some of the courtiers who attended had qualms about Davenant's critique of 'the peoples [sic] giddy fury' as well as the intimations that the king's patience in his subjects is growing thin.[15] In other words, as Martin Butler aptly puts it, 'the appeasement on offer is everywhere subverted by the need to reassert the king's inviolable authority'.[16] In later entertainments, *Macbeth* and the *Tempest* among them, Davenant threaded the political needle more carefully, as he clearly delineated the difference between a despot and a virtuous leader, shoring up the right of the *right* sort of king to rule.

Operatic experiments

Even before he penned *Salmacida Spolia*, pressing political matters thwarted Davenant's theatrical desires. In March 1639 he had obtained a patent from Charles I that authorized him to build a theatre in Fleet Street, 'to exercise Action, musicall Presentments, Scenes, Dancing, and the like', but this plan for a dedicated space to pursue the mixed media spectacle of the court masque on the public stage did not come to fruition until after the Restoration.[17] Soon after the license was granted, Davenant was drawn into the First Bishops' War. Along with other courtiers, he marched north to make a show of force against the Scottish bishops who resisted Charles I's religious authority.

Although he had returned to London by fall, Davenant's energies for the remainder of the 1640s and into the 1650s were primarily consumed by political and military duties.[18] He undertook various roles. He attempted (unsuccessfully) to infiltrate the New Model Army to sway them to the king's side and pawned the queen's jewels in Amsterdam to raise funds for the royalist cause. After the outbreak of hostilities in England,

DAVENANT BEFORE THE DUKE'S COMPANY 13

he served as Lieutenant General of the Ordinance until August 1643. In the same year he was knighted for his 'loyalty and poetry'.[19] He continued to serve the Crown in other capacities, helping to raise funds for the military campaign and serving as a gun runner, conveying arms to royalist forces in the west.[20]

After the defeat of the royalist forces at Naseby in mid-June 1645, things went from bad to worse for Davenant. Like many of his theatre colleagues he had dutifully supported the royalist cause, but, after the king's surrender in 1646, Davenant went into exile with the court of the queen and the Prince of Wales at St. Germain-en-Laye and later stayed with Lord Jermyn at the Louvre.[21] According to the antiquary Anthony Wood, around the time of Charles I's execution in 1649 Davenant converted to Catholicism. The queen tried to help her loyal friend, arranging for Davenant a position in Virginia or Maryland. But his May 1650 trip to the New World was aborted when a parliamentary frigate intercepted his ship, and he was imprisoned, first on the Isle of Wight and then in the Tower of London. Although there was a talk of a trial for treason and possibly execution, he was eventually released on bail in 1652.[22]

A free man in a land whose new rulers were hostile to theatrical entertainments, Davenant persevered and found innovative ways to practice his profession. In 1653 he published anonymously a manifesto, *A Proposition for Advancement of Moralitie*, which argues that theatrical entertainments combining music, scenery, and discourse might educate the populace in civic virtues.[23] Davenant wrote that

> if the peoples [*sic*] senses were charm'd and entertain'd with things familiar to them, they would easily follow the voices of their shepherds; especially if there were set up some Entertainment, where their Eyes might be subdu'd with *Heroicall Pictures* and change of *Scenes*, their Eares civiliz'd with Musick and wholsome discourses, by some *Academie* where may be presented in a Theater several ingenious *Mechanicks*, as *Motion* and *Transposition of Lights*, to

14   SIR WILLIAM DAVENANT AND THE DUKE'S COMPANY

make a more natural resemblance of the great and virtuous actions of such as are eminent in Story; without any scandalous disguising of men in womens habits, as have bin us'd in Playes.[24]

His proposed style of entertainment combined the arts in a syncretic, intermedial fashion to placate and divert the people, an aesthetic that Davenant and others in the 1650s and 1660s would pursue. In 1653, the year that Davenant published his *Proposition*, James Shirley and the composers Christopher Gibbons and Matthew Locke wrote *Cupid and Death*, a masque overseen by the dancing master Luke Channell that gestures toward a new musical-dramatic aesthetic, even as it draws upon the court masques of the past. This masque does not aggrandize the ruler, for there was no longer a king or a court, but it does serve a ceremonial function as an entertainment for the Portuguese ambassador. The playwright Shirley had also written court masques before the outbreak of civil war, most notably *The Triumph of Peace* (1634), and thus was conversant with the form. Like the earlier Caroline masques, *Cupid and Death* combines spoken dialogue, songs, choruses, and dance, but is more dramatically dynamic than its courtly predecessors or Davenant's proposed 'discourses' because it possesses a clear directional plot, in this case drawn from Aesop's fable about the disastrous mix-up of Cupid's and Death's arrows. The masque points the way ahead in a further sense, for it incorporates recitative – modified to suit English – and anticipates a convention seen in later English operas, whereby some characters both speak and sing while other express themselves exclusively in song and dance.[25] Thus, although Shirley's *Cupid and Death* does not entirely bring Davenant's theories to life, it does provide a lively synthesis of music, dialogue, and dance, and perhaps even machine-based spectacle. One stage direction in *Cupid and Death* indicates that '*Mercury* [is] seen descending upon a Cloud', while the printer's preface states that 'The Scaens wanted no elegance, or curiosity for the delight of the Spectator'.[26]

DAVENANT BEFORE THE DUKE'S COMPANY 15

A few years later Davenant had the opportunity to test his theories himself in *The First Days Entertainment at Rutland-House* (1656), an explicitly non-dramatic event carefully designed to avoid the wrath of the antitheatrical government. The work was comprised of 'declamations' with instrumental music and songs staged in the former residence of Cecily Manners, the Dowager Countess of Rutland, which Davenant had managed to acquire.[27] Women, not boys, performed the female singing roles, avoiding the 'scandalous disguising' of the past, and foreshadowing the introduction of actresses on the public stage four years later.[28] Various composers – Charles Coleman, Henry Cooke, Henry Lawes, and George Hudson – provided the vocal and instrumental music, an amalgamated model of creation that would be carried forward into Davenant's other operatic experiments, as he stitched components from multiple creators into a coherent whole. On a practical level, Davenant used *The First Days Entertainment* to further his ambitions, notably through a dialogue between Diogenes and Aristophanes in which the pros and cons of public entertainments, particularly opera, were debated.[29] Indeed, Davenant's entertainment attempted to address the reservations and concerns the government had about music and spectacle, smoothing the way for his next endeavour, the fully sung opera *The Siege of Rhodes*.

Regrettably, the music for *The Siege of Rhodes* has been lost. But by studying the sources that survive – in particular, Davenant's libretto and John Webb's scene designs – we can form a sense of Davenant's vision for musical-theatrical works, a vision that would soon influence his adaptations of Shakespeare. Like the court masque, *The Siege of Rhodes* featured entries in which music and scenic spectacle are combined. Notably, the work's visual and musical elements are explicitly twinned on the title page of the 1656 quarto, which proclaims that the historical event was 'Made a Representation by the Art of Prospective in Scenes, And the Story Sung in *Recitative* Musick'.[30] Yet unlike the court masque, it is based on an actual historical episode of Christian–Muslim conflict, the siege of Rhodes by Solyman the Magnificent in 1522.

16   SIR WILLIAM DAVENANT AND THE DUKE'S COMPANY

Davenant drew on his previous experience writing songs for court masques as well as the expertise of the several musicians who composed the score for *The Siege of Rhodes*. We know the identities of Davenant's composers, for their names are listed in the printed libretto. Many of them had worked on *The First Days Entertainment*, with the notable addition of composer Matthew Locke, who would continue to set Davenant's words to music after the Restoration. We may also glean something of *The Siege of Rhodes*'s music from the libretto. *The Siege of Rhodes* contains songs and choruses, many of the strophic variety (i.e., each verse of poetry is set to the same music), but there are also extensive passages of recitative that drive the dramatic action.[31]

For the rest of the decade, Davenant pursued various theatrical projects that combined music and spectacle, even as he sought to ingratiate himself with the authorities.[32] *The Cruelty of the Spaniards in Peru* (1658) and *The History of Sir Francis Drake* (1659) both address recent historical events, allowing Davenant to contrast the brutality of Spanish *conquistadors* with England's supposedly more humane approach. Such jingoism was designed to curry favour with the government, further evidence of Davenant's ability to adapt his art to current political realities. Writing in 1656 to John Thurloe, Cromwell's Secretary of State, to argue for the necessity of 'morale representations', Davenant mentioned that, 'the first Arguments [in *The Cruelty of the Spaniards*] may consist of the Spaniards' barbarous conquests in the West Indies and of their severall cruelties there exercised upon the subjects of this nation'.[33] The choice of subject was timely, for Cromwell had imperial ambitions; his 'Western Design' was intended to wrest control of the West Indies from the Spanish. Cromwell had mixed success. In April 1655 his troops had failed to take San Domingo in Hispaniola, although they managed to occupy Jamaica in May 1655. Their possession of that island was constantly threatened by Spain, although by 1658 the tide had begun to turn slightly in England's favour. As Janet Clare has argued, *The Cruelty of the Spaniards* enacts

DAVENANT BEFORE THE DUKE'S COMPANY 17

'the objectives, but not the outcome, of [Cromwell's] Western campaign', with Davenant putting a flattering gloss on historical truth.[34] The entertainment ends with a comforting prophecy 'which foretells the subversion of the Spaniards by the English'.[35]

Davenant must have had the support of the government in this 'propaganda war against Spain', for he was able to present *The Cruelty of the Spaniards* at the Cockpit in Drury Lane, where he could reach a broader public than had been possible with the private performances at Rutland House.[36] Like other public theatres, the Cockpit had been officially closed by the authorities. But in 1651 William Beeston had refitted it, with the result that it had better capacity for movable scenery and more space for musicians than the cramped quarters at Rutland House.[37] In short, it was an adequate space for Davenant to experiment with the combination of auditory and visual media. Like *The First Days Entertainment*, *The Cruelty of the Spaniards* uses scenery, speeches, dances, instrumental interludes (to accompany scene changes, reveals, and onstage action), and sung interludes (mostly strophic songs, some with choruses).[38]

The following year, Davenant continued to combine music with drama in *The History of Sir Francis Drake* (1659), also performed at the Cockpit in Drury Lane. Oliver Cromwell had died in 1658, and his son Richard was now in charge, although his grasp on power was tenuous. Still, Davenant strove to flatter the government, as he recycled the propagandistic theme from the previous year's entertainment and even repurposed the scenic frontispiece. He explains that this reuse 'was convenient [. . .], our Argument being in the same Country' (i.e., Peru).[39] *Sir Francis Drake* also has a very similar form to *The Cruelty of the Spaniards in Peru*: instrumental and vocal music, dance, and scenic effect organized in entries. *Sir Francis Drake* may have had the added novelty of being fully sung, given that contemporary reports indicate that it incorporated recitative.[40]

The lasting influence of Davenant's *The Cruelty of the Spaniards in Peru* and *Sir Francis Drake*, both on Davenant's

18 SIR WILLIAM DAVENANT AND THE DUKE'S COMPANY

later intermedial approach to Shakespearean adaptation and to the Restoration musical-dramatic aesthetic more generally, can be traced to Davenant's recycling of these entertainments in *The Playhouse to Be Let* (1663). As they set up these two interpolated entertainments, characters gently mock their musical elements, calling out the inherent artificiality of '*Stilo Recitativo*': 'Suppose I should not ask, but sing, you now a question / And you should instantly sing me an answer; / Would you not think it strange?'[41] Such queries acknowledge the Restoration preference for a performance style that combined spoken dialogue, scenic effect, dance, and instrumental and vocal music, a style later called 'dramatick opera' by Davenant's collaborator John Dryden. It was this distinctive approach that Davenant eventually adopted for his most famous Shakespeare adaptations.[42]

Davenant's 'New World' operas also affected the approach to 'exotic' subject matter in later plays. Dryden's 'American' plays, *The Indian Queen* (1664), a collaboration with Robert Howard, and *The Indian Emperour* (1665) use similar dramaturgical strategies, incorporating substantial musical scenes and even engaging with similar themes, in particular the relationship between colonizer and colonized. In both plays, Dryden (like Davenant) treats the native people somewhat sympathetically. Furthermore, in Davenant's *The Cruelty of the Spaniards in Peru*, the sad downfall of the Indigenous population is predicted by the Priest of the Sun, while in Dryden's plays religious and magical figures provide similarly dire prophecies. *The Indian Emperour* seems particularly indebted to *The Cruelty of the Spaniards in Peru*, for Dryden includes a graphic scene in the final act in which Pizarro tortures Montezuma and his High Priest on a rack, a moment viscerally reminiscent of the torture scene in the fifth entry of Davenant's entertainment, where 'an *Indian* Prince . . . is rosted at an artificiall fire'.[43]

The dance conventions of these entertainments also carry forward into the Restoration theatre. The saraband was associated with the Spanish in *The Cruelty of the Spaniards in*

DAVENANT BEFORE THE DUKE'S COMPANY 19

Peru ('a Sarabrand is plai'd whilst two Spaniards enter . . . and, to express their triumph after the victory over the Natives, they solemnly uncloak and unarm themselves to the Tune, and afterwards dance with Castanietos').[44] The saraband is also associated with Spanish colonizers in *The Indian Emperour*, although in that play the dance distracts them.[45] In a similar way, character dances that originate in Davenant's entertainments from the 1650s also appear in Restoration performances. For example, the monkey dance in *The Fairy Queen* (1692–3), a Restoration version of *A Midsummer Night's Dream* (see Chapter 7), recalls the dance between two apes in *The Cruelty of the Spaniards in Peru*.[46]

As we have argued in this chapter, Davenant's interest in intermedial forms – which he developed to varying degrees in his plays for the King's Men, his court masques, and his operatic experiments of the 1650s – broadly influenced his approach to Restoration performance and in particular his adaptations of Shakespeare. Davenant established conventions that were pursued in Restoration heroic drama and musical entertainments, his vestigial influence even stretching into the early eighteenth-century through Italian operas crafted for London audiences, such as Handel's *Rinaldo* (1711).[47] Davenant was politically adaptable and possessed a keen ability to predict what his audiences would like. These talents would continue to serve him well when the theatres reopened in 1660 and he was granted a patent to form the Duke's Company. Ever the entrepreneur, Davenant would capitalize mightily upon that opportunity.

2

Reopening the Theatres in 1660

Events, as they happen, are messier and more unpredictable than they later appear, after historians have established the narratives into which those events must logically fit. The English Restoration stage is no exception to the conforming pressures of historiography. Just as the closure of the theatres by the Puritans in 1642 curtailed, but never totally suppressed, theatrical activity in London for eighteen years, the reopening of the theatres in 1660 was less a total reopening – public performances were held in London months before Sir William Davenant and Thomas Killigrew received their royal patents – than the imposition upon the English theatrical profession of new regulatory, legal and, most importantly, artistic structures. None of those structures fell easily into place. All were openly resisted.

When Charles II entered London in celebrated triumph on 29 May 1660, his thirtieth birthday, the city's theatrical landscape was not barren, but populated by diverse shoots and saplings eager to grow. In anticipation of the monarch's return – and the inevitable lifting of prohibitions against the theatre – groups of London actors formed themselves into different companies, essentially seeking to revive both the pre-Civil War playhouses and the acting conventions suited to those playhouses. Those conventions formed a strong living

22 SIR WILLIAM DAVENANT AND THE DUKE'S COMPANY

memory for older actors like Michael Mohun, who trained as a boy actor for Christopher Beeston's company at the Cockpit in Drury Lane and later became a member of Queen Henrietta Maria's Men. Mohun, who had faithfully served the royalist cause as a military officer, returned to the theatre in 1659 when he assembled a group of mostly veteran actors – among them, William Wintershall, Robert Shatterall, William Cartwright, Walter Clun, Charles Hart and Nicholas Burt – to perform at the Red Bull in Clerkenwell, an open-air playhouse that recalled the amphitheatre style of the Globe, Rose and Fortune Theatres.[1]

The bookseller John Rhodes, a former wardrobe-keeper for the King's Men at the Blackfriars Theatre, formed a company of young actors – including Thomas Betterton, Edward Kynaston and James Nokes – who staged plays at the indoor Cockpit (or Phoenix) Theatre in Drury Lane. The 1660 production of *Pericles* at the Cockpit, with the young Betterton in the title role, marks the first recorded appearance of Shakespeare on the Restoration stage.[2]

William Beeston (son of Christopher), who had the most experience of all, set up a third troupe at the indoor Salisbury Court Theatre. During the Interregnum, the younger Beeston had unsuccessfully tried to re-establish Beeston's Boys (a popular troupe consisting mainly of boy actors that performed from 1637 to 1642) at the Cockpit and in 1652 had been granted title to what remained of the Salisbury Court Theatre. Located west of St Paul's Cathedral and between the Fleet River and the Thames, Salisbury Court was the last playhouse built before the Civil War. In 1660 Beeston mortgaged his lease to restore the dilapidated theatre and for a while succeeded in reconstituting his company of young actors.

Under what legal authority were these companies established and permitted to give public performances? Prior to 1642, London theatre companies were licensed by the Master of the Revels, an official in the Lord Chamberlain's office who controlled the theatrical profession not just by censoring scripts but also by issuing licenses for acting companies,

REOPENING THE THEATRES IN 1660   23

permitting (or forbidding) the construction of new playhouses, and closing all playhouses during outbreaks of plague. When the theatres were closed in 1642, the office then belonged to Sir Henry Herbert, who had been making a good living from the fees he collected for approving playscripts and licensing acting companies. During the Interregnum, however, the position of Master of the Revels became dormant, such that when Mohun, Rhodes and the younger Beeston formed their companies in anticipation of the restored monarchy, they did so under no authority but their own.

Their freedom did not last long. One of the first positions in the royal household that Charles II re-established was Master of the Revels. On 20 June 1660, less than a month after the king's return – and before the awarding of exclusive patents to Killigrew and Davenant – Sir Henry Herbert was sworn in to resume his former office. Eager to reassert powers that had been in abeyance for eighteen years, Sir Henry demanded that the resurgent companies – which were already staging plays, drawing audiences, and earning money – obtain licenses from him and pay him fees for each play they staged. The acting companies, following the old protocols, dutifully entered into agreements with the reinstated Master of the Revels.

Beeston, who managed an acting company before the Civil War, and thus knew in detail the traditional licensing arrangements, moved quickly to acknowledge Sir Henry's authority. In June 1660 he received a license from the Master of the Revels 'to continue and constitute the said house called Salisbury Court Playhouse into a playhouse', where he was permitted to stage 'comedies, tragedies, or tragi-comedies, pastorals and interludes'. In granting Beeston's license, Sir Henry underlined the continuity of theatrical regulation: 'the allowance of plays, the ordering of players and playmakers [i.e., playwrights], and the permission for erecting of playhouses' have belonged 'time out of mind' to the 'Master of his Majesty's Office of the Revels'.[3] Beeston agreed to pay Sir Henry four pounds a week when his company acted at Salisbury Court. Rhodes did the same for his actors at the

24   SIR WILLIAM DAVENANT AND THE DUKE'S COMPANY

Cockpit. By the end of the summer, Michael Mohun and his troupe at the Red Bull – the most important company, because led by experienced actors – agreed to pay Sir Henry ten pounds for allowing the company to perform, supplemented by payments of forty shillings 'for every new play' and twenty shillings for 'every revived play', consistent with the 'fees anciently belonging to the Master of the Revels'.[4]

In those first exciting months of resumed activity, many aspects of the theatrical profession as it had once been were indeed 'restored': Mohun, Rhodes, and Beeston had all worked in London theatres prior to their closure in 1642; the Red Bull, the Cockpit and Salisbury Court were all pre-Civil War playhouses; Mohun's company consisted mainly of veteran performers; Beeston's troupe revived the earlier tradition of boy and adolescent actors; by necessity, the repertoire was drawn from the old stock of plays; and Sir Henry Herbert once more exercised legal and financial control over London's theatrical world. Nobody was casting actresses. Nobody was constructing elaborate scenery. Nobody was building new theatres. Nobody was adapting Shakespeare. The whole infrastructure of the pre-Civil War theatre seemed poised to resurrect itself. All that would soon change – but not without a fight.

Patents granted to Davenant and Killigrew

Sir Henry Herbert's hopes for a smooth return to the theatrical profession as it had been constituted and regulated prior to 1642 – to say nothing of the aspirations of Michael Mohun, John Rhodes, and William Beeston for their own acting companies – were threatened by Charles II's decision in the summer of 1660 to award patents to Thomas Killigrew and Sir William Davenant, granting them exclusive rights to produce theatre in London. Consequentially, any acting company in the capital not led by Killigrew or Davenant would be shut down.

REOPENING THE THEATRES IN 1660   25

This one unique decision redirected the course of English theatre history for nearly two centuries and guaranteed that the future of the London stage would not look anything like its past.

Why did Charles II impose a monopoly on stage productions in London just as the theatrical profession was emerging from years spent in shadows? Why curtail performances so drastically at the very moment when playhouses regained their freedom? It bears recalling that in the years immediately prior to Parliament's closure of the theatres in 1642 only a handful of acting companies in London were financially viable, a clear sign that theatre was already losing it popular appeal. Upon the reopening of the theatres in 1660, it was, therefore, less a question of artificially capping the number of theatre companies – the numbers had already declined in the pre-Civil War era – than of putting the theatrical profession into close alignment with the reinstated Stuart court.[5] After all, the king, far from being an enemy of the stage (that role had been ferociously undertaken by Puritans) was its great champion and patron. No English monarch has ever been so intimately identified with the professional theatre as Charles II.

The courtier Thomas Killigrew, who in 1647 had followed the future Charles II into exile on the Continent, was rewarded for his loyalty by being named Groom of the Bedchamber in 1660 and also by being granted, along with Davenant, the exclusive right to stage plays in London. Killigrew had written some dramas before the Civil War and, according to Pepys, had played bit roles at the Red Bull in his youth. Yet it was Davenant who boasted the more impressive theatrical pedigree; moreover, he already possessed a claim to a royal patent. The King's Men had performed some of Davenant's early plays at the Blackfriars beginning in the late 1620s (just over a decade after Shakespeare's death) and continuing until 1640. But as we noted previously, it was Davenant's collaboration with Inigo Jones on the lavish and innovative Stuart court masques at the Banqueting House in Whitehall – Jones designed the scenery, Davenant (succeeding Ben Jonson) supplied the words – that proved consequential not just for him personally but for

26 SIR WILLIAM DAVENANT AND THE DUKE'S COMPANY

the future of the English stage.[6] Determined to bring this extravagant theatrical form to a popular audience, he obtained in 1639 a patent from Charles I that authorized him to build a theatre in Fleet Street, a revolutionary new playhouse where the scenic and musical wonders of the court masque could be incorporated into a public performance.[7] Davenant would then form an acting company and oversee the theatre's operations himself. As mentioned in the previous chapter, the impending Civil War prevented Davenant from using his patent, and the innovative public theatre that he championed was not built.[8]

Yet as the performances at Rutland House in the 1650s confirm, Davenant never wavered in his desire – expressed didactically in his anonymous *A Proposition for Advancement of Moralitie* (1653) – to bring theatrical innovation to a wider audience: the people's 'Eyes might be subdu'd with *Heroicall Pictures* and changes of *Scenes*' and 'their Eares, civiliz'd with Musick and wholesome discourses'.[9] The reopening of the theatres gave him the opportunity he had long sought, and he seized it. On 9 July 1660 Killigrew received permission from the king 'to erect one Company of players wch shall be our owne Company' and for all other acting companies 'to be silenced and surprest'.[10] Davenant, unwilling to be overlooked, submitted to the king just ten days later a revised warrant that extended the theatrical monopoly to him. In other words, Davenant tried to resurrect his own royal patent from 1639. The draft revised warrant contained several provisions, including the right to stage performances with music and scenery, to set ticket prices (which might need to be raised to pay for expensive new scenery), and to set actors' wages. The core provision, however, was the establishment of the duopoly and the right of the patentees to build new theatres:

> a Grant unto our trusty and well beloved Thomas Killigrew Esquire, one of the Groomes of the Bed-chamber and Sir William Davenant Knight, to give them full power and authoritie to erect Two Companys of Players ... and to

REOPENING THE THEATRES IN 1660

purchase or build and erect at their charge as they shall thinke fitt Two Houses or Theaters.[11]

Reluctant to nullify a license granted two decades earlier by his own father, Charles II honoured Davenant's hitherto dormant patent. Thus, the monopoly awarded to Killigrew became a duopoly awarded to Killigrew and Davenant. Although it took a few years for the terms to be fully established in law, the central provision – the two courtiers enjoyed exclusive rights to produce theatre in London – was established on 21 August 1660, when Charles II issued a warrant that essentially adopted the terms of Davenant's draft.[12]

The nominal justification for imposing a theatrical monopoly was disingenuously moralistic: to ban performances that featured 'much matter of profanation and scurrility' and to encourage those that 'might serve as moral instructions in human life'. That strategic concession to public morals was intended to mollify Puritan opposition in the City of London, one of the two areas where theatres could be built, the other being the City of Westminster. Yet the real reason for granting the new patent, as we have outlined above, was to repay Killigrew for his service to Charles II and to endorse the old patent granted to Davenant by Charles I. This action cost the new king nothing. Indeed, it shifted the responsibility of paying for lavish theatrical productions from the court to the commercial playhouse. Still, the patents enabled Charles II to reward past loyalty and to make the future theatrical profession an artistic elaboration of the court itself. In one variant or another, the royal patents lasted until they were abolished by the Theatre Regulation Act of 1843.

Fighting for survival and control

Empowered by their royal warrant, Davenant and Killigrew needed to make some important decisions quickly: Who would be their actors? What plays would they perform? Where would

28   SIR WILLIAM DAVENANT AND THE DUKE'S COMPANY

they perform them? How would their theatres be equipped? Making these decisions was not easy or straightforward, not least because (unlike Mohun, Rhodes, and the younger Beeston) neither patentee had ever put together an acting company. However astute in the politics of advancing their own interests in elite circles, they had no experience in the hard graft of running a commercial theatre. They possessed legal authority, but lacked money, infrastructure, and personnel. Yet even before they could make their first move, Davenant and Killigrew faced immediate opposition from the very people who were in a position to help them.

Such opposition was no surprise. After all, the patents that benefited Davenant and Killigrew posed a threat to the livelihoods of Sir Henry Herbert, Master of the Revels, and the companies led by Michael Mohun, John Rhodes, and William Beeston. Sir Henry's authority to license acting companies and to censor plays was now wholly undermined – the patent was itself a permanent license, with Davenant and Killigrew entitled to censor their own plays – while performances at the Red Bull, the Cockpit in Drury Lane, and Salisbury Court were to be suppressed precisely because they infringed upon Davenant and Killigrew's exclusive privileges. As the patent stipulated, 'there shall be no more . . . companies of actors . . . than the two to be now erected by virtue of this authority'.[13] The excluded parties, far from acquiescing to the new theatrical regime, vigorously opposed it. In the end, Davenant and Killigrew came to an understanding with the Master of the Revels and neutralized the rival companies, mainly by absorbing them into their own. Yet it would be misleading to think that the establishment of the patent companies in the early 1660s – the Duke's Company led by Davenant, the King's Company led by Killigrew – was either uncomplicated or unopposed. It was neither.

When Sir Henry Herbert learned that Thomas Killigrew was going to be given an exclusive warrant to stage plays in London and that Sir William Davenant had petitioned Charles II for the same privilege, he leapt into both defensive and

REOPENING THE THEATRES IN 1660   29

offensive action. In a petition sent to the king on 4 August 1660, he argued that the proposed monopoly – an 'unjust surprise' of which he had no 'consent or foreknowledge' – should be rescinded because it was 'destructive' of the 'ancient powers granted' to his office 'under the Great Seal.'[14] As Sir Henry saw it, the king was contradicting himself: Charles II had revived the position of Master of the Revels only to strip it of all power and authority by imposing a theatrical monopoly controlled by Davenant and Killigrew. More aggressively, Herbert tried to discredit Davenant in the king's eyes by linking him to the 'Late Horrid Rebellion', when he had 'obtained leave of Oliver and Richard Cromwell to vent his operas'. Yet Herbert disingenuously failed to acknowledge the theatrical license that the king's own father had granted to Davenant in 1639. Sir Henry, who had resented Davenant ever since a quarrel over censorship in the 1630s, had good reason to put his case strongly: He was, at that very moment, negotiating fee arrangements with Mohun, Rhodes, and Beeston.[15] Were the monopoly to be enforced he would lose valuable income.

Charles II must have taken Sir Henry's objections seriously, because he referred the matter to his Attorney General, Sir Geoffrey Palmer. Despite some initial misgivings – the royal warrant overturned without cause the powers traditionally held by the Master of the Revels – Palmer confirmed in a note to the king dated 12 August 1660 that he found no reason 'to object against the two warrants' for Davenant and Killigrew.[16] Sir Henry's attacks on Davenant failed to change the king's mind. It was true that Davenant (like others at the time) had curried favour with the Cromwellian leadership. But it was also true that Davenant had rendered good service to the martyred Charles I. Sir Henry failed in his attempt to have the warrants revoked. Indeed, they were formally promulgated in late August 1660, diminishing Sir Henry's powers and ordering the suppression of actors at the Red Bull, the Cockpit, and Salisbury Court.

Yet those acting companies were hardly willing to put themselves out of business just because a superseding warrant

30   SIR WILLIAM DAVENANT AND THE DUKE'S COMPANY

had been issued to Davenant and Killigrew. The existence of the warrant was one thing; its enforcement was another. As we have seen, Mohun, Rhodes and Beeston spent the summer of 1660 – a time when nothing was clear about how London theatre was licensed – reconciling themselves to the reinstated authority of the Master of the Revels and negotiating the licensing and censorship fees payable to him. But they felt the ground shifting. In the postscript to his agreement with Herbert, Mohun added the qualifier 'to be made good during the time of acting under the said Master of the Revels', an acknowledgment that Sir Henry's rule was not inviolable. In fact, Mohun's agreement with Herbert fell apart pretty quickly. The Red Bull actors paid him for about a month but then stopped, recognizing that the warrants given to Davenant and Killigrew effectively stripped Sir Henry of his customary powers. Unwilling, however, to let the new patentees obstruct or overthrow them, Mohun and his company staged new and old plays alike at the Red Bull into the autumn of 1660.

For Davenant and Killigrew, these continuing performances were a problem. They could not begin to establish their own companies until they eliminated their rivals. But it was less a matter of shutting their rivals down than of taking them over. After all, the existing companies had what the patentees lacked, but needed and needed fast: actors and theatres. Appealing once more to the Crown, the patentees urged the king to suppress Mohun's company, arguing that it inflated ticket prices, staged morally objectionable plays, and recognized no statutory authority. Killigrew obtained a royal warrant to suppress the Red Bull actors until they entered into an agreement with the new patentees 'to act with women, [in] a new theatre and [with] habits according to [their] scenes'.[17] Killigrew's threat to suppress Mohun's company had its intended effect, because in early October 1660 a new company ('His Majesty's Comedians') was formed under the joint leadership of Davenant and Killigrew. Crucially, this new – and fully legal – company comprised the best actors from the other companies, including Betterton and Kynaston from the Cockpit

REOPENING THE THEATRES IN 1660   31

in Drury Lane. The new company first performed on 8 October 1660 at the Cockpit. Rhodes was the theatre's rightful lessee, but that was a secondary matter. What mattered was that Davenant and Killigrew were now joint managers of the acting company. 'His Majesty's Comedians' would soon split into the two patent companies. But the most important shift had now been made: the actors stayed the same, but new people were in charge. Mohun, Rhodes and Beeston were yesterday's men. The future of London theatre belonged to Davenant and Killigrew.[18]

Meanwhile, the persistent Sir Henry Herbert was fighting a war on two fronts. After the single company was established in October 1660, he harassed the Cockpit actors, demanding payment in return for the preposterous offer of 'protection' from Killigrew's efforts to suppress them. But the actors understood full well that Sir Henry was 'not able' to protect them, precisely because Killigrew (to whom they had already acquiesced) was armed with a royal patent – and they stated as much in their petition to Charles II.[19] At the same time, Sir Henry filed lawsuits against Davenant and Killigrew, accusing the new patentees of obstructing him from collecting his customary licensing fees and, moreover, of undermining his office by setting up acting companies without first obtaining a license from him. The Master of the Revels argued that Davenant and Killigrew should either pay him or be forced out of business. One of the lawsuits was successful, prompting Davenant to protest to the king that Sir Henry's demand for fees was merely 'pretend', because the royal patents that he and Killigrew possessed made any such claim redundant.[20]

After several years of inconclusive lawsuits, Davenant and Killigrew accepted the Master of the Revels as an immutable fact of theatrical life, their own royal patents notwithstanding. Killigrew settled first, in June 1662, agreeing to pay Sir Henry the non-trivial sum of one pound for each old play his company performed and two pounds for each new one, in addition to a one-time payment to compensate Sir Henry for the time and effort he had expended in the matter. In turn, Sir Henry agreed

32 SIR WILLIAM DAVENANT AND THE DUKE'S COMPANY

to surrender his traditional power to license acting companies – henceforth, his only authority would be to license plays – and agreed to forgo any further claim against Killigrew. Revealingly, Killigrew promised 'neither directly nor indirectly to aid or assist Sir William Davenant' or 'his pretended company of players'.[21] By this time, the Duke's Company under Davenant's leadership was performing at its own theatre in Lincoln's Inn Fields, and thus was a direct commercial and artistic rival to the King's Company. Sir Henry, still in dispute with Davenant, wanted to prevent an alliance between the patentees; and so, he exploited the competition between them. Eventually, Davenant came to a understanding with Sir Henry that was similar to what Killigrew had negotiated: the Duke's Company did not require a license from the Master of the Revels but it agreed to pay him to license all the old and new plays that it would perform.[22] This arrangement with the patentees became redundant in 1673, when, after Sir Henry's death, Killigrew purchased for himself the rights to the office of Master of the Revels.[23] The once-powerful position in the Lord Chamberlain's Office survived, but it atrophied within a decade, amounting to little more than a feeble sinecure. Real control of the theatrical profession had shifted to the patentees.

From a historiographical perspective, the legal wrangling among Davenant and Killigrew, Sir Henry Herbert, and the various London acting companies is important not as a narrow account of how the Restoration stage was first licensed and regulated, but as the articulation of a momentous artistic impasse: What would the future of the English theatre be? At stake in the repeated cycle of lawsuits, petitions and warrants was less the powers accorded to sundry individuals than the entire premise of what a theatrical 'restoration' meant for London in the 1660s. Contrary to its literal meaning, this restoration entailed a great deal of innovation. And resistance to innovation in theatre practice was always the sticking point, always the area where disagreements arose in the patent companies. Mohun's actors, when they joined the temporary united company led by Killigrew and Davenant in October

1660, had to be forced to share the stage with women (which meant relinquishing some of their accustomed roles), to perform in new theatres (the surviving pre-Commonwealth playhouses were never going to pass muster), and to make way for painted movable scenery (gone was the non-representational platform stage for which Jonson and Shakespeare wrote). The source of their dissatisfaction was not just the changes in licensing; it was, more generally, the changing nature of theatrical performance and their resistance to that change.

Davenant's reluctance to settle with Sir Henry Herbert was likewise not confined to the narrow issue of theatrical licensing but was a larger protest against the old system in its entirety, the *ancien régime* that had been conclusively overthrown 'by several warrants under your Majesty's royal hand and signet'.[24] Just as Davenant refused to settle for the old ways of licensing and regulating theatre, he refused to settle for the old ways of making theatre. Inspired by a comprehensive vision for the future of the English stage – a vision that the less adventurous Killigrew sometimes claimed for himself, but never consistently executed – Davenant the entrepreneur changed what theatrical performances looked and sounded like, what words were spoken, and who had the final say over the production. Such was the comprehensive vision behind his radical reworkings of Shakespeare, the very productions that secured his legacy. Who better to dictate the legal framework in which this vision unfolded than the visionary himself? Having secured his royal patent, Sir William Davenant did not feel that he needed anyone's permission for anything.

Establishing the patent duopoly

The united company led by Killigrew and Davenant lasted barely a month. The actors from the Red Bull were allied to Killigrew. The patent itself envisaged the establishment of two separate companies in two separate theatres. And most crucially of all, Davenant's expansive theatrical vision could

34   SIR WILLIAM DAVENANT AND THE DUKE'S COMPANY

never be reconciled with Killigrew's willingness to settle for old and accustomed ways of making theatre.

Thus, by early November 1660, the monopoly became a formal duopoly: the King's Company (led by Killigrew) and the Duke's Company (led by Davenant) were now free to follow their own paths.[25] But each company needed its own actors, its own theatre, and its own repertoire. Killigrew, consolidating his earlier arrangement, quickly formed his company from senior actors at the Red Bull, including Michael Mohun and Charles Hart.[26] Their last performance at the theatre on St. John Street – John Fletcher and Philip Massinger's comedy *The Beggar's Bush* (1622) – was on the afternoon of Wednesday 7 November 1660. Twenty-four hours later they presented *Henry IV, Part 1* at their new theatre in Vere Street, Clare Market, just north of the Strand in the City of Westminster. The former Gibbon's Tennis Court, where occasional and clandestine performances had been staged in the 1650s, was speedily converted into something probably like the pre-Civil War Blackfriars: a rectangular indoor theatre lit by candles that accommodated several hundred spectators.[27] As we discuss at greater length in the next chapter, the theatre lacked movable scenery or backstage machines, deficiencies which made it an undesirable performance space within a few years.

Unlike Davenant, Killigrew himself had no special connection with the old Blackfriars, but likely he regarded its traditional form as expedient for the times and suitable for a courtly audience. Having an indoor theatre also meant that his company could perform throughout the year, something not possible in open-air playhouses. Because the King's Company included the older actors – and because it regarded itself as the natural successor to Shakespeare's own company, the King's Men – it held the performance rights to pre-Civil War plays, including those written by Davenant himself. Controlling the old stock drama (as we discuss at length in Chapter 4) gave the King's Company an enormous advantage over the rival Duke's Company because they could put together a rotating schedule of popular plays that could attract an audience day after day.

With the veteran performers firmly under Killigrew's control, Davenant, even though he had greater theatrical experience, had no choice but to form his company largely from the younger actors at the Cockpit in Drury Lane. Yet for Davenant, leading a company of novice performers turned out to be a blessing. Inexperienced actors were more likely to be open to new ways of doing thing – including sharing the stage with women – and were more likely to welcome guidance and instruction from the patentee himself. Had the Duke's Company enlisted the older actors at the Red Bull, Davenant would likely have met with immediate opposition to his theatrical innovations, especially having women's roles played by actual women and using painted movable scenery – the very changes that Killigrew's actors seem to have initially resisted. For a revolutionary like Davenant, leading a company of novices was as much an asset as it was a liability. True, he had to spend time training his actors; but that enabled him to shape the Duke's Company in his own image. We will look more closely at Davenant's approach to acting in Chapter 5.

With the performing rights to the pre-1642 plays belonging to the King's Company and lacking a fresh supply of new scripts for his own company – the market for new plays had essentially disappeared during the Interregnum – Davenant scrambled to find dramatic works that his company could perform. In December 1660 he presented to the Lord Chamberlain his plans for 'reformeinge some of the most ancient Playes that were played at the Blackfriers and of makeing them, fitt, for the Company of Actors appointed under his direction and comand'.[28] In the years before the Civil War, the indoor Blackfriars theatre had been the winter home of the King's Men. Davenant's petition made it clear that not only did he want to perform Shakespeare's plays but that he was already convinced of the need to adapt (or 'reform') them, rendering them suitable for modern day actors and audiences.

Rewriting Shakespeare was thus not a tactic that Davenant arrived at some time after the establishment of his acting company and the opening of his theatre in Lincoln's Inn Fields.

36   SIR WILLIAM DAVENANT AND THE DUKE'S COMPANY

Rather, it was a foundational principle of his artistic leadership, a core element of his vision: to create more and better parts for actresses, to introduce changeable scenery and visual spectacle into the production, to integrate music with the dramatic narrative, to render dramatic plots more agreeable to Restoration literary sensibilities, and to make the text sound more agreeable to the Restoration ear. Davenant knew perfectly well that because he could not immediately compete on repertoire, he would have to compete on production style, changeable scenery and music. Indeed, the Duke's Company's early productions at Lincoln's Inn Fields were so successful that the King's Company was forced in 1663 to build a new theatre in Bridges Street that was likewise equipped with movable scenery. As we will see, it took some time for Davenant to find the right style for his adaptations. But a revisionist intent guided his behaviour from the start.

For Davenant to adapt Shakespeare, he needed first to be granted performing rights to some of Shakespeare's plays. In response to Davenant's petition, the Lord Chamberlain, on 12 December 1660, issued a warrant giving the Duke's Company the right to perform eleven plays, of which nine were by Shakespeare: *Hamlet, Henry VIII, King Lear, Macbeth, Measure for Measure, Much Ado About Nothing, Romeo and Juliet, The Tempest,* and *Twelfth Night*.[29] Davenant was also granted sole rights to perform his own plays from before the Civil War. For a few months, he was allowed to stage six plays (including *Pericles*) that had belonged to Rhodes's company at the Cockpit.

The limitations that Davenant faced in terms of repertoire – he was granted rights to only a small number of old plays, and it would take time for new plays to be written – had two important consequences for his approach to Shakespeare. First, Shakespeare was more prominent in the repertoire of the Duke's Company from the outset of the patent duopoly. In August 1661, eight weeks after the opening of their theatre in Lincoln's Inn Fields, Davenant's company performed *Hamlet* with Betterton in the title role and Mary Saunderson, the leading

REOPENING THE THEATRES IN 1660   37

actor's future wife, as Ophelia. When the new season began the following month, they performed *Twelfth Night* in their first week. Davenant's first Shakespeare adaptation – *The Law Against Lovers*, which mixed *Measure for Measure* with *Much Ado about Nothing* – premiered later that season, in February 1662. By contrast, Shakespeare was never central to Killigrew's repertoire, which slanted heavily toward plays by John Fletcher and Ben Jonson.[30] Second, because Davenant could not attract audiences by the novelty of *which* plays his company performed – comparatively few works were at his disposal – he attracted them by the appeal of *how* those few plays were performed – i.e., with scenery, trap doors, and music. In Chapter 4 we offer a more elaborate discussion of Davenant's repertoire. But for now, it's important to observe that the division of the repertoire between the two companies in 1660 determined in good measure the distinctive path that each company would take. To paraphrase Lady Macbeth, the future was present in the instant.

Although the earliest known performance by the Duke's Company dates from January 1661, in all probability they started acting at the old Salisbury Court theatre on Monday, 5 November 1660.[31] Supplanting his old nemesis Beeston as playhouse manager must have felt to Davenant like sweet revenge. Even so, the arrangement was temporary, only until he could 'provide a new theatre with scenes', as his contract with the actors stipulated.[32] That new theatre would be the converted Lisle's Tennis Court on Portugal Street in Lincoln's Inn Fields.[33] Davenant took his time in renovating his new theatre so that when it eventually opened in June 1661 it immediately surpassed the capabilities of the King's Company at their less well-equipped playhouse in nearby Vere Street.

In setting up their acting companies as legal and commercial entities, Davenant and Killigrew both looked back to how such companies had operated in the 1630s. Senior male actors became shareholders (Shakespeare was a 'sharer' in the King's Men, in addition to being house playwright and part of the acting company), which meant not only that they enjoyed job

38   SIR WILLIAM DAVENANT AND THE DUKE'S COMPANY

security but that they had a material stake in the company's success: their income derived from the profits rather than from individual salaries. Everybody else – actresses, junior male actors ('hirelings'), musicians, wardrobe keepers, doorkeepers, and stagehands – was paid a fixed wage. The patentees determined the number and proportion of shares to be divided among the shareholders, always ensuring that the patentee himself remained in overall control. Shareholding arrangements were abolished by the early eighteenth century and every company member was put on salary, with leading actors and actresses granted a 'benefit' performance to augment their income. But in the early years of the Restoration, a more collective structure existed – at least for the senior men in the company. More than thirty years would pass before a female member of a patent company shared in the profits or took a lead role in company management, a subject we explore in Chapter 7.[34]

On 5 November 1660, Davenant signed articles of agreement with his leading actors and with the scene painter Henry Harris, who later also appeared on the stage. (In 1668, after Davenant's death, Betterton and Harris essentially took over the day-to-day operations of the Duke's Company.) Net profit – that is, total revenue after house charges and wages for the younger male actors had been deducted – was divided into fifteen shares. These shares were to be allocated to the patentee and the senior actors on a 2:1 ratio: ten for Davenant and five to be divided among the other shareholders. The majority stake accorded to Davenant was not just to give him control – though certainly it did that – but also to enable him to cover certain expenses (e.g., scenery, costumes, and actresses' salaries) for which the other shareholders were not liable. Crucially, Davenant's controlling interest in the Duke's Company gave him scope to sell a portion of his shares to investors to raise the capital needed for large expenses, such as converting Lisle's Tennis Court into a modern theatre equipped with the movable scenery that Davenant had long wanted to use in a public playhouse. Although the Restoration stage was firmly allied to the court of Charles II, it was still a private commercial enterprise that would thrive, stagnate, or decline based on how it fared in the marketplace.

From a financial perspective, the new patent companies started from scratch, holding neither physical assets nor capital reserves. They possessed an exclusive royal warrant, but nothing else. To raise capital, Davenant had no choice but to sell a fraction of his shares and invest the money he received from the buyers. Within a year of establishing the Duke's Company he sold several of his shares, with the proceeds (the first sale raised £600 per share) going toward the cost of the new theatre in Lincoln's Inn Fields. This new theatre enabled the Duke's Company to offer precisely the sort of productions that secured its future. To be successful, Davenant had to spend money – a lesson he sometimes failed to apply. When the cast for *Pompey the Great* (1663) appeared 'in English habits', the disappointed audience hissed the actor playing Caesar off the stage.[35]

Whereas Davenant was financially prudent, Killigrew was more reckless, later selling his shares in the Bridges Street Theatre, which the company opened in 1663, to 'adventurers' (as they were disparagingly termed) interested mainly in profits. Killigrew then used the influx of money not for capital investment but to pay off his personal debts. This difference in financial management further reveals why Davenant was the only theatrical pioneer in the years immediately following the reopening of the theatres: He was the only patentee who knew how to manage the money and the only one willing to put the company's interests ahead of his own.

Theatre at the court of Charles II

Never was the English stage more closely tied to monarchy than in the Restoration, when the stage 'was constructed as an agent or surrogate of the crown'.[36] The exclusive patents that recognized two London theatre companies – and outlawed

40 SIR WILLIAM DAVENANT AND THE DUKE'S COMPANY

their competition – were the gift of Charles II to Killigrew and Davenant. As mentioned earlier in this chapter, Killigrew, a courtier, was formally named a Groom of the Bedchamber. The Restoration patent companies were named after their respective royal patrons, King Charles II and his brother James, Duke of York, the future James II.[37] Legally, actors were liveried servants of the sovereign – 'grooms of the chamber' – and so could not be sued for debt without the Lord Chamberlain's permission.[38]

Many of the older actors, who first reassembled at the Red Bull and then eventually joined Killigrew's company, had fought on the royalist side during the Civil War. Most of the new playwrights were aristocratic Cavaliers whose plays of political intrigue, like the Earl of Orrery's tragicomedy *The Generall* (1662), denounced usurpation and affirmed the restoration of rightful monarchs. Davenant's adaptations of Shakespeare – *Measure for Measure*, *Macbeth*, and *The Tempest* – were likewise dominated by themes of sovereignty restored. Once the patent companies started performing, they attracted an audience drawn from courtiers (among them, George Villiers, Duke of Buckingham and John Wilmot, Earl of Rochester) and both the king and his brother were seen in the new playhouses in Lincoln's Inn Fields, the first time an English monarch set foot in a public playhouse. Royalist influence on the theatre and the theatrical profession was unmistakable. It was in those years a partisan enterprise through and through.

Reinstating the tradition of private court performances, Charles II – despite his lack of money – ordered that the disused Cockpit theatre in the Palace of Whitehall be refitted and returned to its former use. (The private Cockpit theatre is not to be confused with the public Cockpit or Phoenix Theatre in Drury Lane.) John Webb, pupil of the great Inigo Jones – who had designed the original court theatre three decades earlier – renovated the small private theatre, transforming it from an actual cockpit dating from the time of Henry VIII into an intimate Palladian court theatre. Among his tasks was to carve out a dressing room for actresses, a feature never before needed. Renovations began in November 1660 and proceeded by fits and starts over several years.[39] But not much could be done. Space was limited, so neither the stage nor the backstage area could expand. Despite the fashionable Palladian style, changeable scenery was impractical in such a tight space. And so, the Cockpit in Court was used for only a few years, until John Webb in 1665 oversaw the creation of a new theatre in the palace's Great Hall.

The first performance in the refurbished Cockpit in Whitehall took place on 19 November 1660 – a mere two weeks after the patent duopoly had been established – when the King's Company presented Jonson's *Epicoene*.[40] George Monck, the newly created Duke of Albemarle, organized the event, whose audience included Charles II. It was fitting that the resumption of theatre at court began with Killigrew's company of older actors – including Mohun, who had fought for the royalist cause in the Civil War – the whole event being a meta-performance of reinstatement and return, both monarchical and theatrical. Much of that self-reflexivity came through in the prologue, doubtless spoken by one of the veteran actors. Though likely written by Sir John Denham, the prologue certainly expressed a view of the relationship between the stage and the throne that Davenant endorsed and promoted. The prologue looks back to the intertwined histories of the stage and the throne, hailing the tradition under Charles I of court performances ('this place / Which *Majesty* so oft was wont to grace'), linking the overthrow of the monarchy with the closure of the theatres ('The *Laurel* and the *Crown* together went, / Had the same *Foes*, and the same *Banishment*'), and affirming that actors remained loyal to the crown during the Civil War ('When by your Danger, and our Duty prest, / We acted in the Field, and not in Jest'). The delivery of the prologue itself was a moment of celebration, a unifying event that could occur only because the stage and the sovereign had been restored together. At each turn in this tragicomic history, theatre and monarchy move in tandem, each supporting the

42   SIR WILLIAM DAVENANT AND THE DUKE'S COMPANY

other, leading the actors to boast, upon their own return, that '[t]hey that would have no *KING*, would have no *Play*'.[41]

In 1663, shortly after being granted his singular patent, Davenant composed a poem addressed to Charles II, cannily attributing to him not just the reopening of the theatres but their necessary *reformation*: elevating public morals and offering the wonders of changeable scenery. With political shrewdness, Davenant banishes his own reforming efforts during the Protectorate and imagines in heroic couplets that the restored theatre owes its existence entirely to the king. And not just its existence, but its flourishing:

> If [the theatre is] to height of Art and Virtue grown,
> The form and matter is as much your own
> As is your Tribute with your Image coin'd:
> *You* made the Art, the Virtue *You* enjoyn'd.[42]

Appealing to common morality was but a platitude, and wholly at odds with the king's libertine personal life. The more revealing aspect of Davenant's panegyric is that it singles out changeable scenery – 'the *Scene* so various now become' – as the 'perfection' of the English stage, that which makes it greater than the theatres of classical antiquity:

> the *Dramatick* Plots of *Greece*, and *Rome*,
> Compar'd to ours, do from their height decline,
> And shrink in all the compass of design.

Having praised his own company's style as the unquestioned summit of theatrical genius – so triumphant that the glories of 'Greece and Rome' fade away – Davenant cannily attributes this genius not to his own artistry but to the king's magnificence. Despite its flattering hyperbole, Davenant's claim carries some truth. When the king returned to England in May 1660, he had brought with him a decided preference for the French way of making theatre: indoor playhouses with proscenium arches, changeable scenery, lavish spectacle, and professional

REOPENING THE THEATRES IN 1660   43

actresses.[43] The company of male actors that performed on the traditional bare platform stage of the outdoor Red Bull theatre in 1660 saw no reason to break with their own tradition. But under Davenant's leadership, the stage was indeed breaking with tradition, by adopting the methods and practices of the finest European theatres. In his poem Davenant took care to credit the king for the rising artistic standards of the English stage. Reversing the political logic of the Stuart court masques, in which the stage enhanced the sovereign – reflecting back to him, through performance, his own absolute power – the Restoration stage proposed, instead, that the sovereign enhances the stage: 'You, in Three years' have led the theatre toward its 'perfection'.

Any courtier who read Davenant's smooth words or who had attended a performance in the small Cockpit theatre in Whitehall Palace knew perfectly well that the restored Stuarts could not compete with the House of Bourbon for artistic prestige. Charles II, unlike his cousin Louis XIV, the 'Sun King', lacked the wealth required to maintain a magnificent court like Versailles, which boasted Molière as the author of theatrical *divertissements*, sometimes created with his musical partner Jean-Baptiste Lully. Nor could the English king set up a public theatre within the walls of his palace at Whitehall, like the Théâtre du Palais-Royal in Paris, where Molière's company began performing in 1660. The Cockpit-in-Court, whose renovation Charles II ordered, was a small and ill-equipped theatre used for private performances only. There was no doubt about it: the Parisian stage far outclassed the London stage. Having been exiled in France, the English king and his courtiers knew the truth of the matter from their own experience. How could it be otherwise, given the eighteen-year closure of theatres in London? But now that theatres had reopened, Davenant was in a hurry to emulate French performance practice and its royal protocols, not least because those practices echoed how his own court masques had been staged before the Civil War. Yet his playhouse in Lincoln's Inn Fields, far from being sumptuous, had first seen life as a tennis court. But what he lacked in resources, he made up for in ambitious eloquence. And thus, Sir William Davenant turned to the ancient art of rhetoric – not just to bind the theatre more closely than ever to the crown, but to claim in words what had yet to be achieved in deeds. After all, that's what theatre does: create realities that exist onstage but nowhere else.

3

New Performance Spaces

It is not possible to understand Davenant's innovative and dynamic theatrical style without considering the actual theatre spaces in which his Shakespeare adaptations were first performed. Indeed, the material characteristics of those spaces – their acoustic and spatial potentialities, their scenic capabilities, and their technologies – determined how Davenant and the Duke's Company developed and perfected a distinctive *mise-en-scène* that successfully integrated drama, music, and spectacle. And so, in this chapter we consider how the theatrical spaces inhabited by the Duke's Company and its rival, the King's Company, shaped their respective aesthetics.

Transitional theatres

By virtue of their royal patents, Davenant and Killigrew were entitled to form their own acting companies. But they had no custom-made theatres at their disposal in which their newly formed companies could perform. Necessity alone compelled the patentees to stage their first productions in older theatre spaces that had been used informally (or illegally) for public performances during the Interregnum and Commonwealth and then to create their own theatres by converting indoor tennis courts into performance spaces.

As noted in the previous chapter, the temporary united company led by Killigrew and Davenant first performed at the

46 SIR WILLIAM DAVENANT AND THE DUKE'S COMPANY

indoor Cockpit (or Phoenix) in Drury Lane in October 1660. Davenant was no stranger to the Cockpit, having staged his operatic experiments *The Cruelty of the Spaniards in Peru*, *The History of Sir Frances Drake*, and *The Siege of Rhodes* there just a few years earlier. The Cockpit, although a throwback to an earlier theatrical tradition, was nonetheless a space conducive to the new aesthetic that Davenant promoted: it accommodated some changeable scenery and, being indoors, it was acoustically suited to instrumental and vocal music. Indeed, one suspects that Davenant himself chose the Cockpit, for the choice implies a certain theatrical sensibility, and it was Davenant rather than Killigrew who had substantial experience in the professional theatre. Even so, the Cockpit was never intended by Davenant as anything other than as a temporary home, because as a theatre structure it could never realize the fullness of Davenant's artistic vision. The immediate problem was that the theatre was too small for elaborate scenic display. John Webb's surviving drawings of scenery for *The Siege of Rhodes* – which John Orrell argues derive from a 1658/9 production at the Cockpit – capture the limitations of the theatrical space.[1] The Cockpit was not originally designed for changeable scenery, and so only very basic stage technology could be used. The Cockpit had a wing and groove system. Stagehands accomplished scene changes by placing wings and shutters in grooves on the stage before the performance began, sliding them on and off as needed. Webb's drawings indicate fixed wings and a grooved frame which, because of the cramped space, could accommodate only three pairs of movable shutters.[2]

Davenant and Killigrew's joint venture at the Cockpit was brief, and by November 1660 the two patentees went their separate ways. Killigrew used the open-air Red Bull as a temporary theatre, while he quickly converted Gibbon's Tennis Court in Vere Street into a Jacobean-style indoor theatre. The King's Men began playing there on 8 November 1660. After briefly taking up residence in the old Salisbury Court, the Duke's Men in June 1661 moved into their new theatre in Lincoln's Inn Fields, a building that first saw life as Lisle's

NEW PERFORMANCE SPACES   47

Tennis Court. Davenant's inaugural production there was one of his own works, the scenery-rich *The Siege of Rhodes*. For the occasion, Davenant transformed his opera into a play with music and added a full-length sequel, with each part performed on alternating days.

Given Davenant's longstanding interest in music, it might seem strange that he pruned the recitative from *The Siege of Rhodes* for the inauguration of his new theatre. Judging from the comments about English antipathy to recitative a few years later in *The Playhouse to Be Let* (1663), it is possible that Davenant did not want to risk staging a through-sung work. From a technical perspective, the space at Lincoln's Inn Fields may not have been conducive to the acoustical demands of fully sung opera. As Michael Burden speculates, there simply may have been 'no easy way of accommodating a band of the sort [*The Siege of Rhodes*] required'.[3] There is scant evidence about the placement of musicians at Lincoln's Inn Fields, but Pepys's diary seems to indicate that the band played either in a small music room situated above the middle of the proscenium arch or in a side balcony over the forestage. When Pepys attended a 1667 performance of Davenant and Dryden's adaptation of *The Tempest*, he groused that he was 'forced to sit in the side Balcone over against the Musique-room at the Dukes-House'.[4] Similarly, when he saw *The Roman Virgin* in 1669 he reported that he sat 'in the side balcony, over against the music'.[5]

From an artistic perspective, Davenant may have converted *The Siege of Rhodes* into a play with music to showcase both the talents of his actors and the features of his new theatre. To present the work as an opera meant that singers such as Matthew Locke or Catherine Coleman had to take on the extra burden of acting and emotional expression, whereas to present the work as a mostly spoken play meant that members of the acting company – including Thomas Betterton, Mary Saunderson, Hester Davenport, and Henry Harris – could undertake some of the principal parts.[6] These fine young performers would have communicated intimately with their audience on the forestage, an area in front of the proscenium

48   SIR WILLIAM DAVENANT AND THE DUKE'S COMPANY

arch. The actor Colley Cibber nostalgically explains the power of the forestage in his *Apology*:

> The usual station of the Actors, in almost every Scene, was advanc'd at least ten Foot nearer to the Audience than they now can be . . . when the Actors were in Possession of that forwarder Space, to advance upon, the Voice was then more in the Centre of the House, so that the most distance Ear had scarce the least Doubt, or Difficulty in hearing what fell from the weakest Utterance.[7]

The appearance of women on the stage was a special effect in and of itself in the early days of the Restoration. The impact that actresses made on audience members may be deduced from Samuel Pepys's reaction to the revised *The Siege of Rhodes*. After seeing Mary Saunderson as Ianthe and Hester Davenport as Roxalana, he thereafter referred to them in his diary not by their own names but by the names of their characters.

Davenant may have eschewed through-sung opera at Lincoln's Inn Fields for a variety of reasons, but his choice to inaugurate his new theatre with a work that combined instrumental and vocal music, spoken drama, and scenic spectacle foreshadowed the aesthetic that Davenant vigorously pursued in his Shakespeare adaptations. Above all, Davenant understood his audience. Through-sung opera may not have been commercially viable in London – it was a genre that usually needed aristocratic subvention to survive and this was something that Charles II could not afford. However, a show with varied *divertissements* of song, dance, and spoken text might thrive in the commercial marketplace, for it appealed to a broader audience.[8]

Changeable scenery

Both Killigrew's and Davenant's converted tennis theatres were small – no larger than 42 feet by 106 feet – and accommodated about 400 audience members.[9] However, the

NEW PERFORMANCE SPACES 49

haste with which Killigrew transformed Gibbon's Court into the Vere Street Theatre meant that the only scenic effect he definitely had at his disposal was the traditional one of candlelight. Like a pre-Restoration private indoor playhouse, Killigrew's theatre had a U-shaped seating plan, possibly on two levels, and a pit with benches.[10] Despite Samuel Pepys's initial praise of the theatre ('the finest play-house, I believe, that ever was in England'), it was hardly a cutting-edge theatrical space.[11]

By contrast, Davenant took more time with his renovation, finding inspiration not in traditional indoor private theatres but in court theatre, a performance venue that he knew intimately and which was better suited to his longstanding interest in mounting productions that integrated visual spectacle with music and drama. To pursue that interest, he needed a theatrical space equipped for changeable scenery. His theatre at Lincoln's Inn Fields, converted from Lisle's Tennis Court, was designed to give him just that.

The scene designer John Webb likely oversaw the transformation of Lisle's Tennis Court into a theatre for the Duke's Company. Davenant and Webb had first collaborated in 1640 on the court masque *Salmacida Spolia* and later on Davenant's operatic experiments in the 1650s, so Webb was a familiar and trusted partner. We have some knowledge of Webb's approach to theatre building because his plans survive for the 1665 renovation of the Hall Theatre at Whitehall. The stage was 39 feet wide by 33 feet deep and 5 feet high at the front, with a raked stage, the elevation increasing to 6 feet at the back shutters. The theatre's scenic capability was modelled on that of Jacobean and Caroline court theatres. Thus, the Hall Theatre featured a proscenium stage and a shutter and groove system similar to what had been used in *Salmacida Spolia*. This included one set of back shutters in grooves, behind which were up to three cut-out relieves – Jocelyn Powell memorably compares them to a child's pop-up picture book, as they provided a greater illusion of depth – in front of a permanent backcloth.[12] In addition, there were four sets of side

50 SIR WILLIAM DAVENANT AND THE DUKE'S COMPANY

shutters in grooves on either side of the stage. Although equipped with changeable scenery, the Hall Theatre did not possess elaborate machines. For example, the absence of a fly gallery meant that a temporary scaffold had to be installed for any flying effects.[13]

Lincoln's Inn Fields had similar dimensions and equipment as Webb's Hall Theatre, for the same sets seem to have been used at both venues.[14] Court records indicate that Webb prepared his scene designs for Roger Boyle's *Mustapha* for a production at the Hall Theatre in March 1665, but the court performance was deferred until October. Instead, the play was given first at Lincoln's Inn Fields in April 1665, presumably with the sets designed for the Hall Theatre.[15]

There are some crucial differences between the theatre at Lincoln's Inn Fields and the Hall Theatre. Lincoln's Inn Fields certainly had a forestage with side doors and adjacent balconies, features absent in Webb's drawing for the Hall Theatre. The stage at Lincoln's Inn Fields was 8 feet deeper than the Hall Theatre stage, and it must have been higher as well to optimize audience viewing and to accommodate at least one trap door, a feature called for in plays performed by the Duke's Company in its early years.[16] On 24 August 1661 Pepys saw Davenant's company perform *Hamlet*, a play that certainly requires a trap for the ghost of Hamlet's father. Pepys also reported that the production was 'done with Scenes very well', confirming the early use of changeable scenery at Lincoln's Inn Fields.[17]

Tim Keenan argues that Davenant's theatre had four wing positions on each side, at most three wing shutters per wing frame, three pairs of lower backshutters in a single frame, and a discovery space. There would probably have been a border to mask the flies, the upper wings, and the shutter grooves, and a backcloth that could be changed as necessary to represent interior or exterior scenes. There is no evidence that Lincoln's Inn Fields had substage machinery to accomplish simultaneous wing and shutter changes. Rather, a crew of stagehands, relying on ropes and pulleys, manually changed the scenery, cued by the prompter's whistle.[18]

Audiences flocked to see the movable scenery at Davenant's new theatre – Killigrew simply could not compete. On 4 July 1661 Pepys reported on the King's Company's falling fortunes: 'I went to the Theatre [in Vere Street] ... But strange to see this house, that use to be so thronged, now empty since the opera begun'.[19] Killigrew's decision to focus on speed of renovation rather than innovation proved fatal to his residency at Vere Street. It might have been easy and expedient to model the space after a pre-Civil War indoor theatre with no capacity for scenic effect, but as an artistic and business strategy, it was woefully misguided. Notably, Pepys had taken to calling Davenant's theatre 'the opera', for opera in England was as much about scenic spectacle as music, and at Davenant's 'house' Pepys and other theatregoers experienced both. Within a year, Killigrew was forced to build a new theatre at Bridges Street, equipped with scenes and machines, to rival the theatre at Lincoln's Inn Fields. Davenant, for the time being, had won the aesthetic battle.

Staging Shakespeare at Lincoln's Inn Fields

Davenant's earliest Shakespeare revivals were first performed at Lincoln's Inn Fields: *Hamlet* 'with scenes' has already been mentioned, but there were other productions in these early years that combined music and spectacle in innovative ways, simultaneously revealing Davenant's aesthetic and the scenic capacities at Lincoln's Inn Fields. To get a sense of how the space at Lincoln's Inn Fields shaped early Restoration Shakespeare, we shall turn to evidence from plays first performed there by the Duke's Company in the 1660s: *The Law Against Lovers* (1662), Davenant's combination of *Measure for Measure* and *Much Ado About Nothing*; *Macbeth* (1664); *The Rivals*, Davenant's revision of John Fletcher and

52 SIR WILLIAM DAVENANT AND THE DUKE'S COMPANY

Shakespeare's *Two Noble Kinsmen* (1664); and Davenant and John Dryden's *The Tempest* (1667).

Davenant began modestly with *The Law Against Lovers*, emphasizing cost-effectiveness over visual splendour. The descriptions of sets and scenery are few and far between in Davenant's posthumous folio, which contains the only Restoration printing of *The Law Against Lovers*.[20] In one stage direction, Beatrice, her sister Viola, and Julietta 'step behind the hangings', perhaps a reference to the changeable backcloth.[21] Other stage directions describe characters who enter 'at several doors' or who 'exeunt several ways', typical staging conventions in the Restoration theatre. In terms of location, the play calls for scenes in a terraced garden as well as a prison, the Duke of Savoy's palace, Beatrice's house, a convent, and the Friar's quarters, all reasonably generic scenes that could be reused in other productions – a necessity in a repertory company. Indeed, one of the scenes in *The Law Against Lovers* involves a siege and some of Webb's designs from *The Siege of Rhodes* may have been repurposed here. Other scenes may have been taken from Davenant's *Love and Honour*, which, like *The Law Against Lovers*, was set in Savoy.[22] In some respects, though, *The Law Against Lovers* is more notable for what is missing than for what is there. Although characters sing and dance, there are neither elaborate musical numbers nor elaborate sets. Davenant seems to have spent most of his energy on the textual elements of the adaptation.

By the time Davenant wrote his next two adaptations, *Macbeth* and *The Rivals*, he was ready to fully exploit the possibilities of the performing space at Lincoln's Inn Fields. The presence of the supernatural musical witches in his *Macbeth* afforded Davenant the opportunity to combine sonic and visual splendour. Pepys famously claimed that *Macbeth* was 'one of the best plays for a stage, and variety of dancing and musique, that ever I saw'.[23] Unfortunately, no documentation about the 1660s staging of *Macbeth* survives beyond the eyewitness account in Pepys's diary, supplemented

NEW PERFORMANCE SPACES 53

by a few scraps of printed music. But a quarto was printed of *The Rivals*. Its descriptions of scenery are more detailed than those in *The Law Against Lovers*, suggesting Davenant paid greater attention to the visual components of the adaptation. The play mentions a citadel, a window, a balcony, a palace garden, and a wood.

The woodland setting plays an integral role in the mad songs presented by Celania (the equivalent of the lovesick Jailer's Daughter in *Two Noble Kinsmen*) and the celebrations of the rural people, who present an entertainment in honour of the prince's birthday. Celania's music breaks no new dramaturgical ground, as inappropriate singing had long connoted theatrical madness; but the rural people's entertainment is far more ambitious, for it combines text, dance, instrumental music (to signify the hunt), and song. It is also quite lengthy, comprising the end of Act 3 and opening of Act 4. The gambit pleased audiences. The prompter John Downes said that that house was full for nine days and singled out the 'very Fine Interlude ... of Vocal and Instrumental Musick, mixt with very Diverting Dancing' for special approbation.[24]

In *The Tempest*, first staged in 1667, Davenant and Dryden also explored the synergistic power of music, dance, stage technology, and changeable scenery to create meaning through performance. This approach is particularly evident in the newly composed Masque of Devils (2.1), which uses disembodied sound and embodied dance to provoke fear and guilt in Antonio, Alonzo, and Gonzalo. The devils are initially heard but not seen, as they sing a dialogue 'within'. Eventually they enter, 'placing themselves at two corners of the stage', which produces additional panic among the usurpers. A series of vices appear, eventually falling 'into a round encompassing the Duke, &c. Singing'. They then perform a dance, presumably in an equally threatening fashion, before vanishing, potentially through a trap, given their infernal nature.[25] Sequences such as this, and the rural entertainment in *The Rivals*, set the template for the Duke's Company's later adaptations of Shakespeare, in

54 SIR WILLIAM DAVENANT AND THE DUKE'S COMPANY

which stage technology combines with 'divertisement' to produce the effect.

The Bridges Street Theatre

Davenant's aesthetic for Shakespeare adaptation proved popular. But the Duke's Company soon found itself competing against Killigrew's custom-built theatre at Bridges Street, which opened in 1663. Killigrew seems to have been more enamoured of machines than Davenant, or at least the Bridges Street Theatre, being newly constructed rather than retrofitted, had more up-to-date technology.[26] As Andrew Walkling has demonstrated, the King's Company at Bridges Street mounted a series of plays that, in addition to changeable scenery, required machine effects. In Dryden's *The Rival Ladies* (late 1663 or early 1664) the gods Cupid, Phoebus, and Mercury fly on wires and Venus and Ceres appear in chariots; in Roger Boyle's *The Black Prince* (1667), masquers float upon two clouds; and in Dryden's *Tyrannic Love* (1669) the spirits Nakar and Damilcar sing on a cloud, and the angel Amariel flies in on a wire.[27]

Judging from stage directions in plays performed at Lincoln's Inn Fields, it does not appear that machines played a significant role in those productions. Dawn Lewcock has argued that the lack of machines in the Lincoln's Inn Fields plays reflects Davenant's rejection of spectacle that served no verisimilar purpose.[28] Citing Davenant's preface to *Gondibert* (1650), Lewcock notes that the playwright specifically maligned the 'descending of Gods in gay Clowds' and the 'rising of Ghosts in Smoake', for the 'best Dramaticks; who in representation of examples, believe they prevail most on our manners when they lay the Scene at home in their own Countrey, so much they avoid those remote regions of Heaven and Hell'.[29] Of course, *Gondibert* was penned during the same period in which Davenant was angling for the return of drama under the guise of moral entertainments; and his preface was dedicated to the ultimate rationalist, Thomas Hobbes. Sceptical statements about machines and verisimilitude must be interpreted within this context.

Still, it does seem clear that Davenant eschewed spectacle for spectacle's sake, and he may even have been suspicious of combining the supernatural with stage technologies.[30] But Davenant did not always practise what he preached with regard to Shakespeare. *Hamlet* features a ghost appearing and disappearing through trap doors; spirits and devils in the *Tempest* likely did the same; and Davenant's adaptation of *Macbeth* expands the role of the musical witches, although we do not know if they appeared on 'gay Clowds' at Lincoln's Inn Fields. Keenan has speculated that Davenant was simply too busy establishing his new theatre to develop an integrated scenic dramaturgy that 'incorporates technical aspects of the new stage within the drama such that they seem interdependent rather than separate and distinct components'.[31] We tend to agree more with Peter Holland, who observes in his analysis of George Etherege's *She Would If She Could* (1668) that the Duke's Company used scenery at Lincoln's Inn Fields to aid 'the audience in their understanding of the play's meaning. It is a primary part of the perception and comprehension of the play'.[32]

As ground-breaking and influential as this hermeneutic approach to scenography proved to be, by the time Davenant died on 7 April 1668 the Duke's Company had fallen behind its competition, particularly with regard to machine-based spectacle. After Thomas Betterton and Henry Harris took over as the guiding artistic forces in the Duke's Company, they quickly responded to this existential threat with productions that immediately began to incorporate more flying and machine effects for supernatural characters.[33] Elkanah Settle's *Cambyses* (late 1670 or early 1671) requires a cloud machine and a wire for a flying spirit. More consequentially, the Duke's Company began planning its move to a newly built theatre at Dorset Garden, a space whose ample backstage machinery would shape the performance aesthetics of Restoration Shakespeare in the years to come.

Scenes and machines in the 1670s

The first flurry of activity for a new theatre began around September 1669, when preliminary negotiations took place on a ground lease in the Salisbury Court area; by the following year a lease had been signed.[34] Around the same time, Thomas Betterton conducted a fact-finding trip to France and, upon his return to London, he applied his newfound knowledge about machines to the construction of the Dorset Garden Theatre. It opened for business in 1671, although it probably wasn't fully fitted for machine productions until 1673.[35] It was Betterton who aggressively adopted and extended Davenant's intermedial house style in Shakespeare productions in the years to come, most notably in the enormously popular productions of *Macbeth* and *The Tempest*, which were both revived at Dorset Garden in the 1670s with machine effects and expanded musical interludes.

Constructing the Dorset Garden theatre cost a princely sum: about £9,000.[36] The French traveller François Brunet visited in 1676 and described its lavish interior, before turning to the seating arrangement and acoustics: 'The pit, arranged in the form of an amphitheatre, has seats, and one never hears any noise. There are seven boxes, holding twenty persons each. The same number of boxes form the second tier and, higher still, there is the paradise'.[37] Robert D. Hume believes that it could have accommodated about 820 spectators, more than twice as many as Lincoln's Inn Fields.[38]

Because of the scarcity of documentary evidence, much remains uncertain about the precise playing dimensions and features of the Dorset Garden theatre. The best evidence regarding the stage and scenery comes from William Dolle's engravings of scenes from Elkanah Settle's *The Empress of Morocco* (1673), a play first performed at Dorset Garden (see Figure 2). Dolle's engravings are printed in the 1673 quarto of Settle's play. Although these images are evocative and detailed, they cannot be considered firm evidence of Dorset Garden's interior because they are stylized representations, not detailed architectural drawings. Extrapolating from Dolle's engravings and other evidence, Edward A. Langhans, John Spring, and Robert D. Hume have all proposed different models for the theatre. Scholarly consensus prefers Langhans's model, which Hume further elaborated.[39] According to Hume, Dorset Garden was a narrow theatre, which featured a substantial upstage scenic area (perhaps as much as 50 feet deep) that could be blocked off with shutters for the performance of plays that did not require elaborate scenery. The proscenium was 30 feet wide and the forestage was probably 18 to 21 feet deep. Hume speculates that there were two doors on each side of the proscenium.[40] The music room was above the stage, as it probably had been at the Lincoln's Inn Fields. Music may also have been played from the balcony, onstage, or on machines.

FIGURE 2 *William Dolle, engraving of scenes at Dorset Garden Theatre, in Elkanah Settle's* The Empress of Morocco *(1673), Folger Shakespeare Library. Reproduced under a Creative Commons Attribution-ShareAlike 4.0 International License.*

58 SIR WILLIAM DAVENANT AND THE DUKE'S COMPANY

For larger operatic productions, the band was sometimes placed between the pit and the stage.[41]

Dorset Garden was well known for its visual splendour and stage technology, so obviously there were shutters and grooves, machines, and traps to accommodate the spectacular performances given there. Langhans argues that there were six wings and two sets of shutters. The first set of shutters were approximately 15 feet beyond the proscenium and the second approximately 5 feet upstage beyond that, thus creating three distinct acting spaces.[42] Opened and closed shutters would have produced different visual and sonic effects; for instance, musicians might be placed out of view of the audience, behind closed shutters.[43] Drawing inferences from stage directions in plays and operas staged at Dorset Garden, Langhans argues that Dorset Garden had at least one small trap on the forestage, two medium traps between the curtain line and the first set of shutters, and two small traps and one large trap upstage of the shutters, possibly between the first and second sets of shutters. Some of the traps, particularly the large one, may have had some kind of elevator rig, which could have been accommodated in the fairly spacious substage area. There must have also been a substantial backstage space, a grid and rigging, fly galleries, as well as complex flying machinery.[44] Some flying effects were simple, involving only a wire capable of flying individual actors. Others involved more substantial machines, such as platforms carrying scenery and groups of performers.

Spectacular performances drew eager patrons to Dorset Garden and, once again, the King's Company struggled to compete. The situation became even more dire when the Bridges Street Theatre caught fire on 25 January 1672 and burned to the ground, destroying the company's stock of scenery and costumes. Ironically, the King's Company was forced to move into the Duke's Company's former theatre at Lincoln's Inn Fields while its new theatre was being built. The Theatre Royal in Drury Lane opened in March 1674 and cost around £4,000, considerably less than Dorset Garden. Despite the nominal backing of the monarch, the King's Company did

NEW PERFORMANCE SPACES 59

not receive any direct financing from the king to build their theatre. The company asked the king to pay fees in arrears for court performances and requested an additional £2,000 subsidy, but there is no record that Charles II made any such payments. Instead, a brief was sent out to parish churches to collect funds for the construction of the theatre.[45]

During their exile at the cramped Lincoln's Inn Fields theatre, the King's Company competed with the Duke's Company by parodying Dorset Garden extravaganzas through satirical prologues, epilogues, and burlesques (which we explore at greater length in Chapter 6). Yet even at Lincoln's Inn Fields they did not eschew spectacle altogether – in fact, they sought to parody the lavish Dorset Garden production style. Their first burlesque was Thomas Duffett's *The Empress of Morocco*, performed in 1673, a parody of Elkanah Settle's tragedy, which includes an epilogue satire on the singing and flying witches in Davenant's *Macbeth* at Dorset Garden. In the parody, the witches appear on broomsticks and in a wicker basket 'machine'.[46] The strategy of ridicule proved so winning that the King's Company pursued it more aggressively after the move into the fully equipped Drury Lane theatre, in Duffett's *Mock Tempest* (1674) and *Psyche Debauch'd* (1675), the latter a spoof on Shadwell's *Psyche*. They also incorporated scenes, machines, and music, and dance in shows with no parodic intent, including revivals of older plays like Dryden's *Tyrannic Love* (1676), and newly written tragedies such as Nathaniel Lee's *Sophonisba* (1675).[47] The King's Company understood the power of spectacular productions at Dorset Garden, even though they could not fully replicate that spectacle at their own theatre in Drury Lane.

Operatic Shakespeare in the 1670s

The aesthetic that the Duke's Company developed for Restoration Shakespeare after its move to Dorset Garden in the 1670s elaborated upon the practice that Davenant had

60 SIR WILLIAM DAVENANT AND THE DUKE'S COMPANY

introduced in the 1660s. The productions of *Macbeth* and *Tempest* that Pepys enjoyed at Lincoln's Inn Fields in the 1660s blended changeable scenery, dancing, and singing. When reviving those productions at Dorset Garden in the 1670s, Betterton amplified the stage spectacle and extended the musical scenes. Pepys had called the theatre at Lincoln's Inn Fields 'the opera' and Davenant's operatic principles lived on at Dorset Garden, with his Shakespeare adaptations providing a template for the genre of musical drama pursued by the Duke's Company in the 1670s: dramatick opera.

A term coined retrospectively by Dryden on the title page of *King Arthur* (1691), 'dramatick opera' combined spoken dialogue, singing, dancing, and spectacle, with these varied components working syncretically to create theatrical meaning.[48] The genre's English roots are found in the Caroline court masques, Davenant's operatic experiments in the 1650s, and even Davenant's transformation of *The Siege of Rhodes* into a play with music and significant scenic effect for the 1661 production at Lincoln's Inn Fields. It was thus only natural for Davenant to continue creating intermedial theatrical productions through Shakespeare adaptations, particularly *Macbeth* and *The Tempest*. After the move to the fully equipped Dorset Garden theatre, Betterton exploited the visual component of Restoration Shakespeare more fully, a practice evidenced in the printed quartos for *Macbeth* (1674) and Thomas Shadwell's revision of Davenant and Dryden's *Tempest* (1674).

Macbeth was revived at Dorset Garden in 1673 and evidence about the staging of this production may be found in the two printed quartos of 1674, which are largely identical.[49] In addition, a manuscript of *Macbeth* survives in the Beinecke Library at Yale University (Gen. MSS Vol. 548).[50] The stage directions in the Yale manuscript are virtually identical to those found in Q1 and, given their emphasis on flying effects, it seems likely that they represent what happened at Dorset Garden rather than at the less well-equipped theatre at Lincoln's Inn Fields, where the play had its premiere around a decade earlier.

NEW PERFORMANCE SPACES

61

John Downes reported on 'Machines' and 'flyings for the Witches' in the 1673 *Macbeth*, and the Yale manuscript and Q1 both indicate that wires, machines, and trap doors were used to accomplish a variety of effects.[51] The play at Dorset Garden opened with the three witches, who departed the stage in dramatic fashion: 'Ex[eunt]. Flying'.[52] The 'weyward sisters' of Davenant's text also made an entrance 'flying' at the beginning of Act 1, Scene 3.[53] After sharing their prognostications with Macbeth and Banquo, the witches exited suddenly, perhaps through trap doors if they had surreptitiously managed to unhook their flying harness during the scene. Alternatively, they could have remained in harness and then flown up and away.[54] Q1 states that the 'Witches vanish' and Macbeth responds with astonishment 'Ha! Gone! ... Th'are turn'd to Air; what seem'd Corporeal / Is melted into nothing'.[55]

Trap effects were also used for ghosts in the play. In Act 3, Scene 5 the stage directions indicate that Banquo's 'Ghost descends' and, a few lines later, he 'rises at his [Macbeth's] feet'.[56] The ghost of Duncan, who haunts Lady Macbeth in Act 4, Scene 4, may have also used a trap for his entrance. Finally, the full range of traps at Dorset Garden were used in a virtuosic series of effects executed in sequence in Act 4, Scene 1: the witches' cauldron sank and they danced and then vanished, their cave sinking after them.[57]

The most spectacular supernatural episode in *Macbeth* occurred in Act 3, Scene 8 during the song 'Hecate, oh come away', a light-hearted ditty performed by Hecate, her spirits, and her coven.[58] The staging at Dorset Garden may have exploited spatial separation for visual and sonic effect, with characters possibly performing offstage, onstage, and in the air, although the stage directions are muddled in Q1. The Yale manuscript clarifies matters: Hecate sings, 'Hark, I am call'd; my lit[t]le spirit see / Sits in a foggy cloud and stays for me', the 'Machine descends', and '1 Sing w^{th}in', beckoning its mistress to 'Come away'.[59] Thus, at Dorset Garden it appears a spirit sang within the descending cloud machine. Hecate and another

62 SIR WILLIAM DAVENANT AND THE DUKE'S COMPANY

spirit may have also flown on individual wires, although such movement is not marked in the text.[60]

The operatic *Tempest* performed at Dorset Garden the following spring exploited music, dance, and spectacle to an even greater degree than *Macbeth*. The epilogue to *The Tempest* acknowledges the production's lavishness and high cost:

> when yo[u] of witt, and sence, were weary growne,
> Romantick, riming, fustian Playes were showne,
> We then to flying Witches did advance,
> And for your pleasures traffic'd into ffrance.
> From thence new Arts to please you, we haue brought,
> And aboue 30 warbling voyces gott.
> Many a God, & Goddesse, you will heare,
> And we have Singing, Dancing, Devills here;
> Such Devills, and such gods, are very deare.
> We, in all ornaments, are lavish growne[.][61]

As mentioned previously, the text had been revised by Shadwell: he expanded musical scenes from the 1667 Dryden/Davenant adaptation and added a new Masque of Neptune in Act 5. Downes reported that the expenditure was worth it: 'not any succeeding Opera got more Money'.[62]

Stage directions in the 1674 *Tempest* quarto are more far more detailed and elaborate than those for the operatic *Macbeth*. Flying, machines, and trap effects were not just used more frequently in the Dorset Garden production but were more consistently incorporated into the dramatic action. The spectacular nature of the production was signalled from the very beginning. An unusually lengthy and detailed stage direction indicates that the band was placed between the pit and the stage because it was so large (see Figure 3). Details of the scenic design are then meticulously described, including a 'new Frontispiece' comprising an arch supported by Corinthian columns and a scene depicting 'a thick, Cloudy Sky, a very Rocky Coast, and a Tempestuous Sea in perpetual Agitation'.

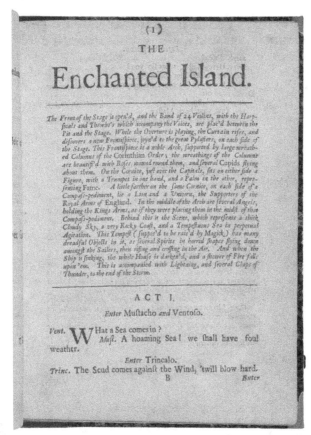

FIGURE 3 *Opening stage direction,* The Tempest *(1674), Folger Shakespeare Library. Reproduced under a Creative Commons Attribution-ShareAlike 4.0 International License.*

There were also flying effects, for the tempest had 'many dreadful Objects in it, as several Spirits in horrid shapes flying down amongst the Sailors, then rising and crossing in the Air'. Finally, sound and lighting effects completed the dynamic picture: the ship sank, the house was darkened, and then the darkness turned to light with a shower of fire accompanied by lightning and 'several Claps of Thunder'.[63] It is likely that

64   SIR WILLIAM DAVENANT AND THE DUKE'S COMPANY

Matthew Locke's 'Curtain Tune' underscored some of this stage action. In this complex synthesis of instrumental music and dynamic stage action in the opening moments of *The Tempest* we see the full flowering of the intermedial aesthetic hinted at in Davenant's Shakespeare adaptations from the 1660s.

The subsequent scenes at Dorset Garden moved from chaos to order, and back again.[64] Act 1, Scene 2 opened 'In the midst of the Shower of Fire'. The set for the opening scene disappeared and was replaced by a vista of a 'Beautiful part of the Island . . . three walks of Cypress-trees, each Side-walk leads to a Cave, in one of which Prospero keeps his Daughters, in the other Hippolito: The Middle-Walk is of a great depth, and leads to an open part of the Island'.[65] It is possible that this stage direction preserves not just how this painted scenery looked at Dorset Garden, but also captures something of what had transpired at Lincoln's Inn Fields in 1667, because in the earlier production Hippolito had also inhabited a cave.[66] In Act 2, Scene 1 visual disorder returned, as the scene shifted 'to the wilder part of the Island, 'tis compos'd of divers sorts of Trees, and barren places, with a prospect of the sea at a great distance'.[67] These two sets were brought back throughout the course of the play.[68]

The 1674 *Tempest* made significant use of traps. For instance, the expanded Masque of Devils in Act 2, Scene 3 combined sonic effects with traps. The musicians were initially placed beneath the stage at Dorset Garden: Alonzo, Antonio, and Gonzalo heard the devils before they saw them, a similar device as the one Davenant and Dryden used when they placed the devils 'within' in 1667. There were flourishes of music, the stage opened 'in several places', and 'Voyces under the Stage' joined the cacophony.[69] The devils then began their song, 'Where does the black Fiend Ambition reside', vocalizing 'under the Stage' until finally emerging through the trap (perhaps on an elevator) as they sang the chorus 'Who in Earth all others in pleasures excel'. The same scene also included various instances of infernal creatures and winds appearing and disappearing through traps to produce astonishment in

NEW PERFORMANCE SPACES 65

onstage and offstage spectators alike. The devils vanished after singing their admonishments, presumably through trapdoors, while another devil rose right in front of Antonio, Gonzalo, and Alonzo before singing to summon the 'subterranean winds', an effect similar to Banquo's ghost appearing close to Macbeth in the banquet scene.[70] As we have seen with the sinking cauldron in *Macbeth*, sometimes set pieces appeared and disappeared via a trap. In Act 4, Scene 2 of *The Tempest* a table rises and sinks through a trap.[71] Finally, traps were sometimes used in conjunction with other modes of entrance. In the dance of the winds that concluded the Masque of Devils, some winds appeared and disappeared through traps, while others walked on in more mundane fashion.[72]

Aerial effects of various kinds abounded in the operatic *Tempest*. In Act 1, Scene 2 Ariel's companion Milcha 'flies down' to assist him and then the two spirits departed together, flying up and crossing in the air, replicating the aerial acrobatics found in the opening storm.[73] Flying and machine effects combined in the spectacular Act 5 Masque of Neptune. 'Neptune, Amphitrite, Oceanus and Tethys appeared in the Chariot drawn with Sea-horses', 'Aeolus descend[ed]', and 'Winds fl[ew] down', perhaps on wires.[74] The masque concluded with yet more aerial display: the scene changed to a 'Rising Sun' followed by the appearance of 'a number of Aerial Spirits in the Air, Ariel flying from the Sun, advances towards the Pit'.[75] Thus, it seems clear that Dorset Garden was not only equipped with flying rigs that allowed actors to move side to side, but they might also have flown out towards the audience: an astounding effect indeed, the Restoration equivalent of the falling chandelier in *The Phantom of the Opera* or the helicopter in *Miss Saigon*.[76]

The 1674 *Tempest* quarto inaugurated an attempt to capture in words the multisensory experience of Restoration Shakespeare. As we have seen, Davenant had a longstanding interest in combining scenic effects, music, and dance in his Shakespeare adaptations. But the extant sources indicate that Davenant could not fulfil his ambition because of the spatial

66 SIR WILLIAM DAVENANT AND THE DUKE'S COMPANY

and technological limitations of his theatre at Lincoln's Inn Fields. Although it is possible that the printed versions of *The Law Against Lovers*, *The Rivals*, and *The Tempest* – all first staged at Lincoln's Inn Fields in the 1660s – failed to describe every scenic effect, Shadwell's quarto translates into words a performance's visual and sonic components, much like the printed descriptions found in Jacobean and Caroline court masques. In the years to come, such detailed description became the norm, as the productions of operatic Shakespeare in the mould established by Davenant were more consistently captured in print, allowing consumers at home to remember what they had seen at Dorset Garden or imagine what transpired there anew. This act of translation from sound and sight to descriptive texts must always be imperfect. Yet in these stage directions we can discover how theatrical space and technology shaped Davenant's intermedial aesthetic at Lincoln Inn Fields and how the Dorset Garden Theatre allowed his successor, Thomas Betterton, to perfect it.

4

Davenant's Repertoire

When formal prohibition of theatrical activity in London began in 1642, the number of professional acting companies was already in considerable decline. Among the adult companies, only the King's Men (Blackfriars, the second Globe), Queen Henrietta Maria's Men (Salisbury Court) and the second iteration of Prince Charles's Men (Red Bull) were still performing, along with the troupe of child actors known colloquially as Beeston's Boys (Cockpit/Phoenix).[1] Whatever survived the long years of playhouse suppression would be a remnant of London's theatrical world as constituted in 1642: these companies, their playhouses, their actors, and their repertoire. As we have seen, much about the theatrical profession changed in 1660, including its licensing regime, the location and architecture of theatre buildings, use of changeable scenery, and the first appearance of actresses. But the parallel fact of continuity in the English theatrical world between 1642 and 1660 cannot be gainsaid; indeed, that continuity determined in good measure how the two patent companies organized themselves, how they operated in their early years, and what plays they performed.

Allocating the old stock drama to the patent companies

The nature of the dramatic repertoire when the theatres reopened in 1660 had little to do with the new licensing scheme – the patents were silent on which plays each company could perform – but everything to do with claims of historical continuity in how the new acting companies were formed. The most decisive claim was that the King's Company under Killigrew's leadership descended directly from the King's Men, the company that had counted William Shakespeare among its sharers and which for decades had dominated London's theatre scene, right up until 1642. This presumption of pedigree did not arise from Killigrew himself, who – unlike Davenant – had no special affiliation with the King's Men.[2] Similarity in name was doubtless suggestive; but any acting company patronized by a male monarch would be so named. Rather, the claim rested primarily upon the links between Killigrew's *actors* and the pre-1642 companies. As we saw in Chapter 2, Killigrew's senior actors were mostly taken from the insurgent company led by Michael Mohun at the Red Bull. That troupe included Charles Hart, Nicholas Burt, and Walter Clun, all of whom began as boy actors with the King's Men before the Civil War, performing women's roles at the Blackfriars. Similarly, Mohun himself had acted with Queen Henrietta Maria's Men and John Lacy had joined Beeston's Boys as a youth in 1639. As the antiquarian James Wright recorded a few decades later in *Historia Histrionica*, the most senior actors in 1660 'were bred up Boys at the *Blackfriers*; and Acted Womens Parts'.[3] With the exception of Davenant himself, the entire cohort that had been active in the pre-Civil War theatre eventually joined the King's Company, not the Duke's Company. As Judith Milhous and Robert D. Hume have compellingly demonstrated, evidence from contemporary Chancery lawsuits confirms that the members of Killigrew's company understood themselves 'as part of an ongoing and unbroken "Socyety of Actors"' who had attempted performances in 1648, and thus served as a bridge between the pre-Civil War King's Men and the Restoration King's Company.[4]

In name, in personnel, and in professional allegiance, the King's Company as established by Killigrew in 1660 was both the embodied and the symbolic remnant not just of the King's Men but also of the larger pre-Civil War theatrical world. It was the sole surviving part of the lost whole. By contrast, the Duke's Company, whose existence was legitimated by the same royal warrant, had no equivalent stake in the theatrical past, apart from Davenant's own career as dramatist and manager. But in one of the great ironies of theatre history, the company with pedigree failed to flourish in the long term, while its upstart rival set the standard for the English Restoration stage.

Having positioned itself as the future of the pre-Civil War theatrical past, the King's Company seems to have laid immediate claim to every play originally acted by the King's Men and perhaps to all English play texts no matter which acting company first owned them. Shrewd from a business perspective, this claim also conformed to theatrical precedent. In the pre-1642 theatre, play scripts belonged to acting companies, who were generally reluctant to publish their scripts for fear of giving ammunition to their rivals. If Killigrew's company was accepted as the rightful successor to the King's Men, then it would logically hold exclusive performance rights to all the plays that had belonged to that company, including all of Shakespeare. That seems to have been the case, judging from the list of 'Old Stock Plays' belonging to the King's Company that appeared in John Downes's *Roscius Anglicanus* (1708).[5] As Deborah C. Payne has observed, nearly every play that Downes attributed to Killigrew's company in its first years – including *Othello*, *Julius Caesar*, *The Merry Wives of Windsor*, *1 Henry IV*, and *Titus Andronicus* – was owned by the King's Men before 1642.[6]

We don't know whether this arrangement favouring the King's Company was formally stipulated in the same way as the theatrical patents. Nor do we know whether Killigrew proactively argued his case for performance rights to older

70 SIR WILLIAM DAVENANT AND THE DUKE'S COMPANY

plays or whether his proprietary claim was assumed to be valid by custom and tradition. We don't know because not a single surviving document explains the *rationale* for how the old stock drama was divided between Killigrew and Davenant. It may well be the case that when the patent companies were established in 1660 no one thought to address the question of repertoire systematically, because the surviving records concern only the allocation of specific plays to one company or the other. Three such documents exist, but just one dates from 1660 – that is, the first moment when the companies needed to know which of the pre-1642 plays they could perform.

These three documents reveal a grossly unequal distribution of the pre-Restoration dramatic repertoire, with the King's Company heavily favoured and the Duke's Company left struggling to acquire any share of the old plays. The first such document is a warrant from the Lord Chamberlain dated 12 December 1660, a month after Killigrew's company began performing independently at its theatre on Vere Street.[7] After the two companies were definitively established as separate and rival entities in the autumn of 1660, Davenant proposed to the Lord Chamberlain (as mentioned in Chapter 2) that the Duke's Company be allowed to 'refor[m] some of the most ancient Playes that were playd at Blackfriers' and 'mak[e] them fitt' for his 'Company of Actors'. Granting that request, the Lord Chamberlain gave Davenant's company sole performance rights to eleven plays, including nine by William Shakespeare: *Hamlet*, *Henry VIII*, *King Lear*, *Macbeth*, *Measure for Measure*, *Much Ado About Nothing*, *Romeo and Juliet*, *The Tempest*, and *Twelfth Night*. Davenant's achievement in bringing Shakespeare to Restoration audiences rested on these plays alone. None of them is known to have been staged by the King's Company in the autumn of 1660, suggesting that the Lord Chamberlain was not so much removing plays from Killigrew's repertoire as safeguarding some of them for the Duke's Company. To end the continuing absurdity of Davenant's older plays belonging to the rival company – the King's Men had performed his 1638 tragedy *The Unfortunate Lovers* on 19 November 1660 – the warrant also granted him exclusive rights to perform his own dramatic works and a temporary right to perform six plays (including *Pericles*) previously acted by Rhodes's company at the Cockpit.[8] The exceptional nature of this dispensation only underlines the point that acting companies still trumped authors in determining who held the performance rights to plays.

Because the Lord Chamberlain's warrant from December 1660 was itself a response to Davenant's protest that he needed more old plays to perform, we can safely infer that the vast majority of pre-1642 plays initially belonged to the King's Company. Clearly, the deck was stacked against Davenant: he had a theatre to run, but few or no plays to perform. He had to fight for just a portion of the many dramatic works that his rival seemed to claim as a theatrical birthright. It would be hard to overestimate just how consequential the unequal division of the pre-Civil War dramatic repertoire was. In 1660 there were essentially no new theatre scripts. The acting companies had no choice but to perform pre-Restoration plays. Nor would any work by a professional playwright (as distinct from aristocratic amateurs like the Earl of Orrery) be consistently available until 1668, when John Dryden contracted with the King's Company to write three plays a year.[9]

The other surviving documents concerning the allocation of the old repertoire date from August 1668 and January 1669, shortly after Davenant's death and when control of the company passed to his widow, Mary. The 1668 warrant grants to the Duke's Company performance rights to twenty-three additional old plays, including *Timon of Athens*, *Troilus and Cressida* and the *Henry VI* trilogy.[10] Most of the plays named in the warrant had initially belonged to acting companies other than the King's Men. For example, James Shirley's comedy *The Bird in a Cage* was first performed in 1633 by Queen Henrietta Maria's Men at the Cockpit, while Beaumont and Fletcher's tragedy *Cupid's Revenge* was first performed in 1612 by the Children of the Revels and by the late 1630s was in the repertoire of Beeston's Boys.[11] The relative absence of plays that first belonged to the King's Men underlines yet again that

72 SIR WILLIAM DAVENANT AND THE DUKE'S COMPANY

Killigrew's company enjoyed proprietary rights to that particular repertoire.

The final document, dated January 1669, lists 108 old plays for which Killigrew's company had exclusive performance rights.[12] They included fourteen plays by Ben Jonson, thirty-eight by Beaumont and Fletcher, and all the works in the First Folio not previously assigned to the Duke's Company. Intriguingly, this document is the only one that grants the King's Company performance rights to specific plays, and it does so with a vengeance: allocating to Killigrew's company dozens more plays than the other warrants granted piecemeal to Davenant's company. The document's full title is significant: 'A Catalog of part of His Majesty's Servants' Plays as they were formerly acted at the Blackfriars and now allowed to His Majesty's Servants at the New Theatre'. This list of plays officially assigned to the King's Company was not meant to be exhaustive ('a part of'), thus implying that Killigrew's company held the performance rights to *other* unnamed plays.[13] This document reinforces the decisive link between the King's Men before 1642 and the King's Company after 1660. In the eyes of the licensing authorities, they were essentially the same company, but separated by a regrettable interruption of eighteen years. Davenant and the Duke's Company were excluded from making any parallel claim to ancestral rights. Thus, we should read the 1669 warrant not as a fresh allocation of dramatic texts – the enumerated scripts were already in Killigrew's repertoire – but rather as formal confirmation of the extreme disparity in playhouse practice that had been in force since 1660: old plays belonged by default to the King's Company, leaving the Duke's Company no choice but to fight for even a slender share of the old repertoire.

Shakespeare in the Duke's Company

Davenant faced a stark reality: his theatrical rival possessed exclusive rights to perform most of Jonson, most of Beaumont and Fletcher, and, indeed, most of Shakespeare. This unequal division of Shakespeare's plays – Davenant's company held rights to just nine of the thirty-six plays in the First Folio, which it gained only after petitioning the Lord Chamberlain – determined to a significant degree not just which plays the Duke's Company would perform but, more importantly, how it was going to compete against the King's Company. Moreover, the relative shortage of new plays in the early 1660s increased Davenant's reliance on the two major elements of his company's repertoire after their new theatre in Lincoln's Inn Fields opened in June 1661: Davenant's own works (*The Siege of Rhodes*, *The Wits*, and *Love and Honour*) and the nine Shakespeare plays allocated to him by the Lord Chamberlain.[14] Davenant's initial reliance on a small number of scripts raises the possibility that his company started out with the performance rights to no plays whatsoever. But it remains beyond doubt that the Duke's Company was seriously disadvantaged from the outset in terms of the range and variety of dramatic works that it could produce.

Within that narrow range, Shakespeare held the predominant place. Yet any account of Shakespeare in the Duke's Company's repertoire – play titles, production dates, frequency of revivals – must begin with the cautionary admission that our knowledge of the Restoration performance calendar is not comprehensive, but the opposite: fragmentary, idiosyncratic, and unbalanced. In 1705 both patent companies began placing advertisements in the *Daily Courant*, a London newspaper first printed three years earlier. These daily theatrical announcements provide a very full performance calendar for the companies from 1705 onward. But for the forty-five years between 1660 and 1705 there is not a single systematic record of theatrical offerings. As Robert D. Hume has meticulously demonstrated, of an estimated 14,067 performances staged by the King's Company and the Duke's Company between 1660 and 1705, we know the play title and date for just 949 performances, with collateral evidence supplying direct or implied information about a further 1,502 performances.[15] In short, we know nothing about 80 per cent of Restoration performances. Pending an

74   SIR WILLIAM DAVENANT AND THE DUKE'S COMPANY

archival discovery of unprecedented magnitude, the full record of Restoration stage performances is forever lost to us.

Moreover, our severely limited knowledge derives from a handful of sources, only some of which (i.e., records from the Lord Chamberlain's Office and the Master of the Revels) are formal or intentional records.[16] Indeed, the best-known source – Samuel Pepys's famous diary – is subjective and covers only the 1660s. Pepys offers information about 342 specific performances, more than any other contemporary source. But his personal account can hardly be considered representative of Restoration theatre, not least because (like many audience members) he returned repeatedly to see favourite productions, including Dryden and Davenant's adaptation of *The Tempest*, and then he repeatedly wrote about them in his diary. Theatre historians often treat Pepys as the first English drama critic even though he aspired to no such status and was unconcerned with providing balanced 'coverage' of London's theatrical scene in his private notes. The most official surviving record, kept by Sir Henry Herbert, Master of the Revels, turns out to be less than revealing. Only fifty-seven performances are noted, all presented by the King's Company and all taking place between 1660 and 1662. Sir Henry's document sheds no light whatsoever on the Duke's Company in those early years. Precisely because these largely disconnected records were never intended to form an integrated whole, they feature significant chronological gaps. As Hume further details, only seven definite play titles and dates are known for the 1669–70 season, while for the 1678–9 season not one single performance can be precisely identified. We simply cannot speak with full confidence about the repertoire of the patent companies in the first half-century of their existence. What we can say with certainty is that the majority of Restoration era performances remain undocumented.

Bearing in mind these profound gaps in the documentary record, what can we still determine about Shakespeare's place in the repertoire of the Duke's Company under Davenant's leadership? In *Shakespeare's Rise to Cultural Prominence* (2018), Emma Depledge compiled a helpful calendar of known

DAVENANT'S REPERTOIRE

or plausibly inferred Shakespeare performances in the patent theatres between 1660 and 1677, relying on information derived primarily from *The London Stage*, an invaluable reference work for all historians of British theatre.[17] The information on Restoration theatre found in *The London Stage* derived primarily from three contemporaneous sources: Pepys's *Diary*, Downes's *Roscius Anglicanus*, and John Evelyn's *Diary*. Based on these combined sources, we can identify forty-four Shakespeare performances staged by the Duke's Company between the opening of its playhouse in Lincoln's Inn Fields in June 1661 and just after Davenant's death in April 1668:

1661–2

Hamlet	24 August 1661
Twelfth Night	11 September 1661
Hamlet	5 December 1661
The Law Against Lovers	15 February 1662
The Law Against Lovers	18 February 1662
Romeo and Juliet	1 March 1662

1662–3

The Law Against Lovers	17 December 1662
Twelfth Night	6 January 1663
Hamlet	9 March 1663
Hamlet	28 May 1663

1663–4

Henry VIII	22 December 1663
Henry VIII	23 December 1663
Henry VIII	26 December 1663
Henry VIII	28 December 1663
Henry VIII	29 December 1663
Henry VIII	30 December 1663
Henry VIII	31 December 1663
Henry VIII	1 January 1664
King Lear	[?] January 1664
Henry VIII	8 February 1664

76 SIR WILLIAM DAVENANT AND THE DUKE'S COMPANY

1664–5

Macbeth	5 November 1664[18]
Macbeth	17 December 1664
Macbeth	28 December 1664

1665–6

London theatres closed in June 1665 due to an outbreak of plague and did not reopen until late November 1666.

1666–7

Macbeth	17 December 1666
Macbeth	28 December 1666
Macbeth	7 January 1667
Macbeth	19 April 1667

1667–8

Macbeth	16 October 1667
Macbeth	6 November 1667
The Tempest	7 November 1667
The Tempest	8 November 1667
The Tempest	9 November 1667
The Tempest	11 November 1667
The Tempest	12 November 1667
The Tempest	13 November 1667
The Tempest	14 November 1667
The Tempest	26 November 1667
The Tempest	12 December 1667
The Tempest	6 January 1668
The Tempest	3 February 1668
The Tempest	14 March 1668
The Tempest	13 April 1668
The Tempest	30 April 1668
The Tempest	11 May 1668

Davenant and Killigrew ran repertory companies whose success depended not upon the steady production of new plays but rather upon revivals of crowd-pleasing works, which for

Davenant included the most popular Restoration versions of Shakespeare. Precisely because new scripts were inherently risky, the Restoration performance repertoire was consistently dominated by those stock plays that had demonstrated their lasting appeal with audiences. An old play that succeeded at the box-office, far from dropping out of the repertoire, became a bankable fixture within it, destined to attract spectators and shore up the company's finances season after season. And yet the most reliable performance calendar that we can put together for the Duke's Company in the 1660s fails to reveal what we know to be true: some Shakespeare plays became central to the company's repertoire, being performed over years and decades. Even though the playhouse longevity of Restoration Shakespeare cannot be fully elaborated in the surviving records, the fact of that longevity is logically implicit in those same records when studied in the aggregate.

Consider, for example, that the calendar lists a mere four performances of *Hamlet*, with none later than 1663. This cannot be anywhere near the full truth. We know from other sources that *Hamlet*, especially with Betterton in the title role, was a successful production for the Duke's Company and later for the United Company, earning a lasting place in the repertoire. John Downes, the prompter for those revivals of *Hamlet*, recalled that '[n]o succeeding Tragedy for several Years got more Reputation, or Money to the [Duke's] Company than this'.[19] When Colley Cibber, in his *Apology* (1740), attempted to 'shew' his readers the 'particular Excellence' of Betterton's acting, he chose Hamlet as the prime example.[20] Cibber, born in 1671, likely never saw Betterton as Hamlet until he joined the United Company as a junior actor in 1690, thirty years after Betterton began acting. Moreover, we know that Betterton played Hamlet for the entirety of his remarkably long career (Figure 4 shows the actor in his signature role). The great tragedian, aged seventy-four, played the Prince of Denmark for the final time on 20 September 1709, nearly fifty years after his first appearance in the role. An abundance of collateral evidence demonstrates the staying power of *Hamlet*

FIGURE 4 *Thomas Betterton as Hamlet*, ink and watercolour drawing, undated. Folger Shakespeare Library, Art Box B565 no. 1. Reproduced under a Creative Commons Attribution-ShareAlike 4.0 International License.

in the Restoration repertoire, even though we have confirmed dates for only a few of the many actual performances.

The lasting popularity of *Macbeth* and *The Tempest* is hinted at in the calendar above – revivals from season to season, performances of the same play on successive days – but even those documented performances fail to capture just how prominent those two plays were in Duke's Company's repertoire, not least because of their lavish scenery and musical interpolations. The number of documented Shakespeare performances in the 1660s is so small that it does not represent either Shakespeare's overall popularity in the Restoration theatre or the box-office appeal of any given Shakespeare play.

Interpreting the performance calendar

What, then, does the performance calendar tell us? Above all, it tells us that Davenant made Shakespeare central to the repertoire of public playhouses in a way that hadn't been true since the 1590s. The Duke's Company performed every last one of the nine Shakespeare plays allocated to it, with just over half appearing in the first six months of the first season at Lincoln's Inn Fields. Davenant's accelerated reliance on Shakespeare – a marked divergence from Killigrew – stands to reason. He had few plays at his disposal and yet his company's success depended upon novelty and variety. The Restoration theatre operated with a rotating repertoire and its audience expected to see different productions, whether the occasional new work or, more typically, revivals of favourite old plays. A different production was offered each day, although a popular one (e.g., the Duke's Company's production of *Henry VIII* at Christmas time in 1663) would be presented several times in succession. A successful new play or adaptation of an older play entered the company's repertoire and would be performed in rotation over succeeding years and decades, giving the company's actors a chance to shine in popular roles and giving audiences productions they enjoyed. By contrast, unpopular productions were quickly withdrawn and disappeared from the repertoire. Thus, Davenant staged different plays in fairly brisk rotation once the Duke's Company began performing at Lincoln's Inn Fields, partly to provide variety for his audiences and partly to determine which plays would become central to his company's success.[21]

The hard pragmatics of setting up and running a repertory company explain why Davenant staged every Shakespeare play at his disposal. But how did he select which ones to perform first? How did those selections relate to his project of 'reforming' old plays and making them fit for his acting company? The performance calendar suggests some answers.

80 SIR WILLIAM DAVENANT AND THE DUKE'S COMPANY

Davenant's first known production of Shakespeare was *Hamlet*, a sensible, obvious and low-risk choice. The title role was already part of Richard Burbage's legend, Davenant had no doubt seen performances of Shakespeare's tragedy at the Blackfriars before 1642, and the play offered a terrific opportunity for Thomas Betterton, the Duke's Company's young leading actor. John Downes recorded that Davenant taught Betterton how to play Hamlet based on his decades-old memory of Joseph Taylor in the role at the Blackfriars.[22] Downes may have exaggerated, but the scenario is perfectly plausible. (We return to this story about actor training in the next chapter.) More importantly, Downes's anecdote suggests a theatrical status for the role of Hamlet that was already in place in the early 1660s.

In revising Shakespeare's play, Davenant moved cautiously but deliberately. The *Hamlet* staged by the Duke's Company in August 1661 was not a full-scale adaptation, let alone a production with interpolated music and dance. Assuming that the 1676 *Hamlet* quarto ('*As it is now Acted at his Highness the Duke of York's Theatre*') was the printed version of the theatrical script that the Duke's Company had been using since 1661, we can see that Davenant's first alterations were conservative yet also predictive of the more radical changes he would make to *Macbeth* and *The Tempest*.[23] The major change to *Hamlet* was reduction: Shakespeare's text (Davenant used Q6, printed in 1637) was shortened by 850 lines and the smaller roles of Voltimand, Cornelius, a Captain, and Reynaldo were written out.[24] Gone were Hamlet's speech to the players and Polonius's advice to Laertes. Hamlet's soliloquies were shortened – as Macbeth's would be a few years later. Phrases deemed vulgar ('grunt') or blasphemous ('by heaven', 'Swounds') were amended or struck out, consistent with the prevailing norms of dramatic censorship. For clarity's sake, plain modern words replaced obscure or archaic ones ('meet / Ophelia here' instead of 'here / Affront Ophelia') while metaphors are toned down or literalized (Hamlet's symbolic 'inkie cloke' becomes a factual 'Mourning cloke'). Aversion to metaphor would soon become a hallmark of Davenant's signature style in adapting Shakespeare.

Playwrights who adapted Shakespeare later in the Restoration were more overtly interested in converting the English history plays and the Roman tragedies into more or less topical political commentaries, especially about the Popish Plot (1678–81) and the Exclusion Crisis (1679–81).[25] Although Davenant was a strong theatrical monarchist – regicide is a major theme in his version of *Macbeth* – his primary concern in adapting Shakespeare was not to tease out contemporary political resonances but rather to 'reform' Shakespeare's plays so that they could succeed on the Restoration stage. Davenant believed that he was modernizing – improving – Shakespeare by changing Shakespeare's texts, making their language relevant and intelligible to his audience, just as using actresses and devising new kinds of scenery were also ways of modernizing the plays in performance. Behind all these changes was a consistent intent: to align the production with the new sensibilities of theatre audiences. For this endeavour he received much praise. As the usually prickly Gerard Langbaine approvingly remarked of *The Law Against Lovers* a few decades later, where Shakespeare's 'Language is rough or obsolete, our Author [i.e., Davenant] has taken care to polish it'.[26]

In the early 1660s, Davenant was more interested in refining a Shakespeare play than in breaking it apart. Thus, his version of *Hamlet* remained structurally the same. Davenant did not invent scenes or create new characters, as he later did in *Macbeth* and *The Tempest*. No changes seem to have been made to accommodate visual or scenic effects. Nor did Davenant think that his *Hamlet* adaptation should replace Shakespeare's prior text. Indeed, the 1676 quarto *retained* the lines omitted in performance, printing them (not always accurately) in quotation marks – as shown in Figure 5 – so that readers could easily distinguish between the adaptation and the original. When the Duke's Company started performing its small share of Shakespeare's plays, it proceeded in the most straightforward and expedient way possible.

Hamlet *Prince of* Denmark.

57

But mad in craft; "'twere good you let him know
" For who that's but Qneen, fair, sober, wife,
" Would from a paddock, from a Bat, a Gib,
" Such dear concernings hide ? who would do so ?
" No, in despight of sense and secresie
" Unpeg the basket on the houses top,
" Let the birds flie, and like the famous Ape,
" To try conclusions in the basket creep,
" And break your own neck down.
    Qu. Be thou assur'd if words be made of breath,
And breath of life, I have no life to breath
What thou hast said to me.
    Ham. I must to *England*, you know that.
    Qu. Alack I had forgot,
'Tis so concluded on.
    " *Ham.* There's letters seal'd, and my two School-fellows,
" whom I will trust as I will Adders fang'd,
" They bear the mandate, they must sweep my way,
" And marshal me to knavery; let it work,
" For 'tis the sport to have the Engineer
" Hoist with his own petar, and't shall go hard
" But I will delve one yard below their Mines,
" And blow them at the Moon : O 'tis most sweet
" When in one line two crafts directly meet.
This man will set me packing,
I'll lug the guts into the neighbour room.
Mother good night indeed, this Counseller
Is now most still, most secret, and most grave,
Who was in's life a most foolish prating knave.
Come Sir, to draw toward an end with you.
Good night mother.   [*Exit.*

ACT IV. SCENE I.

Enter King and Queen with Rosencraus *and* Guildenstern.
King. Here's matter in these sighs, these profound heaves,
You must translate, 'tis fit we understand them :
Where is your son ?
    Qu. Bestow this place on us a little while.[*Exeunt* Ros. *and* Guild.
Ah mine own Lord, what have I seen to night ?
    King. What *Gertrard*, how does *Hamlet* ?

                             Qu. Mad

FIGURE 5 *[Sir William Davenant],* The tragedy of Hamlet Prince of Denmark. As it is now acted at his Highness the Duke of York's Theatre, *1676, Folger Shakespeare Library. Reproduced under a Creative Commons Attribution-ShareAlike 4.0 International License. This page extract shows the dialogue between Gertrude and Hamlet at the end of the closet scene (Act 3, Scene 3). Shakespeare's omitted lines appear in quotation marks.*

DAVENANT'S REPERTOIRE
83

Indeed, Davenant did not immediately rush into writing versions of Shakespeare that blended with the emerging genre of dramatick opera. In 1662, for example, he produced *The Law Against Lovers*, an odd conflation of *Measure for Measure* and *Much Ado about Nothing* that included a few songs for Mary ('Moll') Davis and others. But his most successful and consequential Shakespeare adaptations were not performed until his company's fourth season. The earliest known performance of Davenant's *Macbeth* took place in November 1664 and his version of *The Tempest* (co-written with John Dryden) appeared three years later, in what turned out to be the final season before his death. The other Shakespeare plays staged by the Duke's Company – *Twelfth Night*, *Romeo and Juliet*, *King Lear* and *Henry VIII* – seem to have been staged with little or no textual revision. If Davenant had adapted any of those five plays in any significant manner, the resulting scripts would eventually have been published, either in quarto (as were *Hamlet, Macbeth* and *The Tempest*) or in *The Works of Sr William Davenant K^t* (1673), posthumously published in folio 'Out of the Authours Originall Copies'.[27] But there are no such printed texts, indicating that almost certainly there were no such adapted scripts.

In *Roscius Anglicanus*, John Downes, who had direct knowledge of the Duke's Company's productions, carefully distinguished between performances of Shakespeare's unaltered text ('*Lear*, being Acted exactly as Mr. Shakespear Wrote it') and performances of adaptations (*Macbeth* 'alter'd by Sir William Davenant', 'the *Tempest* alter'd by Sir William Davenant and Mr Dryden').[28] Figure 6 shows the title page of Davenant's adaptation of *Macbeth*, from which the adapter's name is conspicuously absent. Downes referred explicitly to James Howard's lost tragicomic version of *Romeo and Juliet* in which the young lovers survive, remarking that in later years the Duke's Company staged it 'Alternately' with Shakespeare's original tragedy.[29] If Davenant had also adapted *Romeo and Juliet*, then his company would have performed it and Downes would have mentioned it. As the Duke's Company's prompter, Downes copied out the actors' parts; thus, he would have known better

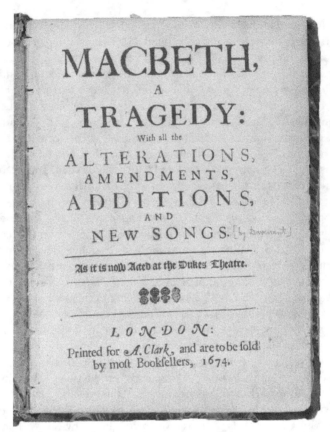

FIGURE 6 *Sir William Davenant, adaptation of* Macbeth, *1674, title page, Folger Shakespeare Library. Reproduced under a Creative Commons Attribution-ShareAlike 4.0 International License.*

than anyone whether a rehearsal script was a new adaption, an old adaptation or essentially the text as found in earlier editions. If Downes did not mention a particular Shakespeare adaptation, we can safely assume that was because it did not exist.

Thus, both direct and indirect theatrical evidence provide a consistent template for how Davenant approached Shakespeare's dramatic works. Most of the nine plays at his disposal were performed more or less unaltered, at least in terms of plot and structure, as we have outlined above with respect to *Hamlet*. Yet when Davenant chose to adapt Shakespeare, he did so imaginatively and vigorously, creating the standout productions of his career. Over decades, theatre history scholarship has skewed our understanding of how textually interventionist Davenant's Shakespeare repertoire actually was. Much scholarship (including our own, in this book) has focused on *Macbeth* and *The Tempest*, partly because they were his most radical versions of Shakespeare and partly because they survived in the playhouse for well over a century. This makes sense: such adaptations are interesting from a dramaturgical perspective, were popular with audiences, and generated a long documentary trail. By contrast, scholarship has paid much less attention the other seven Shakespeare plays that Davenant staged in the 1660s. The historiographical result is the misimpression that Davenant radically adapted *every* Shakespeare play that his company performed. The truth is more circumspect: Davenant rewrote about half the Shakespeare plays belonging to Duke's Company and developed his approach over a number of years.

Looking at the matter from a business perspective can be enlightening. The wholesale adaptations of Shakespeare for which Davenant remains best known demanded an enormous investment of his time. The modest cuts made to *Hamlet*, Davenant's first Shakespeare adaptation, were thoughtful, not arbitrary. When he merged portions of *Measure for Measure* and *Much Ado about Nothing* to create *The Law Against Lovers*, Davenant could hardly have created that hybrid play without considerable planning and discernment. In addition to revising the poetry of *Macbeth*, which required surgically precise revisions to hundreds of lines, Davenant wrote four new scenes (including two between Macduff and Lady Macduff, who never meet in Shakespeare's play) and cut the Porter's scene. In the version of *The Tempest* that he wrote with Dryden, just under a third of Shakespeare's Folio text survives. Nor could he have created additional or expanded roles for actresses – a necessity in the Restoration – in a casual

86   SIR WILLIAM DAVENANT AND THE DUKE'S COMPANY

or haphazard way. These amended scripts were not the work of an afternoon. It took the luxury of time for Davenant to adapt Shakespeare's dramatic poetry in a way that would appeal to Restoration audiences.

Yet time was precisely what Davenant lacked, especially in the first year or so after he received the royal patent. He had patrons to flatter. He had financing to secure.[30] He had lawsuits to fight. He had a theatre to build. He had scenery to construct. He had actors – and actresses – to train. He had rehearsals to run. He had audiences to attract. The last thing a busy theatrical patentee could afford was to spend weeks revising a single script. Particularly in the summer and autumn of 1661, expediency must have been a paramount virtue for Davenant. In those demanding first years, he was content to trim a Shakespearean text, but not remake it. Only later, when the frenetic pace of running a theatre had slackened a bit – because the Duke's Company finally had a sufficient number of reliable productions in its performance roster, each ready to be staged on short notice – could Davenant devote the necessary time to preparing the two Shakespeare adaptations for which he is best remembered and which in his own time were box-office gold.

A contrast with Shakespeare's place in the King's Company's repertoire for the same period is instructive. It bears remembering that Killigrew's company enjoyed a wholly disproportionate share of the pre-1642 repertoire, including twenty-seven of the thirty-six works in the First Folio. According to Depledge's tabulation, the King's Company staged the following Shakespeare plays between November 1660 and the end of the 1667–68 season:

1660–1

1 Henry IV	8 November 1660
The Merry Wives of Windsor	9 November 1660
The Merry Wives of Windsor	5 December 1660
Othello	8 December 1660
1 Henry IV	31 December 1660
1 Henry IV	4 June 1661

DAVENANT'S REPERTOIRE

1661–2
The Merry Wives of Windsor	25 September 1661
Hamlet	27 November 1661

1662–3
A Midsummer Night's Dream	9 September 1662

1663–4
No recorded performances of Shakespeare

1664–5
No recorded performances of Shakespeare

1665–6
London theatres closed in June 1665 due to an outbreak of plague and did not reopen until late November 1666.

1666–7
Sauny the Scot [*The Taming of the Shrew*]	[?] April 1667

1667–8
The Merry Wives of Windsor	[?] August 1667
Sauny the Scot	1 November 1667
1 Henry IV	2 November 1667
1 Henry IV	7 January 1668

Davenant held the rights to nine Shakespeare plays and staged them all, with forty-four different performances documented. Killigrew held the rights to twenty-seven Shakespeare plays but staged only six of them, with just fourteen different performances documented. John Downes reliably listed *Julius Caesar* and *Titus Andronicus* among the old dramas acted by the King's Company, even though other records fail to supply any precise date for any performances of those two plays.[31] Taking those additional plays into account, Killigrew's company seems to

88 SIR WILLIAM DAVENANT AND THE DUKE'S COMPANY

have performed only eight of the twenty-seven Shakespeare plays allocated to it. Davenant's repertoire included some Shakespeare every season, with *Henry VIII*, *Macbeth*, and *The Tempest* being clear favourites with the audience. The surviving record (patchy, admittedly) suggests that Killigrew's interest in Shakespeare in the same period was far less consistent. There are fewer recorded performances of Shakespeare by the King's Company overall, with none in the seasons of 1663–4 and 1664–5, the precise time when the Duke's Company was mounting its successful and lavish productions of *Henry VIII* and *Macbeth*. This does not mean that Killigrew's company staged no Shakespeare whatsoever in those two seasons. But the disparity in the surviving records would imply a corresponding disparity in how much Shakespeare each company performed. We don't know the exact number of performances; but even so, the evidence suggests that the Duke's Company always performed more Shakespeare than its rival company did.

One reason why the King's Company staged Shakespeare less often (perhaps far less often) than the Duke's Company was because, as we have seen, it possessed the acting rights to many other pre-1642 plays. In picking and choosing from among the many old plays available to him, Killigrew sidelined Shakespeare. Indeed, he much preferred the works of Beaumont and Fletcher, which had been more popular than Shakespeare's in the decades before 1642. In other words, Killigrew was reinstating the pre-Civil War hierarchy of dramatists. On this precise matter the archival record is unusually plentiful. As Master of the Revels, Sir Henry Herbert kept a list of every play acted by the King's Company between November 1660 and July 1662 so that he could determine the licensing fees payable to him, a factor that argues for the list's accuracy. In those first two seasons, the company staged at least fifty-eight plays, of which twenty were by John Fletcher, seven by James Shirley, three by Ben Jonson and three (*1 Henry IV*, *The Merry Wives of Windsor*, *Othello*) by Shakespeare.[32] Downes's *Roscius Anglicanus* corroborates this imbalance in his list of the King's Company's 'Principal Old Stock Plays', which likewise shows Fletcher as predominant.[33]

Killigrew staged Shakespeare less frequently than Davenant did because he had (so it seemed to him) many better alternatives. Davenant staged Shakespeare more frequently than Killigrew did for precisely the opposite reason: other than his own plays, he had few alternatives. Because Killigrew had little reason to put Shakespeare at the heart of his company's repertoire – indeed, he never did so – he had little reason to be much interested in adapting Shakespeare for performance. Davenant revised or adapted five of his nine Shakespeare plays, whereas Killigrew staged Shakespeare's own text almost exclusively. John Lacy's *Sauny the Scot* (1667), a prose version of *The Taming of the Shrew*, marks the one time that the King's Company performed a Shakespeare adaptation. As we will see in Chapter 6, the only other time when the King's Company experimented with Shakespeare was in the 1670s, when it staged parodies of the spectacular operatic versions of *Macbeth* and *The Tempest* produced by the Duke's Company at Dorset Garden Theatre.

An unusual irony of Shakespeare performance history is that during the Restoration, the company that felt itself to be the successor to the King's Men, and on that basis secured the acting rights to three-quarters of the plays in the First Folio, actually performed very little Shakespeare. The self-proclaimed lineal descendant of Shakespeare's own company demonstrated little desire to claim its full inheritance. By contrast, the company with access to a limited share of Shakespeare's dramatic works was the one that invested in them heavily. Davenant was the one who made Shakespeare central to his company's repertoire and reputation. It was he who devoted time and ingenuity to crafting his up-to-date versions of Shakespeare. It was he who from the start performed Shakespeare with movable scenery. It was he who made Shakespeare lucrative. He did all that with just nine plays.

SIR WILLIAM DAVENANT AND THE DUKE'S COMPANY

Restoration Shakespeare at court

Thus far, we have considered the Shakespeare repertoire – to the extent that it has been documented – for public performances staged by the patent companies in the 1660s. But the tradition of private court theatricals that existed under Elizabeth I, James I, and Charles I was soon revived by Charles II. Like their pre-Civil predecessors, the Restoration acting companies were invited to perform at court some of the plays from their public repertoire, both new works and revivals. The first such documented performance took place on 19 November 1660, when the King's Company staged Jonson's *Epicoene* at the Cockpit-in-Court.[34] In her impressive archival study of Restoration court theatre, Eleanore Boswell estimates that about twenty performances annually were staged at Whitehall during the reigns of Charles II (1660–85) and James II (1685–8), first in the Cockpit-in-Court and later in the Hall Theatre.[35] As evidenced in the Lord Chamberlain's papers, a good share of those performances included pieces presented by visiting companies of foreign actors, mainly French and Italian.[36]

The old tradition of court masques, which reached its high point during the reign of Charles I, when Ben Jonson collaborated with Inigo Jones, was likewise revived in the Restoration. Under Charles II, however, such private entertainments were, in the main, staged less frequently and without the expensive scenes and machines that Jones had designed decades earlier for the Banqueting House at Whitehall. Davenant was a living embodiment of that rich tradition, and thus could have revived the practice in the 1660s. So why were court masques generally less popular in the Restoration? A main reason is that Charles II was not awash in money. The young monarch could not afford to pay for bespoke theatrical extravaganzas staged one time only for a coterie Whitehall audience. Moreover, there was no reason for the king to pay repeatedly for theatrical spectacle when he could easily find it in the playhouses. Charles II was the first English monarch to watch a play in a public theatre and at a time when the patent companies made increased use of the changeable scenery, visual effects, and musical interpolations previously seen only in court masques. Why should a cash-strapped court subsidize theatrical marvels when the patent companies staged them at their own expense? This 'outsourcing' of lavish production values and dramatick opera to the public theatres was especially true for the Duke's Company and all the more so after its move to Dorset Garden in 1671.

Just as our knowledge of the public repertoire for the Restoration acting companies is largely incomplete, our knowledge of the court repertoire for the same period is likewise fragmentary. Boswell uncovered documentary evidence for 135 of the 159 known or conjectured performances at Whitehall between 1660 and 1700, which she estimated as no more than one-quarter of the total number of such performances. Bearing in mind that what we know about Restoration court theatre may not reflect the totality of actual performances, we can nonetheless draw some reasoned conclusions. An immediate observation is that the imbalance in the public theatre repertoire was only exaggerated in court theatre. Among the thirty-four 'old' plays likely to have been performed at Whitehall, comedies outnumbered tragedies and tragicomedies. Beaumont and Fletcher were the most frequently performed dramatists, with fourteen of their works presented at court. Shakespeare came second, lagging well behind Beaumont and Fletcher but only barely ahead of Ben Jonson and James Shirley. We know conclusively that five Shakespeare plays – all tragedies – were performed at court: *Macbeth* (December 1666), *Hamlet* (April 1686), *Othello* (November 1686), *Julius Caesar* (April 1687), and *King Lear* (May 1687, February 1688). No doubt other plays were acted at court, possibly some by Shakespeare. But among the surviving records in the Lord Chamberlain's Office, there is evidence for these five plays only, amounting to a mere six performances in total.

The Shakespeare plays selected for performance and the dates of the performances are both revealing. As discussed

92   SIR WILLIAM DAVENANT AND THE DUKE'S COMPANY

earlier in this chapter, Shakespeare was not an important pre-Civil War playwright for the King's Company. We cannot therefore be surprised that according to the surviving records they staged not a single work by Shakespeare at court. But we might be surprised that Shakespeare's central and lasting place in the Duke's Company's repertoire – although based on a small number of highly popular plays – was not reflected in command performances at Whitehall. Indeed, *Macbeth* is the only play by Shakespeare known to have been acted at court during Charles II's entire reign.[37] This neglect was certainly not because Shakespeare (as adapted in the Restoration) was unpopular with elite audiences. The king and his retinue witnessed the premiere of the Dryden-Davenant version of *The Tempest* at Lincoln's Inn Fields on 7 November 1667, with Pepys observing that 'the house [was] mighty full'.[38] Moreover, most of the Shakespeare plays frequently revived by the Duke's Company – *Hamlet*, *Macbeth*, and *The Tempest* – featured plots that condemned usurpation and celebrated the return of rightful kings, themes inherently pleasing to a formerly exiled monarch.

Shakespeare's near invisibility in Restoration court theatre must have been because the Cockpit-in-Court and the Hall Theatre were both inadequately equipped (as we discussed in the previous chapter) to present Shakespeare with the scenic effects and musical episodes that were integral to the most successful productions staged by the Duke's Company in their own theatre. Davenant's *Macbeth* was performed in the Hall Theatre the same year it opened to acclaim at Lincoln's Inn Fields. Indeed, its public success was likely the reason Charles II commanded a private performance. No doubt some movable scenery was used in the Hall Theatre, because it was built to accommodate painted wings and shutters. Betterton and his fellow actors from the Duke's Company would have taken their customary acting and singing roles, with music played by violinists from the court band. Yet as Pepys unhappily observed, 'the House, though very fine, [was] yet bad for the voice – for hearing'.[39]

With serious acoustical defects, the Hall Theatre was not an ideal venue for the spectacular and operatic versions of Shakespeare pioneered by Davenant at Lincoln's Inn Fields and taken to new heights by Betterton at Dorset Garden. Tellingly, the 1666 performance of Davenant's *Macbeth* is the only recorded instance of 'blockbuster' Shakespeare attempted at court. The other tragedies chosen for performance at Whitehall – *Hamlet*, *Julius Caesar*, *King Lear*, and *Othello* – lacked musical episodes and could have been performed with minimal scenery. Although it remains a matter for conjecture, it seems reasonable enough to conclude that Restoration Shakespeare as a distinctive performance genre was a phenomenon that belonged wholly to the commercial public theatre.

5

Acting Restoration Shakespeare

The term 'classical theatre', often reduced to Shakespeare, denotes a niche segment of the theatrical profession today. We speak of leading classical actors like Harriet Walter and Kenneth Branagh, visionary classical directors like Katie Mitchell and Thomas Ostermeier, and prestigious classical theatre companies like the Royal Shakespeare Company in Stratford-upon-Avon and Shakespeare's Globe in London. Drama students the world over worry about their classical audition monologue. A defining element of classical drama is that it feels different from modern or contemporary drama in practically every way: narrative, structure, characterization, language, ideology, and the demands it makes upon actors and directors. Today, working in classical theatre is rhetorically constructed as the worthy but poorly recompensed alternative to the tarnished but lucrative experience of appearing in soap operas or action movies. Being a Shakespearean remains a mark of esteem and prestige in the entertainment industry, a last holdout of Bardolatry's cultural capital. If you want money, land a role in a sitcom. If you want respect, play Cleopatra. A piteous predicament, as Juliet's Nurse would say.

But it's our predicament. It never arose in the Restoration, when acting and staging Shakespeare were not so very different from acting and staging any other type of play. It bears recalling

96   SIR WILLIAM DAVENANT AND THE DUKE'S COMPANY

that every dramatic work performed in the Restoration – old, new, or adapted – was written within a fairly narrow chronological span. Fewer than fifty years separate Shakespeare's last play written for the King's Men from Davenant's first production for the Duke's Company. In the 1660s, Shakespeare's plays were old enough to feel behind the times – hence, they needed revising – but not so old as to have petrified into unalterable classics or forgettable relics. True, Dryden lauded Shakespeare as one of the 'Gyant Race, before the Flood'.[1] But the destructive flood waters of the Interregnum had at last receded. Now was the moment to restore Shakespeare to the London stage, which meant adapting his plays to become good vehicles for modern actors and receptive to interpolated music and intermedia spectacle.

In adapting Shakespeare's plays to align with Restoration theatrical sensibilities, Davenant showed that he was not fixated on reviving an 'authentic' Shakespeare. Indeed, the normative discourse of Shakespearean authenticity that has characterized a fair amount of theatre scholarship and theatre practice over the past century did not exist in the Restoration. For the founder of the Duke's Company, the question was not how to return to Shakespeare but how to *recycle* Shakespeare so that (as we discussed in the previous chapter, on repertoire) his plays could channel the imagination and energy of the Restoration stage. In his 1663 poem addressed to Charles II, Davenant made clear his ambition to 'reform the publick Mirrour' – his preferred image for the stage – so that the 'Dead' may teach 'their living Race'.[2] Making good on that vow, Davenant preserved Shakespeare for posterity by making Shakespeare his contemporary, thus establishing a precedent whose artistic vitality and timeliness have never waned.

In a corresponding way, Davenant seems to have felt no driving obsession to recreate how actors performed Shakespeare's roles in Shakespeare's time, assuming (which we do not) that such specific knowledge survived into the 1660s and beyond. Cherished anecdotes about Davenant teaching Betterton to act Hamlet in the same way that Shakespeare

ACTING RESTORATION SHAKESPEARE 97

taught actors in the King's Men are less empirical realities than meditations on the Restoration theatre's historiographical fragility, an argument we elaborate later in this chapter. After all, how could Davenant's new scenes in *Macbeth*, new characters in *The Tempest* and new plot in *The Law Against Lovers* recuperate a performance precedent? The material was new, so by definition there was no precedent.

If acting Shakespeare had been the secret of success for a Restoration theatre company, then surely Killigrew would have produced more of the many Shakespeare plays for which his company held the performance rights. But the very idea of a 'Shakespearean' actor would have made little sense to performers like Thomas Betterton and Mary Saunderson or to spectators like Samuel and Elizabeth Pepys. There were good plays, there were bad plays. There was good acting, there was bad acting. That Shakespeare eventually became the standard by which great acting was judged speaks to the exceptionality of Shakespeare the dramatist as articulated and reinforced by the cultural nationalism of Bardolatry that David Garrick advanced in the second half of the eighteenth century. But for a Restoration actor, performing Shakespeare was not something exceptional. And so, in this chapter we contend that Davenant, instead of being guided by a particular vision for acting Shakespeare, was guided by a grand holistic vision for the theatre that could be realized in part by acting Shakespeare.

The acting company

Restoration acting cannot be usefully discussed in the abstract, because it was mostly undertaken by a small, precise, and knowable group: the successive members of the Duke's Company and the King's Company. In the late autumn of 1660, the new patentees dissolved their short-lived united company and set about forming their own separate companies. Davenant (as discussed in Chapter 2) gravitated toward the cohort of younger and less experienced male actors who had

98   SIR WILLIAM DAVENANT AND THE DUKE'S COMPANY

been performing under John Rhodes's management at the Cockpit in Drury Lane. On 5 November 1660, he formally engaged his new recruits: Thomas Betterton, Thomas Sheppey, Robert Nokes, James Nokes, Thomas Lovell, John Mosley, Cave Underhill, Robert Turner and Thomas Lilleston. Henry Harris, although not part of Rhodes's company, was named in the contract as both actor and painter. The agreement stipulated that these men – who became sharers in the new company – would perform 'all manner of tragedies, comedies and plays' in any theatre in the Cities of London and Westminster 'until the said Sir William Davenant shall provide a new theatre with scenes'. While Davenant prepared his scenic theatre in Lincoln's Inn Fields, his newly assembled company took up residence in the old Salisbury Court Theatre and began acting there no later than 29 January 1661, when Pepys saw a performance of John Fletcher and William Rowley's *The Maid in the Mill*.[3]

But the Duke's Company was lacking something: women. Through his involvement with court masques in the 1630s and early 1640s – productions in which female royalty, courtiers, and singers took the stage – Davenant first learned how to create performances that included women. Queen Henrietta Maria, adorned in a Caroline version of Amazonian dress, played the heroine in *Salmacida Spolia* (1640), a character who wondrously appears descending from heaven in a stage machine designed by Inigo Jones.[4] In the dedicatory letter addressed to the Duke of York in the 1673 folio edition of Davenant's works, Mary Davenant respectfully notes (as we observed in Chapter 1) that the late queen consort 'often smil'd upon his Endeavours'.[5] In the 1656 private staging of *The Siege of Rhodes* at Rutland House, Catherine Coleman sang the role of Ianthe and a still unidentified woman appeared as Roxalana. Thus, when the patent companies established themselves in 1660, Davenant enjoyed the advantage of being the only person in the London theatre world with significant experience of collaborating with women and creating dramatic characters expressly for them. This expertise markedly influenced his Shakespeare adaptations, which are notable for

ACTING RESTORATION SHAKESPEARE 99

their expanded opportunities for female performers, including new scenes for Lady Macduff and Lady Macbeth and new female roles in both *The Tempest* (Milcha, Dorinda, and the breeches role Hippolito) and *The Law Against Lovers* (Viola, younger sister to Beatrice). Among Davenant's first group of actresses, Mary Saunderson played Lady Macbeth, Jane Long acted Lady Macduff and in all likelihood Hippolito, while Mary ('Moll') Davis as Viola sang 'Wake all ye dead!' and danced a lively saraband with Benedick, Balthazar, and Beatrice to the percussive rhythm of castanets.[6] The invented role of Viola added little to the hybrid plot of *The Law Against Lovers* – but added a great deal to the performance.

The presence of women on the Restoration stage was neither guaranteed nor universally welcome. Women are not mentioned in the initial royal warrant of 21 August 1660. No evidence suggests that the insurgent companies at the Red Bull, Salisbury Court and the Cockpit in Drury Lane included actresses in the spring and summer of 1660. The young actor Edward Kynaston, praised by Pepys as 'the loveliest lady that ever I saw in my life', successfully reprised the Elizabethan convention of boy actors by playing female roles at the Cockpit in the summer of 1660.[7] Indeed, the first reference to a female performer in the English Restoration theatre is a complaint from the older men in the King's Company – who all started as boy actors before the Civil War – that Killigrew had 'obliged' them to 'act with women'.[8]

Davenant, however, was always committed to including women in his company, and in 1664 mounted a novel production of *The Parson's Wedding* with an all-female cast, no doubt seeking to exploit the sexual charms of the actresses. His initial terms of agreement with the male actors granted him ten out of fifteen shares in the Duke's Company in recognition of the costs he would incur for looking after and training all the 'Women that are to performe or represent Womens parts'.[9] William and Mary Davenant welcomed four of the new actresses – Hester Davenport, Mary Saunderson, Mary Davis and Jane Long – into their home, built adjacent to

100 SIR WILLIAM DAVENANT AND THE DUKE'S COMPANY

the new theatre at Lincoln's Inn Fields. The female recruits lacked not just experience, but role models: there were no legendary predecessors to learn from because they themselves were the first generation. No one understood this unusual circumstance better than Davenant, who took it upon himself to instruct the women and, effectively, to become their guardian, in a female version of the traditional male apprentice system. The fact that Mary Saunderson, one of the Duke's Company's first female actors, married Thomas Betterton, one of the Duke's Company's first male actors, speaks to the household sensibility that Davenant fostered, in which unity triumphed over division.

Davenant's close custody of his actresses may now seem paternalistic, but his methods were unquestionably successful. Whereas Killigrew soon quarrelled with his senior actors, Davenant inspired confidence and loyalty in the Duke's Company's actors. A good number of Davenant's first cohort of male actors were tradesmen or shopkeepers. Having come of age as apprentices, they understood the need for an acknowledged 'master' craftsman to train the rising generation. They would have brought to the theatre the bonds of solidarity and fraternity inculcated in them by London's venerable livery companies. Granted, some turnover in actors was a fact of life in the Restoration theatre, especially when younger women married or became mistresses to aristocrats or even to a monarch.[10] But because Davenant's company was well-managed, it enjoyed greater stability in personnel than did Killigrew's company.

The long-term value of stability in the acting ensemble cannot be underestimated, because the Restoration theatre, for all its visual display and machine marvels, was essentially an actor's theatre. Every new play performed by the Duke's Company – whether Davenant's semi-operatic version of *Macbeth* (1664), George Etherege's comedy *Love in a Tub* (1664), or the Earl of Orrery's tragedy *Mustapha* (1665) – was written or adapted with particular actors in mind. Indeed, the same quartet of leading actors appeared in all three productions:

Thomas Betterton (Macbeth, Lord Beaufort, Solyman the Magnificent), Mary Saunderson (Lady Macbeth, Graciana, Roxalana), Henry Harris (Macduff, Sir Frederick Frolic, Mustapha), and Jane Long (Lady Macduff, Widow Rich, Zarma). Davenant knew that scripts had to accommodate actors, not the other way around. Shakespeare had known the same, because his plays had also been written with specific performers in mind. As a theatrical vehicle, a Restoration play – like a pre-1642 play – was a function of who would perform it. Such bespoke dramaturgy is especially apparent with actresses. Davenant created the role of Beatrice's younger sister Viola in *The Law Against Lovers* so that Mary Davis could play to her strengths: singing and dancing. According to Pepys, Davis was so talented that her presence in the Duke's Company made up for the loss of Hester Davenport, whose departure risked 'spoil[ing] the house'.[11]

A few years later, in 1664, Davenant needed a new play with a pair of contrasting female roles to compete with the success of Sir Robert Howard and John Dryden's *The Indian Queen*, a heroic tragedy embellished with music, dance and supernatural spirits. (The King's Company had produced *The Indian Queen* to compete directly with the Duke's Company's lavish and successful production of *Henry VIII*.) The result was his adaptation of *Macbeth*, which featured a greatly enhanced role for Lady Macduff, who becomes not just the moral counterpoint to Lady Macbeth but an eloquent dramatic heroine in her own right. The breeches role of Hippolito in Davenant and Dryden's version of *The Tempest* – a character whose scenes are replete with sexual innuendo – was doubtless invented as yet another opportunity to showcase the erotic appeal of women on the Restoration stage, as was Davenant's decision to cast a woman as Ariel. It cannot be emphasized enough that when Davenant adapted Shakespeare he did so with his own actors in mind – their strengths, their limitations, their allure, their temperament – a collaborative awareness that led him to expand some roles, eliminate others, and invent new ones altogether. He knew – as Shakespeare before him

102 SIR WILLIAM DAVENANT AND THE DUKE'S COMPANY

knew – how to create productions that showcased his company's actors.

Davenant did not live to see the full results of his artistic leadership, one of which was the enduring popularity of star performers. Some of the greatest Restoration actors – Thomas Betterton, Anne Bracegirdle, Elizabeth Barry – held the stage for decades, regularly appearing several times each week. Retaining favourite actors was important for a company's success because their appeal was a major reason why audiences returned to the theatre, often watching multiple performances of the same play. Pepys, who saw Davenant's *Macbeth* at least four times in eleven months, always noted with disappointment when Betterton did not perform: 'I was vexed to see Young (who is but a bad actor at best) act Macbeth in the room of Baterton [*sic*], who poor man is sick!'[12] Pepys's regret that Betterton did not play Macbeth captures something of the aura that encircled Restoration theatrical stars, who became identified with the roles they acted.[13]

Whether low comedian or tragedy queen, a Restoration actor's claim to a role was ironclad. Once cast in a part, an actor would normally continue to play it in subsequent revivals. In a repertory system, where any of twenty or thirty plays might be performed on short notice, the link between actor and role (as we have previously noted) was less a tribute to individual performers than a practical necessity.[14] In Betterton's last full theatrical season, he was still performing Shakespeare's great tragic heroes: Hamlet, Macbeth, Othello, and Lear. The role of Hamlet belonged especially to Betterton throughout his long career, as noted in the preceding chapter. That his ageing figure and weakened form were eventually incongruous with the youthful Prince of Denmark was poignantly apparent to every spectator. That Betterton's physique was less than heroic – 'short thick neck', 'stooped in the shoulders', 'corpulent body', 'thick legs with large feet', as detailed in Anthony Aston's unsparing head-to-toe inventory – had always been apparent.[15] Yet none of these incongruities mattered when compared to the unshakeable bond between the greatest actor and his greatest part. Indeed, the main reason we have multiple eyewitness accounts of Betterton as Hamlet – beginning with Pepys the spectator writing in his diary in 1668 and ending with Richard Steele the critic writing pseudonymously as 'Mr Greenhat' in *The Tatler* in 1709 – is that Betterton owned the role for decades. Nor was the link between actor and role limited to a handful of company members. Cave Underhill played the First Gravedigger in *Hamlet* for the Duke's Company in 1661 and then for decades afterward, reprising the comic role for his benefit at Drury Lane in 1709.

The difficulty of performing so many different roles on short notice – and having to perform on 200 days during a season that ran from October to June – was reduced by the highly efficient custom of actors specializing in a 'line of business': heroine, hero, villain, lover, fop, ingénue, or clown. '[E]very significant actor in the Restoration,' as Peter Holland has observed, 'had some clearly defined type of role in comedy and another in tragedy at each stage of his [or her] career'.[16] Thus, Betterton played Hamlet and Falstaff in the same season, an unlikely scenario for an actor today. Far from restricting opportunities, lines of business ensured that certain kinds of roles would always be available to certain kinds of actors. When Davenant and Dryden adapted *The Tempest*, they knew from the outset that Betterton was destined to play Prospero – the ruler, the protagonist – while Henry Harris was well-suited for Ferdinand – a lover who could sing John Banister's charming 'Echo Song'. Jane Long, skilled in breeches roles, would have been the logical choice for Hippolito, a sexually titillating role that would never have been played by the stately Mary Saunderson. In this way, Restoration actors built up a repertoire of physical behaviours, emotional comportment, and vocal expressions that matched the types of characters they regularly played. Thus, when learning a new part, Restoration actors did not start from scratch; rather, they drew upon their own embodied repertoire to create a new character. In turn, accumulated expertise in character types reduced a company's need for lengthy rehearsals. A Restoration actor – just like their

104 SIR WILLIAM DAVENANT AND THE DUKE'S COMPANY

Elizabethan and Jacobean predecessors – could easily play four different roles over six days, with not much notice as to which play was going to be performed and when.

Diversity in the Restoration theatrical repertoire – tragedy, comedy, tragicomedy, history, dramatick opera – reminds us that the real fault line in productions was *genre*, not playwright and not whether a play was old, new, or adapted. For actors, it didn't much matter if a tragedy was written by Shakespeare, Davenant, or the Earl of Orrery. What mattered was knowing that the play was a tragedy and not a comedy. Thus, for Betterton, playing the title role in Shakespeare's *Henry VIII* and Solyman the Magnificent in Davenant's *The Siege of Rhodes* (Parts 1 and 2) and Orrery's sequel *Mustapha* were all of a piece: each character was a monarch, each play a tragedy, each production rich in music and lavish in scenery and costume. Genre itself determined how an actor approached the script and performed a character, drawing on the kinetic and expressive conventions of a particular line of business. This consistent pattern of theatrical practice resists any easy assumption that acting Shakespeare in the Restoration was a distinctive or exceptional undertaking.

Training

The master–apprentice system of training boy actors – who, in time, became adult actors – worked well for the theatre of Shakespeare and his contemporaries. All instruction was conducted in-house and over a sufficiently long period to ensure a reliable supply of future talent.[17] Yet what worked before the Civil War would not work after the Restoration. As Davenant surely understood, resuming old ways of actor training was not viable. Boys were no longer needed. Women, who were needed, could not legally become apprentices. And yet the women in the Duke's Company had to be instructed by someone because they had no experience whatsoever. Appointing stage veterans to train the beginners was no easy task, because almost all the

ACTING RESTORATION SHAKESPEARE 105

experienced actors – that is, the middle-aged men who had begun their careers as squeaking boys – belonged to the King's Company. Davenant's male actors had little experience: for the most part, just several months of performances under John Rhodes at the Cockpit.[18] Neither company could afford to spend years grooming the next generation of performers. Sooner rather than later, Davenant and Killigrew needed performers they could confidently put on the stage. There were princes and princesses to act.

Over time, senior members in both companies would be expected to train and mentor novices. In the final decade of his career, Betterton was paid the handsome sum of fifty pounds per annum – in addition to his earnings as actor and manager – for teaching younger members of the company. Mary Saunderson is particularly remembered for successfully training the young Anne Bracegirdle. Many newcomers eventually learned the art of acting by playing first in Dublin or the English provinces, with the most talented being hired by the London theatres. But all that lay in the future. In 1660, no such career paths existed. Yet theatres were open for business, and their managers needed actors.

Killigrew, who had no experience in supervising actors, seems to have rushed to open the doors of his theatre on Vere Street, putting women on the stage before they were ready to perform in public. In January 1661, Pepys complained that the King's Company's production of Middleton's *The Widow* was 'wronged by the womens [*sic*] being much to seek in their parts', meaning that their performances left much to be desired.[19] By contrast, Davenant seems to have been as meticulous in actor training as he was in every other aspect of theatre management. The Duke's Company waited, perhaps for months, before it started performing at Salisbury Court, its initial home while Lisle's Tennis Court in Lincoln's Inn Fields was turned into a theatre. Logic alone suggests that Davenant used this interval to prepare his less experienced company. His decision to have several actresses lodge in his home – a paternal act recalling the inclusion of boy apprentices in a master's

106 SIR WILLIAM DAVENANT AND THE DUKE'S COMPANY

household – made sense from a practical standpoint. By eroding the boundary between private and professional life for his female actors, Davenant was better able to instruct them in the art of playing, helping them to 'improve themselves daily'.[20]

Evidence suggests that early on Davenant worried about not having a sufficient number of actors. In August 1662 a warrant was issued compelling the actor John Richards, who had accepted an engagement with a Dublin theatre, to 'return at once' to the Duke's Company in London. The order's legal basis was Richards' position as a servant to the Duke of York; but the reason for demanding his return was that Davenant needed him in the company (even though Richards played mostly minor parts) and was anxious about further defections.[21] Indeed, both patentees recognized a longer-term need to develop future talent. Their solution was to create an acting school that was allied to the patent companies but also sufficiently distanced from them. This new establishment for teaching young actors was called a nursery: a place set apart where 'infant' actors could be 'nursed' until they were ready to join the professional companies.

The history and practice of Restoration nurseries is sketchy, but a rough outline emerges in the surviving documentation. In 1663, Davenant and Killigrew cheated their rival George Jolly out of his theatrical patent – given to him separately in December 1660 by Charles II, who had enjoyed Jolly's performances at the Frankfurt Fair in 1655 – and then used the appropriated patent to establish the first Nursery.[22] By the following spring, they had persuaded the Attorney General to grant them a license:

> to erect and make a theatre, and to gather together boyes and girls and others, to bee instructed in the nature of a Nursery, for the trayneing upp of persons to act playes, to bee from time to time approved by the said Thomas Killigrew and Sir William Davenant.... [and to] remove the said boyes and girls and other actors soe to bee there instructed, for the supply of each of their said companies....[23]

ACTING RESTORATION SHAKESPEARE

107

From the outset, the Nursery was intended to be a public theatre (though of lower status) whose sole purpose was to supply the patent companies with trained actors. In a final move toward consolidating the patent duopoly, the license further stipulated that Jolly's anomalous patent was to cease. Eventually, the aggrieved George Jolly settled for being paid to run the Nursery on the patentees' behalf.

In the summer of 1664, not long after the Attorney General issued his license, Killigrew told Pepys that he intended to set up a Nursery in Moorfields where plays and operas would be performed, the latter with singers recruited from Italy.[24] Nothing came of Killigrew's bold plans. But we know from a reprinting of James Shirley's *The Constant Maid* that a Nursery operated in Hatton Garden no later than early 1667.[25] It might have lasted there only a few years, because in the spring of 1669 Elizabeth Pepys told her husband that she attended a performance at the 'New Nursery', relocated to Killigrew's original theatre in Vere Street.[26] In 1671, the widowed Mary Davenant moved the Nursery to the Barbican over the objections of the local residents in the parish of St. Giles-without-Cripplegate.[27] The Barbican nursery lasted at least until the late 1670s, when Dryden satirized it in his *MacFlecknoe*:

> . . . a Nursery erects its head,
> Where Queens are form'd, and future heroes bred;
> Where unfledg'd actors learn to laugh and cry,
> Where infant punks their tender voices try,
> And little *Maximins* the gods defy.[28]

Dryden's mockery of juvenile actors failing to impersonate great dramatic characters was anticipated by Samuel Pepys, who on his first visit to the Nursery in Hatton Garden in 1668 praised the music and the theatre itself for being 'better than we looked for', but lamented that the acting in Thomas Kyd's tragedy *Jeronimo is Mad Again* was 'as bad as could [be]'. Indeed, he and other audience members openly '[made] sport

108 SIR WILLIAM DAVENANT AND THE DUKE'S COMPANY

at the folly of their Acting' during the performance. Upon more charitable reflection, Pepys decided that the Nursery was worth visiting, if only to witness 'the different growth of people's abilities by practice'.[29] He returned the next day, curious to discover whether the novice actors 'did a comedy better then [sic] a Trajedy [sic]'. He discovered that 'they do it both alike, in the meanest manner'.[30] The comedian Joseph Haines, one of the few well-known Restoration actors who began their career at the Nursery in Hatton Garden, delivered part of the prologue to the King's Company's production of Thomas Duffett's *The Mock-Tempest* (1674), a satire of the Dorset Garden production (which we discuss in Chapter 6).

The nursery system of actor training seems to have died out by the early 1680s, which stands to reason. In 1682 the companies merged to form the United Company, thus consolidating all theatrical activity under a single management. Colley Cibber recalled that when he joined the United Company in 1690, 'young persons desirous to be actors' were required to serve a probation of six to twelve months during which they received no salary.[31] With more than two decades of professional experience behind them, the company's senior members were well-equipped to make actor training a primarily internal matter.

Rehearsal

The chequered history of actor training in the Restoration was separate from the instructions given to actors in rehearsal.[32] After the company's manager selected a new play to perform, the manuscript was read aloud to the entire company by the author or adapter. Roles were then assigned to the acting ensemble, usually based on seniority and customary lines of business. The company's prompter then prepared the 'book': the annotated full script, detailing entrances and exits, scene changes, music and sound cues, and directions for any special effects. Each actor received his or her 'part' – cues and lines for

ACTING RESTORATION SHAKESPEARE 109

their character, written on a roll of paper – but not the full script.[33] (The same practice had been followed in the pre-Civil War theatres.) Because most Restoration plays were performed before they were printed, Davenant's actors did not have access to the full text of any new or adapted play. In the 1660s, the lag time between performance and publication was often years. Pepys saw Davenant's *Macbeth* in 1664 but the adaptation was not printed until 1674, likely in response to a quarto version of Shakespeare's *Macbeth* printed a year earlier that falsely advertised itself as 'Acted at the Duke's Theatre'.[34]

When it came to plays by Shakespeare, members of the Duke's Company could in theory get a sense of the full play by reading it in the bulky and expensive folio text or (where applicable) the smaller and less expensive quarto text. But in practice such return to the textual source was unlikely, given that Betterton himself seems not to have owned a single Shakespeare play text until 1709 – a year before his death – when he acquired a copy of Nicholas Rowe's six-volume edition of the plays.[35] As Barbara Murray has argued, in the 1660s it was not so easy for anyone – reader, actor, playgoer – to acquire direct knowledge of Shakespeare's dramatic corpus.[36] Moreover, Davenant's adaptations were often so thorough and so inventive that the Shakespearean source text would have been only moderately useful to the Duke's Company's actors and perhaps a downright hindrance, given that Davenant routinely made small changes in diction that substituted the denotative for the connotative: 'the last *minute* of record time,' 'out *short* candle,' as Restoration Macbeth precisely soliloquized. If you were cast as Lady Macduff in Davenant's version of *Macbeth*, the folio text gave you almost no idea of the five scenes in which you appeared because Shakespeare never wrote them. The situation was worse if you played Hippolito or Milcha in the Dryden-Davenant *Tempest*: those characters appear nowhere in the folio text because they were invented by the adapters. But the situation was not much better if you played Prospero or Miranda, because just under a third of Shakespeare's text survived in the adapted version.[37] If you

110 SIR WILLIAM DAVENANT AND THE DUKE'S COMPANY

acted in *The Law Against Lovers* you would struggle to find the exact source text, because Davenant's play mixed *Measure for Measure* with *Much Ado about Nothing*. Thus, even when performing Shakespeare, Restoration actors developed their characters mostly by relying on their 'parts', without fully knowing the larger narrative, the relationships between characters, and whether the words they spoke were written by Davenant or Shakespeare.

When Davenant gathered his company for group rehearsals, much of the time was likely devoted to practicalities of staging: marking out entrances and exits; working out songs, dances, and fights; running through scene changes; and setting up any 'discoveries' – that is, pictorial groupings of actors placed behind upstage shutters who were 'discovered' onstage at the beginning of a scene when the shutters were pulled back into the wings.[38] Pepys once attended an early evening rehearsal of the King's Company during which they staged the dances for the next day's performance.[39] Surviving evidence suggests that there was little directorial blocking in the modern sense. Generally, actors entered and exited through the traditional proscenium side doors, taking focus in a scene when it was their turn to speak and retreating when another character spoke. As we described in Chapter 3, much acting took place on the forestage, the area closest to the audience and with the best lighting (chandeliers and a row of candles placed across the front of the stage). Yet the scenic area at Lincoln's Inn Fields – a more intimate venue than the later Dorset Garden Theatre – was close enough to the audience that it could also be used for acting. As Tim Keenan has noted, no stage direction in any play written for performance at Lincoln's Inn Fields indicates that actors moved down to the forestage after a discovery.[40]

When actors did not speak for a considerable stretch of time, they might break character. Betterton, a scrupulous performer, complained that actors in secondary roles took themselves out of the performance, 'whispering to one another, or bowing to their Friends in the Pit, or gazing about'.[41] He did not exaggerate: Elizabeth Pepys was mightily irritated that the

ACTING RESTORATION SHAKESPEARE 111

actress and singer Elizabeth Knepp kept winking and smiling at her husband during the King's Company's performance of *The Heiress*.[42] The liberties that some Restoration actors took during a performance suggests that the purpose of collective rehearsal was less to craft an ensemble production than to ensure that the company knew how to get through the play: cues and lines, entrances and exits, musical episodes, and staging for group scenes likes dances or swordfights. Precision in performance was not always achieved. Pepys's occasional complaint that some actors didn't know their lines reflects both the pressures of a repertory system and perhaps reluctance to memorize lines from a play that might last only two or three performances and then vanish from the repertoire. Disappointed with the Duke's Company's first performance of *Romeo and Juliet* in 1662 – none of the actors had memorized all their lines – Pepys vowed never again 'to see the first time of acting'.[43]

An actor's detailed character work was best accomplished not in group rehearsals but in what Restoration actors called private 'study'. Charles Gildon, in his pseudo-biographical *The Life of Mr. Thomas Betterton* (1710), purports to quote the late actor reflecting on the importance of such study:

> When I was a young Player under Sir *William Davenant*, we were . . . obliged to make our Study our Business, which our young Men do not think it is their duty now to do; for they now scarce ever mind a Word of their parts but only at *Rehearsals*, and come thither too often scarce recovered from their last Night's Debauch; when the Mind is not very capable of considering so calmly and judiciously on what they have to study, as to enter thoroughly into the Nature of the Part, or to consider the Variation of the voice, Looks, and Gestures.[44]

The Betterton quoted here is a figure of Gildon's creation, but the comments are nonetheless revealing. When 'Betterton' championed private 'Study', he did not mean anything bookish or theoretical. Rather, he meant the process by which an actor

112 SIR WILLIAM DAVENANT AND THE DUKE'S COMPANY

charted a dramatic character's sequential emotions ('passions', 'humours') throughout the play and the corresponding embodied signifiers – gestures, poses, facial expressions, movements and vocal intonations – that best expressed those emotions.[45] Good actors worked diligently at this task, bringing to group rehearsals a sufficiently worked out physical and vocal plan for their character. The actor's 'study', which no doubt was refined or adjusted in rehearsal, was accomplished without much knowledge of the full play, let alone familiarity with how fellow actors crafted their own performances.

This approach to acting was not so much applied to play scripts as derived from them. Restoration playwrights, because they presumed the power and significance of an actor's overt emotional display, created characters who recognized the emotional states of others more by the outward physical signs of those emotions than by their representation in language. In a scene created by Davenant for his *Macbeth* adaptation, Lady Macduff and Macduff encounter witches who sing joyfully about regicide. (We discuss this scene at greater length in the next chapter.) After the witches disappear, Lady Macduff notices – before her husband utters a word – that the witches have frightened him: 'Why are you alter'd, Sir? Be not so thoughtful'.[46] Her words respond to Macduff's changed appearance and attitude, and thus depend on the actor playing Macduff shifting his expression from confident to rattled *before* Lady Macduff speaks. In a similar way, the guilty Alonzo in Davenant and Dryden's version of *The Tempest* is distraught after witnessing the haunting Masque of Devils: '[T]hey have left me all unman'd; / I feel my sinews slacken'd with the fright, / And a cold sweat trills down o're all my limbs'.[47] Such lines are a gift for a Restoration actor – precise instructions – because they explain not just the character's emotion at a particular moment ('fright'), but also what that emotion feels like to the character ('unman'd', 'a cold sweat') and what it looks like to other characters and to the audience ('sinews slacken'd'). Davenant knew how to write for actors: he gave them lines that made their work easier.

For any Restoration actor, guidance received from the playwright, the company manager, or a senior actor was valuable. Betterton was proud that he and Elizabeth Barry, his leading lady from the 1680s onwards, always 'consult[ed] e'en the most indifferent Poet in any Part we have thought fit to accept of'.[48] Davenant was known for tutoring his actors individually; and although hard evidence is scarce, it seems plausible that rehearsals under Davenant were not cursory. The comparatively small number of plays allocated to the Duke's Company in 1660 meant that Davenant could devote more time to rehearsing each play, including treating multiple performances as rehearsals in front of an audience. As Deborah C. Payne has observed, the performance calendar in *The London Stage*, although incomplete, suggests that the Duke's Company staged two or three plays a month in the early 1660s while the King's Company presented six or eight plays a month.[49] In his biography of Betterton, Gildon constructs Davenant's leadership of the Duke's Company as a lost golden age of discipline and high standards in the acting profession. In 1710, a young actor might get away with showing up hungover and unprepared at a morning rehearsal. But not in the 1660s, when Davenant was the controlling figure in the room, especially when rehearsing his own adaptations of Shakespeare.

Considered together, the importance of an actor's private study, the reliance on 'parts', the rhetorical features of acting, and the absence of a modern stage director yield a crucial insight: Restoration theatrical performance was not primarily about actors creating an illusory dramatic world to which audiences surrendered. If anything, Restoration theatrical experiences were richly performative and inclusive: actors sometimes didn't know their lines; the dramatic text was bracketed by prologues and epilogues addressed directly to the audience; the production was infused with music and dance; actors shifted their attention from the stage to the audience and back again; the prompter calling the cues with bells and whistles was heard throughout the entire theatre; changes of scenery were not just visible but enjoyable to the audience;

114 SIR WILLIAM DAVENANT AND THE DUKE'S COMPANY

candles in the auditorium were never extinguished, turning the entire playhouse into an arena for performances by both actors and spectators, each commenting on the other. Within this holistically performative world, the dramatic text was but a single component. It was no accident that Pepys's highest praise for Davenant's *Macbeth* was neither for the play nor the acting, but for the entire production's 'variety' and 'divertisement' [*sic*].[50]

Acting Shakespeare in the Restoration

Critics and commentators in the eighteenth century tended to look back disdainfully on Restoration actors, with the exception of celebrities like Elizabeth Barry or Thomas Betterton. In 1759, Thomas Wilkes regretted that Restoration performers had mistaken 'turgid vociferation' and 'unnatural rants' for 'the best display of the heroic and tender passion'.[51] John Haslewood, despite having been born during the reign of George III, complained that Restoration tragedians 'strutted and bellowed, in a tone as far from the manner of life as the language [they] recited'.[52] Such critics insisted that the 'natural' style of acting realized in their own time first by Charles Macklin and then by his famed successor David Garrick best captured histrionic excellence. Because 'the established maxim of our modern Stage is always to keep Nature in view', Wilkes proudly elaborated, 'Acting is in a far greater perfection than it ever was in the days of our forefathers'.[53] Persistent comparisons between the greatness of 'our modern Stage' and the embarrassing defects of 'our forefathers' can hardly be surprising. After all, which theatrical era ever promoted itself by claiming that the best actors were the dead ones? The long history of acting criticism does not reveal which style is superior, as if any such transtemporal judgement could be credibly reached. Rather, it reveals that acting has a *history*, as does dramatic literature and scenography and theatre architecture. Like all histories, the history of acting provokes disagreements.

When understood through historiography, generations of judgements about acting style become less compelling, not least because style is necessarily timebound and ephemeral: 'so far out of the reach of Description', as Cibber lamented in 1740 when he tried to recreate on the page the famous actors that he had first seen in 1690.[54] We know from eyewitnesses that Henry Harris played Cardinal Wolsey with 'State, Port, and Mein'; that Thomas Betterton was 'the Muse of *Shakespear* in her Triumph'; and that 'to the last', Mary Saunderson was 'the Admiration of all true Judges of Nature, and Lovers of *Shakespear*' (Figure 7 depicts Harris as Wolsey).[55] Yet if such testimonies felt insufficient to those who wrote them – 'how shall I shew you *Betterton*?', Cibber agonized – then how

FIGURE 7 *Henry Harris as Cardinal Wolsey in Shakespeare's Henry VIII, print by Henry Edward Dawe, 1820. Folger Shakespeare Library, Art File H314 no. 1. Reproduced under a Creative Commons Attribution-ShareAlike 4.0 International License.*

116 SIR WILLIAM DAVENANT AND THE DUKE'S COMPANY

much less sufficient must they be for posterity.[56] When it comes to the question of what acting Shakespeare in the Restoration entailed, the interesting answers look beyond matters of style and focus on the values, epistemologies and cultural assumptions that made a historically specific acting method intelligible and meaningful to its historically specific audience. As Joseph Roach has observed, the theory and practice of acting are 'right and natural for the historical period in which they are developed and during which they are accepted'.[57]

One assumption about Restoration acting that we explore in this chapter is that Shakespeare offered Davenant and the Duke's Company a way to place the Restoration theatre into a historical narrative that bridged the gap of the Civil War and the Interregnum. This narrative emerges in *Roscius Anglicanus*, particularly in the passages when John Downes fixates on the story of Davenant teaching Betterton how to act Shakespeare. Downes was responsible for promoting in print the oral tradition that Betterton's performances could be traced back to Shakespeare's instruction to the actors in the King's Men who created the parts.[58] Writing in 1708, the retired Duke's Company's prompter recalled not just the afternoon performances but also the morning rehearsals for *Henry VIII*, first staged by Davenant at Lincoln's Inn Fields in 1663:

> The part of the King was so right and justly done by Mr. *Betterton*, he being Instructed in it by Sir *William*, who had it from Old Mr. *Lowen*, that had his Instructions from Mr. *Shakespear* himself, that I dare and will aver, none can, or will come near him in this Age, in the performance of that part.[59]

We have no idea on what basis John Downes believed that William Shakespeare taught John Lowin who taught William Davenant who taught Thomas Betterton, but the story is possible. Lowin, who lived until 1653, was still with the King's Men in 1635, when he spoke the prologue to Davenant's *Platonic Lovers* at the Blackfriars. Tradition claims that Lowin, one of the principal actors named in the First Folio, played the title role in *Henry VIII* when it was first performed at the Globe in 1612 or 1613. And surviving documents – such as the cast list for Jonson's *Catiline* (1611) – place the actor with the King's Men around that same time.

But what matters about this passage from *Roscius Anglicanus* is not the accuracy of how it maps lines of theatrical inheritance but the reason why that particular mapping was needed. The importance of genealogy to historians at the time was not to settle points of scholarship but to provide something socially useful: a sense of self for individuals or institutions. Thus, what mattered in Downes's genealogy of Shakespearean acting was less its clarification of past theatrical practices than its clarification of present-day mentalities. What matters for the Restoration theatre was that an appeal to ancestral wisdom could restore a normative theatrical past. It wasn't just that theatre was once again part of public life and leisure; it wasn't just that performances resumed after an eighteen-year hiatus; but rather, theatre was being restored in a particular way. In the strut and fret of the Restoration actor, Downes insisted, acting as Shakespeare knew it – as Shakespeare created it – could be seen. Theatres had been closed for nearly two decades, yet nothing was lost.

At least for Downes, acting Shakespeare was always normative. It wasn't simply that an actor must act well, but that acting well meant to act 'justly'. In his account of *Hamlet* – a play famously fixated on ghosts, surrogation, and 'counterfeit presentments' – Downes's language was stronger still. Davenant taught Betterton 'every Particle' of the role; and it was by the younger actor's 'exact Performance' of what he learned that his reputation rose:

The Tragedy of *Hamlet*; *Hamlet* being Perform'd by Mr. *Betterton*, Sir *William* (having seen Mr. *Taylor* of the *Black-Fryars* Company Act it, who being Instructed by the Author Mr. *Shaksepeur*) taught Mr. *Betterton* in every Particle of it; which by his exact Performance of it, gain'd him Esteem and Reputation, Superlative to all other Plays[.][60]

118 SIR WILLIAM DAVENANT AND THE DUKE'S COMPANY

Roscius Anglicanus insisted that there was something prior to the actor, something foundational that demanded his or her loyalty. It wasn't that Betterton relied on a pre-existing script; indeed, Davenant's rewritings of Shakespeare call into question the very idea of a continuous textual tradition. Rather, the point was that Betterton, when instructed by Davenant, relied on a continuous *performance* tradition, an embodied repertoire handed down from actor to actor like a family heirloom. In this uninterrupted line of theatrical succession, Davenant was the crucial link between past and present.

Why would it be necessary for the theatrical present to look like the theatrical past? Because Downes was trying to do something more than compile a calendar of Restoration performances. He was trying to shape a theatrical canon. And for a canon to possess integrity and authority, it must amount to more than a miscellany. As John Guillory has reminded us, canons are functions not of texts but of the institutions that safeguard and promote them.[61] The Duke's Company under Davenant's leadership must be understood as a canon-forming institution. Gerard Langbaine, in *An Account of the English Dramatick Poets* (1691), described himself as a 'Champion in the Dead Poets Cause', defending Shakespeare, Jonson, and Fletcher.[62] We might call Downes a 'Champion in the Dead Actors' Cause', in that he presented the actors who first performed Shakespeare as having inaugurated an unbroken tradition that lived on in the Restoration. No details of that embodied tradition are specified, but it doesn't matter. What matters is the assurance that, whatever its substance, this tradition was exemplified in the person of Thomas Betterton, the actor who learned the art of acting from Sir William Davenant. From this rhetorical perspective, the most important attribute of acting Shakespeare in the Restoration was not what it looked like but what it achieved. Its achievement was to answer the urgent historiographical question posed by the closure, suppression, and reopening of the theatres: What would be *restored* in the Restoration theatre?

6

Case Studies: *Macbeth* and *The Tempest*

In 1666 Samuel Pepys went to Lincoln's Inn Fields to see the Duke's Company perform one of his favourite plays, Davenant's adaptation of *Macbeth*. He described it as 'a most excellent play in all respects, but especially in divertisement, though it be a deep tragedy; which is a strange perfection in a tragedy, it being most proper here and suitable'.[1] What did Pepys mean by 'strange perfection'? What particular combination of elements did Davenant create in his popular Shakespeare adaptation that bewitched audiences and proved so lucrative for his company for so many years? This chapter seeks to understand Davenant's 'strange perfection': how it worked in his two most successful adaptations, *Macbeth* and *The Tempest*; how it was taken up by Thomas Betterton and transferred to the new theatre at Dorset Garden; and, finally, how the rival King's Company responded to and critiqued the Duke's Company's aesthetic in the 1670s.

Macbeth

Davenant made many textual changes when he adapted Shakespeare, although most Restoration playgoers would not have noticed. Shakespeare had not been played onstage for

120 SIR WILLIAM DAVENANT AND THE DUKE'S COMPANY

many years, so, quite simply they had no point of comparison. Still, Davenant, a consummate man of the theatre, keenly understood what his audience desired, and it was not an unexpurgated *Macbeth*. Thus, Davenant modernized the language, regularized the meter, avoided mythological or classical allusions, and cut obscure or archaic language. He eschewed metaphors, eliminated any smut, cursing, or blasphemy, and drew sharper distinctions between vice and virtue, focusing particular attention on the ethics of ambition.[2]

Davenant wasn't afraid to tinker with plot and characters: in *Macbeth* he streamlined the plot and clarified character motivations, reduced the number of roles, and amplified the opportunities for the women in his company. To showcase his actresses, he expanded the role of Lady Macduff, who served as a moral foil for the immoral Lady Macbeth, and increased the number of speaking witches from three to four (some of these roles may have been played by women). He also reduced the number of roles to 'right-size' the play for his company, eliminating ten characters, including the comical Porter.[3]

And yet it is wrong-headed to think of Davenant's *Macbeth* as simpler or less multivalent than Shakespeare's version. He carefully pruned Shakespeare's poetic language to make space for a complexity accomplished through intermedial rather than textual means. In Davenant's *Macbeth*, the costumes, the changeable scenery, and the 'divertisement' of dancing and music worked together to enrich the drama, a 'strange perfection' that rendered the tragedy whole and complete.[4]

Our chapter on theatrical space and technology examined what little we know about the scenic and technical aspects of *Macbeth* as staged by the Duke's Company in the 1660s and 1670s. In this chapter we focus primarily on how music for *Macbeth* provided 'divertisement', how it functioned with other elements to produce a 'strange perfection'. A few pieces of music by Matthew Locke survive that were used in the 1660s productions of *Macbeth*. These old tunes enjoyed staying power, for they seem to have been carried over, potentially in expanded form, into the 1670s productions at

MACBETH AND THE TEMPEST 121

Dorset Garden. Indeed, one dance from the 1660s score was even transplanted into Richard Leveridge's musical setting from 1702, a setting we discuss in Chapter 7. To explore the intermedial variety of Davenant's adaptation, and how it was taken up and expanded in the 1670s by Betterton, we shall focus on two of the musical witches' scenes in *Macbeth*: Act 2, Scene 5 and Act 3, Scene 8.

In Act 2, Scene 5 Davenant highlighted the slippery nature of music: are the witches funny, horrific, or a bit of both? The Macduffs are likewise unsure what to make of them, for one of them hears strangeness, while the other hears hell. Upon Duncan's murder, an apprehensive Lady Macduff flees the court with her children and servants and arranges to meet her husband on a secluded and barren heath. Shortly after their reunion, the Macduffs are taken aback by the sudden appearance of witches, who extol regicide in their song 'Speak, sister, speak'.[5] Matthew Locke's early setting of the song does not survive, but the text suggests that it began with recitative dialogue among the witches, followed by a chorus of 'rejoicing' when 'good king's bleed'. This musical interlude provokes divergent reactions from the Macduffs. Although Macduff is terrified by the witches' evil celebration, Lady Macduff gently chastises him, reminding him that he is a courageous warrior: 'This is most strange: but why seem you affraid? / Can you be capable of fears, who have so often caus'd it in your enemies?' Macduff defends himself, explaining 'It was an [*sic*] hellish Song: I cannot dread / Ought that is mortal; but this is something more'.[6]

Davenant revealed 'something more' about the mysterious witches in the second song, 'Let's have a dance'. The music for a dance tune associated with *Macbeth* survives in various publications from the late 1660s and, as Robert Moore has shown, the words of 'Let's have a dance' fit this melody, which potentially allows us to reconstruct what Davenant's audience (and the onstage audience, the Macduffs) heard (see Figure 8).[7] There is nothing overtly threatening about the sound of this song, although the jig rhythms allude to a longstanding

122 SIR WILLIAM DAVENANT AND THE DUKE'S COMPANY

FIGURE 8 *Locke, 'Let's have a dance' reconstruction, opening. Score reconstructed from contemporary sources by Amanda Eubanks Winkler.*

connection between witchcraft and sexual profligacy. In the early modern period, a jig could be either a comic song-and-dance full of low and bawdy humour or a dance with a lilting rhythm that complemented its leaping movements.[8] The audience for Davenant's *Macbeth* would have been aware of the sexual and comical associations with the jig, and these conventions would have shaped impressions of the jaunty tune in a major key tune with dark and violent lyrics: 'Let's have a dance upon the Heath; / We gain more life by *Duncan's* death'.[9] Thus, through the juxtaposition of music and lyric, the witches are both disturbing and entertaining.

While the offstage audience were probably horrified and enchanted in equal measure by the witches' antics, Davenant's onstage couple also reacted to what they saw and heard, revealing both the Macduffs' admirable courage and their weakness of perception. Lady Macduff remains unperturbed by the witches. Her 'vertue' protects her; she is too good, too 'innocent', to tremble at a silly jig or fall prey to infernal musical manipulation. Her husband approvingly exclaims:

Am I made bold by her? how strong a guard
Is innocence? if any one would be
Reputed valiant, let him learn of you;
Vertue both courage is, and safety too.[10]

Sadly for the Macduffs, having a healthy marriage based on mutual respect provides no exemption from tragedy: quite the opposite. Despite Lady Macduff's admonition to her husband that 'Messengers of Darkness never spake / To men, but to deceive them', Macduff still asks the witches to tell his future, engaging in the same folly as Macbeth.[11] And while Lady Macduff might accurately understand the sound of the witches' music, she seems to miss the very real menace of their lyrics. She is actually wrong about their powers – they may indulge in comedic and grotesque song and dance, but they accurately foretell the Macduffs' doom. Thus, Lady Macduff's behaviour (and that of her husband) is simultaneously wrong-headed and laudable.

These divergent onstage reactions to the witches' music also foreshadow a fissure in the Macduff's relationship that will reach its apex in the following act. Macduff's downfall comes when he once again fails to listen to his wife and misreads a situation, leading to dire consequences. In Act 3, Lady Macduff warns her husband to resist the siren song of ambition, suggesting that his desire to wrest the throne from Macbeth would make him no better than the usurping tyrant himself. A few scenes later, when preparing to flee the court, Macduff completely misjudges the danger to his wife and children because he erroneously thinks that Macbeth would not be so cruel as to kill the weak and helpless. Lady Macduff, more perceptive in this case than her husband, accurately predicts the slaughter of her family.

Davenant's witches may actually be menacing, they may wield real and dangerous powers, but it is all too easy to be diverted by their charming sounds. Whereas their songs in Act 2 directly participate in the drama as they celebrate the regicide of King Duncan, in Act 3, Scene 8 they show up with little dramatic provocation, simply to provide the 'divertisement' that Restoration audiences craved. Here we see another facet of Davenant's pragmatic and practical approach to adaptation. Rather than writing another completely new musical scene, he stitched together various pre-existing materials. Early in

124 SIR WILLIAM DAVENANT AND THE DUKE'S COMPANY

Macbeth's performance history, scenes from Thomas Middleton's *The Witch* featuring the comical hag Hecate and her tuneful spirits were interpolated into Shakespeare's *Macbeth*: in a sense, Davenant's insertions of song, dance, and spectacle elaborated upon the way *Macbeth* had already been played before the Restoration.[12] Davenant, who may have been unaware that these songs were not by Shakespeare, retains this Jacobean performance tradition by including Hecate's jolly song, 'Hecate, oh come away'.[13] Because no musical setting from the 1660s or 1670s survives for 'Hecate, oh come away' by Matthew Locke or anyone else, Davenant's witches may have actually sung Robert Johnson's Jacobean setting of the tune.[14] As noted in Chapter 3, spectacle was added to the mix when 'Hecate, oh come away' was performed at Dorset Garden in 1673. There, the sequence combined machine effects with music to cast Hecate as a flighty creature (literally and figuratively) who delegates the hard work of witchery to her minions, while she gallivants with her spirits.

It is difficult to interpret this scene as anything other than a comical diversion from the main plot – a feast for the eye and ear. But for Restoration theatregoers it was precisely these light-hearted moments that contributed to the 'strange perfection' of the tragedy, providing a needed respite from bloodshed, unbridled ambition, and tyranny. But the respite is temporary indeed, as the plot winds its way towards the inevitable, bloody conclusion, a conclusion spurred on, in part, by these highly entertaining witches. Thus, by interpreting all the components of these scenes – visual, auditory, and kinetic – by understanding how music, dance, and drama work together, we begin to understand the complexity of these characters.

The Tempest

We know more about the genesis of the 1667 *Tempest* than the 1664 *Macbeth* because Dryden described his collaboration with Davenant in the preface to the 1670 quarto. According to

MACBETH AND THE TEMPEST

125

Dryden, Davenant instigated key elements of the adaptation. The veteran playwright was the one who suggested adding the role of Hippolito to Shakespeare's play, and he also invented and for the most part wrote 'the Comical parts of the Saylors'. Davenant also edited his collaborator: Dryden remarked that his 'writing received daily his amendments'. It is possible that Dryden was being deferential to the memory of his esteemed colleague (Davenant had died in 1668), but his regard for Davenant and his theatrical instincts appears sincere. Indeed, Dryden believed that Davenant had not gotten his due; thus, he decided to fully credit his collaborator rather than passing 'by his name with silence in the publication of it [i.e., the play], with the same ingratitude which others have us'd to him'.[15]

Davenant does seem to be the controlling voice in this revision. Mongi Raddadi has analysed the language of the revised *Tempest* and identified textual modifications similar to those in Davenant's other Shakespeare adaptations. As with *Macbeth*, oaths and other offensive language have been eliminated, Shakespeare's grammar has been regularized, modernized, and clarified, references to classical deities have been excised, and lengthy speeches have been compressed and stripped of complex syntax and poetic language.[16] Familiar structural changes were also made: Davenant and Dryden added roles for women, inserted more music, and drew connections between Prospero's plight and the recent past of civil war and unlawful usurpation. *The Tempest* also features the parallelisms that Davenant so favoured in *Macbeth*. The lusty new character of Hippolito (likely played by Jane Long in breeches) was a man who had never seen a woman, while Miranda and her sister Dorinda (another new character) were women who had never seen a man. The quartet pairs off romantically, with Hippolito and Dorinda serving as comical foils to the more serious Miranda and Ferdinand. Completing the symmetry of character that Davenant always emphasized, Caliban acquires a sister, Sycorax (in Shakespeare's text, the name was used for Caliban's unseen mother), and Ariel gets a companion, Milcha.

126 SIR WILLIAM DAVENANT AND THE DUKE'S COMPANY

Davenant and Dryden did not completely reinvent the wheel in their *Tempest*, for they retained the texts of some of Shakespeare's songs. In the 1670 quarto, Ariel sings 'Come unto these yellow sands' and 'Full fathom five' with little textual alteration from the First Folio, although the earlier musical settings by Robert Johnson were discarded in favour of new compositions by John Banister.[17] Other songs retained in the 1670 quarto are the rustic number sung by Trincalo, 'I shall no more to sea' and 'The master, the swabber, the gunner, and I', and Caliban's 'No more dams I'll make for fish' and 'We want music, we want mirth'. Actors in Shakespeare's time and in the Restoration may have improvised these songs on the spot; may have used aurally transmitted, simple tunes, passed down from one generation of actor to the next; or, possibly, they sang these lyrics to well-known ballad tunes.

Other scenes, such as the Act 2 Masque of Devils; Ariel's Act 3 song, 'Dry those eyes'; and Ferdinand and Ariel's echo duet later in the same act, 'Go thy way', embroidered upon ideas found in Shakespeare's *Tempest*. As Claude Fretz has shown, the Masque of Devils serves a similar dramatic purpose as Ariel's harpy scene.[18] 'Dry those eyes', sung by Ariel to comfort Alonzo, Antonio, and Gonzalo, is analogous to the magical banquet in Act 3, Scene 3 of Shakespeare's play, and the lyric almost directly quotes from the masque presented by Prospero in Act 4, Scene 1 ('all want shall shun you, Ceres blessing so is on you').[19] 'Go thy way' takes another approach. Avoiding direct textual allusion to Shakespearean source material, it complicates the relationship between Ariel and Ferdinand through an entirely new and charming duet.

A key part of Davenant's adaptation strategy involved altering and expanding roles to showcase the talents of his performers, as we have already noted. 'Go thy way' was crafted to display the skills of Henry Harris (Ferdinand), an actor with proven musical abilities and a reputation as a fine romantic leading man, and Mary ('Moll') Davis, a performer known for her musical and terpsichorean talents as well as her sex appeal, who most likely took the role of Ariel.[20] As has been discussed

MACBETH AND THE TEMPEST 127

in the previous chapter, Restoration actors played 'lines': types of roles for which they were known.[21] In the case of 'Go thy way', the audience's knowledge of the performers would have fostered an erotic interpretation of the dynamic between Ariel and Ferdinand, although it is possible that their relationship had this resonance in Shakespeare's day too, for boy singer-actors were often the objects of desire.[22]

Harris and Davis's performance must have been effective, for it piqued the interest of Samuel Pepys. When he saw the play on 7 November 1667, he called 'Go thy way' a 'curious piece of Musique in an Echo of half-sentences, the Echo repeating the former half, while the man goes on to the latter, which is mighty pretty'.[23] He so enjoyed the song that he used his connections to obtain a copy. Pepys had cultivated a friendship with Harris, and he was also acquainted with the composer John Banister. In March 1668, he invited both men to his house for dinner and on 7 May he asked Banister to 'prick me down the notes' to the duet (see Figure 9).[24] On the 11th of the same month, he attended the theatre once again, and tried to write down the lyrics during the play without success: 'but when I had done it, having done it, without looking upon my paper, I find I could not read the blacklead'. Luckily, he had an inside source, for 'between two acts, I went out to Mr Harris, and got him to repeat to me the words of the Echo, while I writ them down'.[25] Thus, persistence paid off, and Pepys got his song.

Fortunately, this music survives in a printed pamphlet called *The Ariels Songs in the Play call'd the Tempest*, which, in combination with the 1670 quarto, allows us to analyse the scene's dramaturgy.[26] When Ferdinand and Ariel enter, the spirit is 'invisible', a stage direction that Davenant and Dryden take from Shakespeare, where Ariel frequently enters unseen by the other characters. It seems likely that Ariel is actually visible, for she leads and entices Ferdinand, and this stage action would have lent the scene a certain *frisson*, if the audience observed Ferdinand fruitlessly seeking the source of the voice. Despite the flirtatious undertones of his interaction

FIGURE 9 Banister, 'Go thy way' from The Ariels Songs *(1674/5)*.
© *The British Library.*

MACBETH AND THE TEMPEST   129

with the spirit, Ferdinand's mood is melancholic. He laments
the death of his father, albeit in melodious terms, transmuting
his sighs of grief for his father into a 'burthen', a heavy weight
and a musical refrain. He then proclaims his desire for death:
'Fain I would go to shades, where / Few would wish to follow
me'.[27] In keeping with the echo conceit, Ariel repeats
Ferdinand's words 'Follow me' – with a twist, making them an
imperative – but speech fails to persuade. At this moment,
Davenant and Dryden shift to the heightened register of song,
as Ferdinand wonders if the spirit will 'answer when I sing',
and indeed Ariel does.[28] As before, Ariel speaks Ferdinand's
own words back to him, but endows them with new meanings.

As with *Macbeth*, music conveys crucial dramatic
information, both to those onstage and those in the audience.
Ferdinand initially asserts power over the spirit, as he establishes
the tune that Ariel must follow; but at the end of the song, Ariel
wrests control from his interlocutor and sings a new, independent
melody line, promising that 'kind fortune' will smile upon
Ferdinand, if only he will follow him. Ferdinand is ravished by
what he hears; the song convinces Ferdinand to take Ariel's
'word for once'. 'Lead on Musician', he cries, a testimony to the
power of Ariel's, and perhaps Moll Davis's, voice.[29] This
sequence also demonstrates how the collaboration between the
actors, the playwrights, and the composer enriched meaning, in
this case through the dramatic device of an invisible/visible
musician, a potentially flirtatious dynamic between a musically
proficient actor and actress, and a song by John Banister that
moves the drama forward, as Ariel shifts from being an echo to
having his own persuasive musical rhetoric.

As we have established, in Restoration Shakespeare traces
of textual and performative pasts remain in the adapted texts.
In a corresponding way, Restoration Shakespeare, far from
being static, was itself adapted in later years, decades, and
sometimes even centuries. As we discuss in the next chapter, *au
courant* composers penned new music for the witches in turn-
of-the-century revivals of *Macbeth*. And just seven years after
the first performance of *The Tempest*, an adapter, probably

130 SIR WILLIAM DAVENANT AND THE DUKE'S COMPANY

Thomas Shadwell at the prompting of Thomas Betterton, revised the Davenant/Dryden text for Dorset Garden, amplifying the musical and visual components to showcase the possibilities of the new theatre. John Banister's songs for Ariel were retained from the 1667 production, but Shadwell expanded the Masque of Devils and added a brand-new Act 5 extravaganza with machine effects, the Masque of Neptune, briefly described in Chapter 3.

To ascertain how Shadwell and probably Betterton elaborated upon the 1667 *Tempest*, amplifying the multisensory 'divertisement' established by Davenant, we shall focus on the Masque of Devils, which was newly set to music in 1674 by Pelham Humfrey and Pietro Reggio.[30] In both the 1667 and 1674 versions of *The Tempest*, a spoken exchange sets up the *raison d'être* for the sung masque: it is designed to prick the conscience of the usurpers. Alonzo, Antonio, and Gonzalo appear, discussing their unhappy situation. Gonzalo encourages his companions to cheer up, for they survived the shipwreck, but Alonzo remains distraught, for he believes his son, Ferdinand, might be dead. He also regrets his and Antonio's respective usurpations of the dukedoms of Mantua and Milan and posits that their lamentable state might be punishment for their crimes.

Anxious speech soon dissolves into horrid sound. In both versions of the masque, the devils initially make their presence known through auditory, not visual, means, but the placement of the devils in 1674 reveals how the Dorset Garden Theatre allowed Shadwell to expand upon the 1667 *Tempest*. The stage directions for Davenant and Dryden's *Tempest* call for 'Musick within' and mention 'A Dialogue within sung in parts'.[31] In Shadwell's version the devils are located in Dorset Garden's ample substage area, their eerie vocalizations originating in 'hell'.

The lavish score of the 1674 *Tempest* needed experienced musical personnel to execute. Thus, Charles II allowed the participation of singers from the Chapel Royal.[32] The involvement of Chapel Royal singers in the Dorset Garden production makes it likely that boys took the high-voiced devil

MACBETH AND THE TEMPEST 131

roles.[33] Even if fluting trebles played some of the devils, they genuinely terrified Alonzo, Antonio, and Gonzalo, judging from the trio's exclamations. These onstage reactions would have potentially guided the offstage audience's emotional response to the infernal creatures. Indeed, it is possible that the youthful devils were meant to be frighten the audience, just as children playing evil characters in horror films frighten audiences today. And yet, boys singing the devils' roles may have also undermined their menace, allowing Restoration audiences to dismiss their threat, allowing them to distance themselves from, even feel moral superiority to, the guilt-ridden usurpers who are so frightened by their music. Just like the witches in *Macbeth*, it's possible that these creatures signified as both humorous and repulsive, an effect produced by the combination of dramatic performance and musical sound.

Theatrical technologies also combine with music and drama in this scene. We have already mentioned the subterranean sounds of the devils as they lurk beneath the stage. The devils actually begin their opening musical number 'Where does the black fiend ambition reside' in this substage 'hell'. After a sung dialogue in which devils individually explicate the cost of ambition ('Who in Earth all others in pleasures excel, / Must feel, the worst torments of Hell'), the creatures rise through the trap(s), and echo these sentiments in homophonic chorus (i.e., sung in block chords), set for maximum audibility and effect.[34] This is considerably more impressive than Davenant and Dryden's version, where the fiends simply stroll on, appearing at 'two corners of the Stage'.[35]

Later in the masque, dance and feats of vocal virtuosity are added to the performance. A devil, most likely played by Pietro Reggio, appears suddenly from a trap and sings an elaborate Italianate song of his own composition, 'Arise, ye subterranean winds'. Reggio's heavily embellished aria would have provided the audience with another kind of pleasure – Humfrey's score is French influenced, but this song showcases the considerable capabilities of an Italian singer and composer. Something of the way this song may have sounded is captured in a manuscript copied by organist and composer Daniel Henstridge. As Rebecca Herissone has argued, it appears that Henstridge notated what he heard when Reggio performed, including ornaments not found in other sources and a phonetic transcription of the singer's Italian-accented English (see Figure 10).[36]

'Arise, ye subterranean winds' also aligns dramatic purpose with a performer's talents, for the devil/Reggio uses the power of his voice to instigate a spectacle: two infernal winds appear through trapdoors and ten more enter to perform a dance. The music for this dance, written by another Italian immigrant, Giovanni Battista Draghi, does not survive; however, the winds certainly would have used a grotesque and menacing musical and gestural language, for the scene concludes with them driving Alonzo, Antonio, and Gonzalo offstage.

Notably, the denouement of the masque at Dorset Garden was far more elaborate than its analogue in the 1667 *Tempest*, which included neither Reggio's virtuosic song nor any trapdoor effects. Instead, dancers probably performed to an instrumental version of the devil's concluding chorus 'Around, around we pace', in keeping with typical English theatrical practice.[37] By expanding the masque, inserting a new song, trapdoor effects, and a custom-fitted dance, Shadwell and his collaborators built upon Davenant and Dryden's sturdy scaffolding. This dramaturgical model would serve Betterton

FIGURE 10 *Reggio, 'Arise, ye subterranean winds', Lbl Add. MS 29397, fol. 78v (inv).* © *The British Library.*

MACBETH AND THE TEMPEST 133

and the Duke's Company well as they developed the genre of dramatick opera.

Burlesques of *Macbeth* and *The Tempest*

The popular appeal of the visually and musically elaborate Shakespeare adaptations pioneered by Davenant at Lincoln's Inn Fields, and then extended by Betterton at the new theatre in Dorset Garden, is further documented by contemporary satires of the Duke's Company's productions, two of which relate to the case studies for this chapter. In the 1670s, as its audiences declined, the King's Company staged the earliest known Shakespeare parodies: *The Mock-Tempest* (1675) and a farcical version of Elkanah Settle's *The Empress of Morocco* (1673) whose epilogue mocked the witches in Davenant's *Macbeth*. Both burlesques were written by Thomas Duffett, sometime milliner in the New Exchange, and later dismissed by Langbaine as a 'Wit of the third-rate'.[38] His burlesques are unembarrassed comic distortions of Shakespeare's (adapted) dramatic narrative, treating serious subjects in a ludicrous manner: e.g., Prospero is not the exiled Duke of Milan but the Keeper of Bridewell prison, the notorious workhouse for London prostitutes. Even so, F.J. Furnivall was wrong when he regretted, two centuries later, that '[a]s pearls before swine, so were Shakspere's plays in the eyes of the hog Duffett'.[39] Understood in their Restoration context, Duffett's ribald plays are not parodies of Shakespeare as canonized in the First Folio so much as parodies of how Shakespeare was adapted and staged by Davenant's successors in the Duke's Company.[40]

In 1672, the King's Company, after its theatre in Bridges Street was destroyed by fire, relocated to the smaller theatre in Lincoln's Inn Fields that had been used by the Duke's Company from 1661 to 1671, before it moved to the new and larger theatre at Dorset Garden. At Dorset Garden, the Duke's Company enjoyed vastly superior resources, including elaborate perspectival scenery and stage machines of the kind

134 SIR WILLIAM DAVENANT AND THE DUKE'S COMPANY

formerly seen only in court masques. Making a virtue of a necessity, the King's Company realized that while it could not duplicate the rival company's production style – the fire had also destroyed the King's Company's accumulated stock of costumes and scenery – it could certainly parody their style. Such parody was a disingenuous revenge – though no less effective for that – because the King's Company envied the box-office success that its rival enjoyed. Thus, the first burlesque of Davenant's adaptation of Shakespeare was performed in the very theatre where that adaptation had been first staged, a theatre whose construction had been overseen by Davenant himself. The mocking irony would have been unmistakable to any reasonably well-informed spectator.

In December 1673, the King's Company satirized the elaborate witches' scenes in Davenant's *Macbeth*, then being performed at the Dorset Garden theatre in a production famously described by John Downes as 'being drest in all it's [*sic*] Finery, as new Cloath's, new Scenes, Machines, as flyings for the Witches; with all the Singing and Dancing in it'.[41] All that 'Finery' was ridiculed in Duffett's 'Epilogue Spoken by Hecate and three Witches'. In the customary inversion of parody, the witches are not supernatural beings but contemporary London prostitutes who crack jokes about tricking and robbing their clients. The comic sketch begins conventionally, with special effects of thunder and lightning to herald the entrance of Hecate and the witches. Yet as the stage directions indicate, the boom of thunder and the flash of lightning were produced not behind the 'Painted Tiffany' (silk or fine fabric used for scenic effects) that seduced spectators at Dorset Garden, but 'openly, by the most excellent way of Mustard-bowl, and Salt-Peter'.[42] In this vignette, Thunder and Lightning were emblematic characters played by Cardell Goodman and Nathaniel Kew. Mocking the elaborate hidden technology at Dorset Garden, the burlesque resorts to more primitive but openly displayed techniques which it presents in a laughable manner: Goodman as Thunder beats a wooden bowl while Kew as Lightning sets off a flash in a pan of gunpowder.

MACBETH AND THE TEMPEST 135

At Dorset Garden, Hecate descends in an extravagant 'Machine' operated by unseen stagehands.[43] In Duffett's version, the 'Glorious Charriot' that carries Hecate down to the stage turns out to be a homespun 'large Wicker Basket'. In a clear dig at the extended musical and vocal set pieces in Davenant's version of Shakespeare's tragedy, the witches' chorus of mewling cats is listed alongside the company's musicians in the dramatis personae, a snide reference to the witches' second song in Davenant's *Macbeth*: 'Sometimes like brinded Cats we shew, / Having no musick but our mew'.[44]

Confined to a small and under-equipped temporary home in Lincoln's Inn Fields, the King's Company opted to perform several meta-theatrical parodies, knowing that its audience would appreciate the topical caricature. The resulting parodies were always selective, taking aim primarily at the scenic extravaganzas mounted at Dorset Garden: 'the garnish'd Dishes [that] delight your Eyes, / And give you nought but Vermine in disguise', as Duffett tartly remarked in a 1673 prologue for the King's Company.[45] As Judith Milhous has helpfully observed, '[n]o ordinary play' staged by the Duke's Company in this period was ever satirized by the King's Company.[46] And so, the *Macbeth* burlesque sets up a particular fault line in the sensibilities of Restoration theatre audiences, acknowledging that its simple production values can 'hardly please' those who 'adore the Ghosts and Devils yonder' – that is, at Dorset Garden – where rival actors 'roar like Drum in battle' yet somehow never manage to make 'Plot and Language' clear.

Duffett's decision to write a *Macbeth* parody might have been inspired by the satiric epilogue that John Dryden had composed in July 1673 for the King's Company's performance of Jonson's *Epicoene* during its annual summer residency in Oxford. Facetiously explaining why 'our Poetic train' seeks 'refuge' from the 'infected Town', Dryden inventories the theatrical plague that has gripped London: French actors ('Hot *Monsieurs*'), Italian comedians ('Stout *Scaramoucha*'), and the Duke's Company's machine-driven *Macbeth*: 'But when all fail'd, to strike the Stage quite Dumb, / Those wicked Engines

136 SIR WILLIAM DAVENANT AND THE DUKE'S COMPANY

call'd Machines are come. / Thunder and Lightning now for Wit are Play'd, / And shortly Scenes in *Lapland* will be Lay'd'.[47] Despite having successfully collaborated with Davenant and the Duke's Company on the first adaptation of *The Tempest* less than a decade earlier, Dryden now openly criticized the company (then under Betterton's leadership) for promoting theatrical gimmickry at the expense of dramatic poetry.

The King's Company had a vested interest in satirizing the Duke's Company, but it was hardly alone in taking a dim view of theatrical spectacle at Dorset Garden. In the same year that Duffett's *Macbeth* parody was first performed, an anonymous writer lamented in a theatrical epilogue that

> Now empty shows must want of sense supply,
> Angels shall dance, and Macbeths Witches fly:
> You shall have storms, thunder & lightning too
> . . .
> Damn'd Plays shall be adorn'd with mighty Scenes
> And Fustian shall be spoke in huge Machines.[48]

In this epilogue, Davenant's most successful and most enduring Shakespeare adaptations – *Henry VIII*, *Macbeth*, and *The Tempest* – are ridiculed in just a few lines. Dancing angels appeared in the vision of Queen Katharine in *Henry VIII*, a staple in the Duke's Company's repertoire and first performed in 1663. So memorable was that moment in the blockbuster production that the playwright Bayes in George Villiers' satire *The Rehearsal* (1672) upbraids his hapless actors by telling them that 'you Dance worse than the Angels in *Harry the Eight*'.[49] He continues the insult by likening their stumbling movements to the 'fat Spirits in *The Tempest*, egad'. When Villiers' first drafted the play around 1664 he based the character Bayes partly on Davenant, which certainly explains the precision of Villiers' theatrical satire. Next in line for attack are the flying witches in *Macbeth*, a well-documented novelty in the Dorset Garden production. The last allusion combines the extravagant storm depicted in the opening scene of

MACBETH AND THE TEMPEST   137

Shadwell's reworking of the Dryden-Davenant adaptation of *The Tempest* with the customary thunder and lightning that accompanied the witches in *Macbeth*. This anonymous epilogue mocking the 'empty shows' produced by the Duke's Company suggests that such criticism was less a disingenuous harangue issued by a marketplace rival seeking to gain advantage and more a topic of lively debate and dissent within the small theatrical world of Restoration London.

After moving to its rebuilt theatre in Drury Lane in March 1674, the King's Company continued to satirize the Duke's Company's elaboration production values, notably through Duffett's other Shakespeare burlesque, *The Mock-Tempest*. Langbaine, although he held Duffett in low esteem, nevertheless understood the precise inter-theatrical 'Design' of his burlesque: 'to draw the Town from the Duke's Theatre, who for a considerable time had frequented the admirable revis'd Comedy call'd *The Tempest*' – that is, Shadwell's popular operatic treatment of Dryden and Davenant's version of *The Tempest*.[50] Indeed, rivalry between the patent companies is written into Duffett's script. As we noted in Chapter 3, Shadwell's lengthy description of the opening scene calls for a 'tempestuous Sea in perpetual Agitation' with 'several Spirits in horrid Shapes, flying down amongst the sailors, then rising and crossing in the Air'.[51] Duffett infamously reimagined Alonzo's ship overtaken by surging waves as a brothel in modern-day London besieged by lusty clients – Alonzo and the noblemen – who 'clime the Walls like Cats'.[52] As with Thunder and Lightning in the earlier *Macbeth* parody, the actors play not just their characters but also comic personifications of scenic effects. Thus, the burlesque begins not with the howling winds and crashing waves indicated in Shadwell's script, but with 'breaking Doors' and 'breaking Windowes', while the drunken lords cry not 'Ahoy, ahoy' but 'Whore, a Whore'.[53] The horrid spirits are not flying devils but the City Watch, London's official guardsmen charged with keeping the peace, a responsibility that extends to quelling boisterous rabbles. Mocking the 'shower of Fire' in the Duke's Company's

138 SIR WILLIAM DAVENANT AND THE DUKE'S COMPANY

production that descends upon the sailors as they abandon their sinking ship, Duffett's burlesque calls for a shower of 'Fire, Apples, [and] Nuts' that rains down on the 'Rabble' apprentices who seek to overtake the 'Wenches'.[54]

With unerring comic precision, Duffett's play ridicules the two scenes (one serious, one comic) with vanishing banquet tables in the Duke's Company's production of *The Tempest*. First comes the aristocratic serious scene, when two spirits bring in 'a Table furnish'd with Meat and Fruit' to tempt Alonzo, Antonio and Gonzalo. As the men reach hungrily for the food, 'Two Spirits descend and flie away with the Table (3.3)'.[55] The low comedy counterpart occurs in the next act, when Caliban calls forth music for Trinculo and his fellow mariners. 'A Table rises', followed by the entrance of 'four Spirits' who place 'Wine and Meat' on the table, and then dance upon it. When they stop dancing, the 'Bottles vanish, and the Table sinks agen (4.2)'.[56] *The Mock-Tempest* conflates these two scenes into one hyperbolic comic episode. In the burlesque, Prospero and Ariel conspire to deceive Alonzo and his entourage in a scene that openly spoofs the Duke's Company's spectacular production of *The Tempest*:

PROSPERO

[. . .] Well, *Ariel* go let a Table be brought to them furnish'd with the most sumptuous Cates, but when they try to eat, let two great Babboons be let down with ropes to snatch it away.

ARIEL

O Sir *Punchanello* did that at the Play-house.

PROSPERO

Did he so – then bend thy ayry ear . . . Then do as I commanded, but make hast least the Conjurers to'ther [*sic*] House steal the Invention – thou know'st they snatch at all Ingenious tricks.

ARIEL

I fly most Potent Sir.

Exit ARIEL *flying.*[57]

MACBETH AND *THE TEMPEST* 139

Ariel rejects Prospero's initial idea that two baboons could descend to the stage on ropes and then carry the banquet table offstage, shrewdly noting that 'Sir *Punchanello* did that at the Play-house'. As Andrew Walkling has helpfully observed, burlesque Ariel seems to be alluding to either the puppeteer Anthony Devoto (elsewhere referred to by Duffett as 'Author Punch') or to the troupe of Italian comedians based in Paris who visited London in the spring and summer of 1673, or even both.[58] From 1667 to 1675, Devoto performed *commedia dell'arte* style drolls and interludes at a booth theatre in Charing Cross. The Italian troupe, led by Tiberio Fiorilli ('Scaramouche'), came to England likely at the invitation of Charles II, before whom they performed on 29 May 1673, the king's birthday. Although not known for their use of stage machines, the troupe often used stage traps and favoured striking scenic effects. This context of contemporary harlequinade performances enables us to understand Duffett's first line of satiric attack. The Duke's Company, in its never-ending pursuit of novelty, is not original, but embarrassingly derivative, reduced to mimicking the eye-catching tricks of Italian puppeteers and commedia troupes. Their approach to performing Shakespeare is to plagiarize from Italian clowns. Thus, burlesque Prospero taunts the Duke's Company by commanding Ariel to execute the whispered plan quickly, lest the 'Conjurers' at the rival theatre, who 'snatch at all Ingenious tricks' because they can design none of their own, decide to 'steal [his] Invention'.

Yet the satire has barely commenced, because the eventual banquet scene in *The Mock-Tempest* is a *tour de force* of comic inter-theatricality. As Duffett's stage directions indicate, two devils on wires descend to the stage with a table laden with food and drink. As the shipwrecked men reach for the food, Gonzalo and Antonio 'are snatch'd up into the Air' by the devils, while Alonzo 'sinks with the Table out of sight'.[59] This is a theatrical moment of out-Heroding Herod. The King's Company's burlesque mocks the Duke's Company's astounding stage effects not by diminishing them (as with old-fashioned

140 SIR WILLIAM DAVENANT AND THE DUKE'S COMPANY

Thunder and Lightning in the earlier *Macbeth* parody) but by expanding them: the Devils take the surprised Gonzalo and Antonio with them as they fly away.

We can be sure that the extended comic rebuke of the Duke's Company was not lost on the King's Company's audience at Drury Lane. Theatregoers in Restoration London, having only two companies from which to choose, freely attended performances at both playhouses. Precisely because they were familiar with the various productions staged by the rival companies, they would have immediately understood – and enjoyed – the humorous topicality of Duffett's script. The King's Company was so confident that its audience would understand *The Mock-Tempest* that three months after the first performance it published the doggerel lyrics of the production's songs as an obvious parody of the published libretto for the Duke's Company's semi-operatic version of *The Tempest* that was being sold to Dorset Garden audiences.[60] Burlesque is perhaps the most ephemeral of all dramatic texts, given that its intelligibility depends upon a prior understanding of its equally ephemeral precursor text. Today, the satiric allusions in *The Mock-Tempest* and the parody of *Macbeth* need to be explained through theatre history scholarship. But the original audience possessed the first-hand experience and knowledge that made any exegesis redundant. In short, they got the joke.

The satiric edge of Duffett's play was so pointed that John Dryden, who had written the adaptation of *The Tempest* with Davenant, defended himself in verse nearly a decade after the burlesque was first performed:

> The dull Burlesque appear'd with impudence,
> And pleas'd by Novelty, in Spite of Sence.
> . . .
> The dullest Scriblers some Admirers found,
> And the Mock-Tempest was a while renown'd:
> But this low stuff the Town at last despised,
> And scorn'd the Folly that they once had pris'd.[61]

MACBETH AND THE TEMPEST   141

Montague Summers cited this diatribe against 'dull Burlesque' as evidence that Duffett's plays were ineffectual even in their original context.[62] But surely the opposite inference is more persuasive: Dryden's indictment of *The Mock-Tempest* well after its premiere – and after Duffett's theatrical career had ended – tells us that 'dull Burlesque' remained quite sharp. Dryden's retrospective attack on burlesques did not focus on their cutting parody of theatrical spectacle because he himself was suspicious of extravagant stage machinery, as evidenced in his 1673 epilogue written for the King's Company in Oxford (see above). Rather, he reserved his invective for what he regarded as the burlesque's deplorable desecration of poetic beauty: 'Disguis'd Apollo chang'd to Harlequin'. In blaming the burlesque simply for being a burlesque – a low treatment of a high subject – Dryden avoided confronting a critical point that animated *The Mock-Tempest*: the real travesty of Shakespeare was that the Duke's Company buried his plays under the weight of scenes and machines, thus giving audiences superficial novelties instead of dramatic substance.

In this chapter we have looked in-depth at some of the Duke's Company's most successful Shakespeare productions: Davenant's *Macbeth*, Davenant and Dryden's *The Tempest*, and Shadwell's embellishment of the Davenant-Dryden version of *The Tempest*. We have focused on these productions not just because they were popular and held the stage well into the eighteenth century – for *The Tempest*, even longer – but because they represented the fulfilment of the intermedial performance style that Davenant first pioneered at Lincoln's Inn Fields in the 1660s. The fact that most Restoration adaptations of Shakespeare, including those staged by the Duke's Company, were not as elaborate or successful as *Macbeth* and *The Tempest* does not detract from the significance of those productions but rather emphasizes it through their singularity. These particular productions exemplify the theatrical aesthetic of Restoration Shakespeare that began (but did not end) with Sir William Davenant in its most adventurous, its most innovative, and its most consequential incarnation. Like any ground-breaking artistic experiment, these productions provoked strong negative reactions from within the theatrical profession itself. As we have seen, such reactions took the quintessentially metatheatrical form of burlesque. Duffett's parodies of Shakespeare are not just doggerel mockeries but critical enunciations in their own right, an instance of the Restoration theatre bluntly commenting on itself. We cannot appraise the unusual significance of the Dorset Garden productions of *Macbeth* and *The Tempest* without recognizing the extreme reactions these productions incited: on the one hand, enthusiastic audiences in season after season; on the other hand, ferocious attacks mounted by the rival King's Company. When it came to Davenant's vision for how Shakespeare could be performed, a vision that was enlarged by his managerial successor Thomas Betterton, it was impossible to stay neutral.

7

Davenant's Legacy

William Davenant pursued a vibrant style of performing Shakespeare in the 1660s, a style tailored to his theatrical space and the talents of his youthful acting company that appealed to the eye as well as the ear. Davenant's style survived the man himself, for it was taken up and expanded by Thomas Betterton in the 1670s. At the Dorset Garden Theatre, Betterton and his collaborators increased the use of spectacle, expanded the opportunities for music, and tailored the plays to showcase the company's strengths. The dynamic performance style that the Duke's Company fostered found lasting acclaim with generations of audiences. The musicalized *Macbeth* and *Tempest* were revived into the nineteenth century. Other Shakespeare adaptations such as *The Fairy Queen* (1692–3) and Charles Gildon's *Measure for Measure* (1700) built upon Davenant's legacy. As we discuss below, such productions were artistically satisfying but never enjoyed the same financial success as Restoration Shakespeare in the 1660s and 1670s.

Purcell, Shakespeare, and the United Company

By the late 1670s, both patent companies were in financial trouble. Theatre attendance had plummeted during the Popish Plot (1678–81) and Exclusion Crisis (1679–81). This drop in

144 SIR WILLIAM DAVENANT AND THE DUKE'S COMPANY

audience numbers, compounded by mismanagement at the King's Company, led to the merger of the two companies in 1682. The United Company, as the new theatrical entity was known, seemed poised for success: it had a talented company of actors, including Thomas Betterton; it had two relatively new theatres at its disposal, the Theatre Royal for plays and Dorset Garden for performances requiring a high-level of spectacle; and, after 1688, it profited from the services of the highly talented composer Henry Purcell.

Purcell possessed prodigious musical gifts. He began his musical education as a choir boy in the Chapel Royal and, after his voice broke in 1673, received instruction from John Blow and Christopher Gibbons. Matthew Locke, who was deeply involved in the development of English opera from the Interregnum onwards – and who created the earliest score for Davenant's *Macbeth* – was likewise a significant influence on the young composer. By 1677 Purcell had a comfortable royal appointment. Ostensibly the composer for the violins at court, he actually spent most of his time writing sacred music. Over the next few years his career at court flourished: he became the organist at Westminster Abbey in 1679 and three years later was admitted as a Gentleman of the Chapel Royal.[1] Purcell's ascendency ended when James II, a Roman Catholic, significantly reorganized the court musical establishment upon his succession in 1685, an event that significantly diminished the importance of music for Protestant worship. Purcell's fortunes at court foundered even more after William and Mary began their joint reign in 1689. On 2 May 1690 the king asked the Lord Chamberlain to cut positions from the Royal Household; one of Purcell's appointments – his position as harpsichordist – was eliminated. Although he continued to compose some music for the court, after this point Purcell turned his attention almost wholly to the theatre.[2]

From 1690 onward Purcell worked on various operatic projects for the United Company, including one notable adaptation of Shakespeare: *The Fairy Queen*, a reworking of *A Midsummer Night's Dream* first performed in 1692. *The Fairy*

DAVENANT'S LEGACY 145

Queen was part of a series of dramatick operas mounted by the United Company, which expanded upon the template established by Davenant and his successors in the 1660s and 1670s. Although this anonymous adaptation sometimes has been assigned to Elkanah Settle, we follow Andrew Walkling in suspecting that Betterton supervised or executed the reworking of the text and planned the production.[3] The dances were choreographed by Josias Priest, who had worked with Purcell previously on *Dido and Aeneas* (*c*. 1688), the famous short opera first performed at Priest's school for young ladies in Chelsea, as well as Purcell's previous two dramatick operas, *Dioclesian* and *King Arthur*. *The Fairy Queen* was revived almost immediately in 1693, probably with additional music.[4]

The Fairy Queen adaptation mostly follows the strategies established by the Duke's Company in the 1660s and 1670s. The language of the text (taken from the 1685 Fourth Folio) is modernized, and scenes are reshuffled and sometimes cut to allow more time for the music, but the essential plot structure remains the same.[5] In terms of the placement of music, *The Fairy Queen* also followed some of the same techniques found in Davenant's earlier adaptations. Sometimes songs were carried over with little or no lyrical alteration. Bottom's unaccompanied 'The Woosel Cock', is one such example, although as with similar songs from *The Tempest*, no musical setting survives. In other cases, Shakespeare's play formed the scaffolding upon which new and more elaborate musical episodes were built. Titania's protection charm/lullaby in *A Midsummer Night's Dream* (2.2) is transformed in Act 2 of *The Fairy Queen* into an extended self-contained masque featuring Night, Mystery, Secrecy, and Sleep. In Purcell's opera (3.2), Titania summons a rustic entertainment to please the transfigured Bottom, a dilation of his request for the 'tongs and the bones' in *A Midsummer Night's Dream* (4.1).[6]

Many scholars have noted the self-contained nature of masques, what Walkling has called an 'almost total quarantining', which has been viewed as a dramaturgical departure from previous Shakespeare adaptations and earlier dramatick

146 SIR WILLIAM DAVENANT AND THE DUKE'S COMPANY

operas.[7] Michael Burden has suggested that practical reasons may have informed this choice. A letter written by Katharine Booth to her mother in May 1692 indicates that the roles of 'the Fairy King and the Queen' were taken by 'little children of about 8 or 9'. Perhaps the children needed additional time to practice their parts or perhaps past experience had taught the team at Dorset Garden that musical rehearsals were best conducted separately from dramatic ones.[8]

Burden's explanation for *The Fairy Queen's* structure is certainly plausible. But we would argue, *pace* Walkling, that the 'quarantining' of the masques is not, in fact, absolute. Nor do the masques necessarily impede dramatic momentum. As Burden has noted, 'a masque, by definition, needs to be "presented" to an audience on whose conduct its themes in some way reflect'.[9] In other words, the masques reflect the character and affect the behaviour of those who see them. Thus, Bottom gets a comical rustic entertainment. Titania is presented an elaborate masque of sleep, fit for a queen at bedtime. Oberon provides the evening's final masque, a celebration of love and marriage directed both to the happy lovers onstage and royal spectators offstage, with its prominent display of orange trees (William of Orange/William III). In the case of *The Fairy Queen*, the reactions of the onstage audience as they witnessed the spectacle would have continued the dramatic trajectory of the play. Such reactions are essential components of the overall performance, even if they were improvised and even if they went unrecorded in the published quartos. In turn, such reactions must have guided the response of the real-life audience, amplifying and reflecting back the wondrousness of what they saw and heard.

Indeed, the difference between the entertainments in *The Fairy Queen* and earlier Shakespeare adaptations (or earlier non-Shakespearean dramatick operas) is one of degree, not kind. Dramaturgically, the masques in *The Fairy Queen* are similar to the moments in Davenant's adaptations where an onstage audience reacts to a musical interlude, such as the Masque of Devils in *The Tempest*, or the interlude in

Macbeth (2.5) where the Macduffs watch as the witches sing and dance. Other sequences in *The Fairy Queen* expanded upon previous instances of machine-spectacle at Dorset Garden, such as the Masque of Neptune in the 1674 *Tempest*, which brilliantly synthesized and harmonized various media. Although printed stage directions do not always reflect reality, one such intermedial sequence was almost certainly staged as described in print, the opening of the Masque of Seasons in Act 4 of the opera. A symphony by Purcell survives to accompany the descent of the machine that opens this sequence:[10]

> The Scene changes to a Garden of Fountains. A Sonata plays while the Sun rises, it appears red through the Mist, as it ascends it dissipates the Vapours, and is seen in its full Lustre; then the Scene is perfectly discovered, the Fountains enrich'd with gilding, and adorn'd statues: The view is terminated by a Walk of Cypress Trees which lead to a delightful Bower. Before the Trees stand rows of Marble Columns, which support many Walks which rise by Stairs to the top of the House; the Stairs are adorn'd with Figures on Pedestals, and Rails and Balasters on each side of 'em. Near the top, vast Quantities of Water break out of the Hills, and fall in mighty Cascade's to the bottom of the Scene, to feed the Fountains which are on each side. In the middle of the Stage is a very large Fountain, where the Water rises about twelve Foot.[11]

Walkling has surmised that water might have been piped in from the Thames to feed the fountains. This dynamic water effect coupled with the mist, Purcell's regal instrumental music scored with trumpets and kettledrums, and the descending machine would have created a feast for the eyes and the ears – an entertainment fit for royalty.[12]

But this sensory feast did not come cheaply. *The Fairy Queen* cost a princely sum to produce, by some accounts as much as £3,000.[13] It was certainly the most expensive and elaborate Shakespearean dramatick opera of its time. We might view *The Fairy Queen* as a cautionary tale, for it pushed the practical limits of the Duke's Company's aesthetic beyond what was financially prudent. The prompter John Downes explained that *The Fairy Queen* was superior in 'Ornaments' to other dramatick operas and that 'The Court and Town were wonderfully satisfy'd with it; but the Expences in setting it out being so great, the Company got very little by it'.[14] Thus, despite *The Fairy Queen*'s considerable charms, it did not turn a significant profit, due to the level of spectacle and the elaborate musical forces involved (not supplied by kingly decree as they had been for *The Tempest*). *The Fairy Queen* might have proved to be a good earner in revivals, but the score was lost *c*. 1695 and was not recovered until the twentieth century.[15]

Shakespeare and theatrical chaos in the 1690s and beyond

1695 was a tumultuous year in the London theatre scene and the missing *Fairy Queen* score was the least of the United Company's worries. Dissension in the company had increased after Christopher Rich took control in 1693. As explained previously, Betterton and Harris had run the Duke's Company after Davenant's death in 1668. But within a decade Harris began to pursue politics more vigorously, and by 1681 he transferred his managerial duties to William Smith. Betterton and Smith jointly managed the Duke's Company from that point forward and likewise took control of the United Company after it was formed in 1682. This arrangement lasted until 1687, when Alexander Davenant bought out his brother Charles's shares with money secretly obtained from Sir Thomas Skipwith and Christopher Rich. In true nepotistic fashion Alexander appointed his brother Thomas, aged twenty-three, as nominal manager, although Betterton and Smith served as a shadow government, advising the inexperienced Thomas. The dramatick operas of 1690–3, including *The Fairy Queen*, were partially motivated by Alexander's desire to pay off his creditors, a scheme that was unsuccessful and led him to flee to the Canary Islands after an unfavourable chancery audit of his finances. He defaulted on his loans to Skipwith and Rich, who now owned Alexander's shares and patent outright, bringing them on equal footing with Charles Killigrew, Thomas Killigrew's heir and fellow patentee. Skipwith remained uninvolved, but Rich, with the support of Killigrew, set about putting the financial house in order – limiting spending, cutting salaries, and reassigning roles to less well-paid younger actors. Betterton might have retired around this time had he not lost his entire fortune in an unhappy investment on the cargo of a ship captured by the French. Unwilling to be at the mercy of tyrannical management, Betterton and several of his fellow actors deserted the United Company and resolved to start their own acting company. Emboldened by the Lord Chamberlain's support, the rebel actors – led by Betterton, Elizabeth Barry, and Anne Bracegirdle – received a hearing before William III in 1695 and were allowed to set up a separate company at their former theatre in Lincoln's Inn Fields, the very theatre where Davenant had led the Duke's Company.[16]

The breakaway company ultimately did not succeed, but it did have well-known actors, proficient singers and dancers, and a popular house composer, John Eccles. These considerable assets would reveal their value as the troupe embraced Davenant's intermedial aesthetic in new productions and revivals of Shakespeare's plays. As Milhous aptly noted, 'these people had in common not only their repertory and training but the philosophy of company management inherited from Sir William Davenant, which put the good of the company above the profits of the owners', a refreshing change from Christopher Rich's self-serving tactics.[17] The fledgling company's move to Lincoln's Inn Fields was a kind of homecoming, because the theatre had been occupied by the Duke's Company in the 1660s and early 1670s, before it moved to more elaborate premises in

150 SIR WILLIAM DAVENANT AND THE DUKE'S COMPANY

Dorset Garden. The return to Lincoln's Inn Fields was more about expediency than nostalgia, however, because the old theatre had been converted back into a tennis court. Once again, the building needed to be adapted for theatrical use. The new company's retrofitted theatre did not include much machinery, but it seems to have had trapdoors, a substage area where music could be played, and an apparatus for flying effects.[18] The breakaway company could not afford to rival the resources of Dorset Garden because its income was restricted to the funds provided by the actor-sharers and, as their official agreement states, 'publique Receipts'.[19] The lack of spectacle coupled with the theatre's small seating capacity ultimately caused the company at Lincoln's Inn Fields great financial difficulty.[20]

Sometime in the midst of this chaos, *Macbeth* – always a crowd-pleaser – was revived with a new score by John Eccles, although it is not clear if the production opened before or after the breakaway company established itself at Lincoln's Inn Fields.[21] Regardless of when Eccles's score was first performed, *Macbeth* proved popular with both companies during this period. We know that Lincoln's Inn Fields revived *Macbeth* with Eccles's score in the early eighteenth century because the names of basses in the first layer of annotations are crossed out and replaced with Cook, a singer at Lincoln's Inn Fields in the early eighteenth century. Another singer in this second layer of annotations, Short, also worked at Lincoln's Inn Fields in the early eighteenth century.[22] Indeed, performances of Eccles's *Macbeth* at Lincoln's Inn Fields may have spurred Christopher Rich's company to retaliate in 1702 with a new setting of the witches' music composed by Richard Leveridge.

Leveridge's and Eccles's scores reveal two different approaches to the witches' scenes, one more economical than the other. Eccles's setting is lavish, drawing on the extravagant mode of Purcell's dramatick operas from the 1690s. His score calls for double soprano-alto-tenor-bass (SATB) chorus, a string orchestra with continuo group (likely a harpsichord, theorbo, and bass violin), and the unusual instrument of the serpent, a low-pitched wind instrument shaped like a snake. Soloists may have been drawn from the chorus, although it is clear that Hecate was performed by a separate bass singer. Despite the quality of Eccles's music, it fell out of favour, perhaps because of the expense involved with hiring the necessary personnel. Leveridge's music, on the other hand, requires more modest resources: a single SATB chorus and string orchestra with continuo, although the role of Hecate still required a separate bass singer. (The earliest manuscript of Leveridge's score indicates that in one production the composer himself, a talented comical singer, took the part.) Perhaps because it was less expensive and less taxing for singers to perform, Leveridge's music endured. Commonly known and advertised as the 'Famous Music', it was used in *Macbeth* productions well into the nineteenth century.

The Tempest also proved popular with audiences around the turn of the century. When Rich's company revived it in 1695, the production seems to have retained the music and text from the 1674 operatic production. Purcell was commissioned to provide a new song, 'Dear pretty youth', sung by Dorinda to Hippolito (4.3) after her beloved was wounded by Ferdinand.[23] Rich's company also mounted a revival with an entirely new score, perhaps hoping to replicate the success they had enjoyed with Leveridge's *Macbeth*. Margaret Laurie has speculated that John Weldon, Purcell's pupil, may have composed the music, given that his setting of *The Tempest* was advertised in the *Daily Courant* as being performed at Drury Lane in July 1716.[24] As with the *Macbeth* revivals from the 1690s and early eighteenth-century, the music for this later production uses up-to-date devices: in this case, florid text setting inspired by Purcell and da capo aria forms imported from contemporary Italian opera.[25]

In the revivals from the 1690s and early 1700s, Davenant's adapted text remained largely unchanged, although the music was updated to suit new tastes. Thus, the dramaturgy established by Davenant and his followers in the 1660s and 1670s remained: the syncretic combination of scenic effects,

152 SIR WILLIAM DAVENANT AND THE DUKE'S COMPANY

dance, music, and drama created meaning in performance. And Davenant's influence proved long-lasting. Although his textual approach to Shakespeare ultimately lost its appeal in the eighteenth century, these interpolated musical scenes from *Macbeth* and *The Tempest* remained popular.

New adaptations at Lincoln's Inn Fields

Between 1698 and 1700 the halcyon dream of a theatre company run cooperatively by the actors at Lincoln's Inn Fields had transformed into a nightmare. Colley Cibber gossiped, 'Experience, in a Year or two shew'd them, that they had never been worse govern'd, than when they govern'd themselves!'[26] Negligence and selfishness reigned, and the audience defected to Rich's better-organized troupe.

In addition to the aforementioned *Macbeth* revival, the company at Lincoln's Inn Fields mounted several other Shakespeare adaptations in quick succession: Charles Gildon's *Measure for Measure* (1700); George Granville's *The Jew of Venice* (1701), a reworking of *The Merchant of Venice*; and William Burnaby's *Love Betray'd* (1703), an adaptation of *Twelfth Night*. Describing the rationale for this spate of revivals and adaptations, the anonymous author of *A Comparison between the Two Stages* (1702) imagined Betterton praying to Shakespeare for deliverance: '*O* Shakespear, Shakespear! *What have our Sins brought upon us! We have renounc'd the ways which thou hast taught us, and are degenerated into Infamy and Corruption*'. After beseeching the Bard for help, 'he falls to work about his Design, opens the Volume and picks out two or three of *Shakespears* Plays; and now, says he, I'll feague it away ifaith'.[27] In response, so the author tells us, Drury Lane turned to their own 'god', Ben Jonson, and the 'Battel continued a long time doubtful, and Victory hovering over both Camps, *Batterton* Sollicits for some Auxiliaries from the same

DAVENANT'S LEGACY

Author, and then he flanks his Enemy with *Measure* for *Measure*'.[28]

These productions deploy a combination of old and new strategies. Playwrights adapted the texts in a similar fashion to what Davenant and the Duke's Company had done decades earlier: they modernized and streamlined Shakespeare's texts, and simplified moral complexities. Moral clarity was even more important in this period, given that authors at the turn of the century were keen to pay lip service to the virtues of the theatre in the wake of Jeremy Collier's *A Short View of the Immorality and Profaneness of the Stage* (1698). Admittedly, many playwrights continued to write smut, but Collier's attack did influence Gildon's and Granville's thinking.[29] Thus, while both Davenant and the turn-of-the-century adapters felt that morals must be clearly communicated, the early eighteenth-century adapters were responding to a specific recent controversy.

Practical exigencies drove another set of strategies in these turn-of-the-century adaptations. The company at Lincoln's Inn Fields, although it could not match the technological resources of Dorset Garden Theatre, possessed some key strengths in the musical component of theatrical production: John Eccles, the company's house composer; Anne Bracegirdle and John Bowman, both experienced actor-singers; and Thomas Betterton, who had been involved with many of the elaborate musical extravaganzas staged by the Duke's Company and United Company. Thus, music continued to be an essential feature of these new Shakespeare adaptations, whether as one-off songs or as masques performed for onstage audiences.

For the first of these adaptations, Betterton and company had a secret advantage – they possessed a relatively unknown musical score by the recently deceased Henry Purcell: his opera *Dido and Aeneas*. The only known performance of *Dido* was sometime around 1688 at Josias Priest's boarding school for girls, so it was hardly a well-known work to London audiences.[30] Charles Gildon, who wrote the aforementioned biography of Thomas Betterton, interpolated Purcell's music and Nahum Tate's libretto for *Dido* into Shakespeare's *Measure*

154 SIR WILLIAM DAVENANT AND THE DUKE'S COMPANY

for Measure.[31] Gildon seems to have been familiar with Davenant's *Law Against Lovers*, a conflation of *Measure for Measure* and *Much Ado About Nothing*, for he includes some of the same material, even though his adaptation is generally closer to Shakespeare's text.[32] While Gildon drew upon a pre-existing work for the music, the music functions in a similar fashion as the Shakespeare adaptations from the 1660s and 1670s that had newly composed scores. For instance, Purcell and Tate's allegorical prologue becomes a celebratory Act 5 masque (similar to the 1674 Masque of Neptune in *The Tempest*).

Like Davenant before him, Gildon is also concerned with the slippery signification of music and the unintended consequences of hearing it, questions that are explored through the embedded masques performed for an onstage audience.[33] These masques consist of interpolations from *Dido*, presented by Escalus to 'sweeten' the 'Sour temper' of his master Angelo in the hope that the 'Power of Harmony' might cause him to 'relish Mercy, more than Justice'.[34] This is a very old notion – that musical harmony arouses a parallel harmony in the listener. But in the play, Escalus' plan to temper Angelo's mood does not succeed because Escalus misjudges the music and Angelo's nature. At the outset of the first entertainment, Angelo expects a 'Diversion' and hopes that music will 'chase Away the Guilty Image' provoked by Isabella's plea that he show mercy to her brother Claudio.[35] But the interpolated Act 1, Scene 1 of *Dido* is ill-suited for soothing a troubled breast, as Dido sings a lament over an oscillating, obsessive repeated bass line, revealing her tormented passions. Her anguished and lovestruck exclamations, the encouragement of her courtiers to pursue the Trojan Prince, and Aeneas's disingenuous declaration to Dido, 'Aeneas has no Fate but you', only stoke Angelo's lust for Isabella. Watching the opera does not spur him to internal 'harmony'.

The most striking disconnect between Escalus's desired outcome and the music he selects comes in Act 3, when Escalus prepares Angelo's 'Thoughts for pleasing Slumbers' by presenting

Dido's desertion by Aeneas and her subsequent death. The tragic subject matter is clearly not designed to promote sleep, particularly as in the previous act Angelo had drawn a parallel between Isabella and himself and Dido and Aeneas.[36] Angelo notices Isabella's presence immediately after he hears *Dido*'s closing number, a choral lamentation for the dead queen ('With drooping Wings you Cupids come'). The juxtaposition of the visual and the sonic – Isabella's appearance and the musical sighs of Purcell's composition – might have encouraged Angelo to sympathy if he were less immoral. But Angelo cannot feel anything but desire. When he spies his 'Ev'ning Star of Love', he resolves that he will take her by 'Force, if fair means fail'.[37]

We should not view Angelo's reactions as a haphazard or inept dramatic choice on the part of Gildon, for at the outset of the play the courtier Balzathar is sceptical that Escalus's plan to soften Angelo's heart through music will succeed: 'Musick, Shew, and Opera's; those Seldom please, where Cruelty presides'.[38] Angelo is just that kind of cruel man; he experiences only base passions in response to music that urges him to nobler sentiments. His depraved reaction only reinforces the audience's view of him as a brute.

Gildon's *Measure for Measure* points towards the structure used in subsequent Shakespeare adaptations at Lincoln's Inn Fields, for many of them included embedded masques. Such masques, often on mythological topics, had been a staple of the breakaway company's offerings almost from its inception. However, the music for many of these productions has been lost, suggesting that they were not set at all, or at least they did not enter the repertory.[39] Such is the case with the masques in George Granville's *The Jew of Venice*, his adaptation of *The Merchant of Venice*, and William Burnaby's *Love Betray'd*, his adaptation of *Twelfth Night*. In his preface, Burnaby griped that his play suffered because his celebratory Act 5 masque was not set to music.[40] And Granville's masque of Peleus and Thetis from Act 2 of his play may have been excised early in its performance history, given that Granville's adaptation held the

156 SIR WILLIAM DAVENANT AND THE DUKE'S COMPANY

stage for the next forty years and yet the musical entertainment was never subsequently advertised or mentioned in critical commentary.[41]

The masque libretto for Peleus and Thetis allows us to assess its relationship with the plot of Granville's *Jew of Venice*. Unlike Gildon's *Measure for Measure*, it is difficult to draw clear parallels between the characters in the masque and the characters in Granville's drama. Prometheus could be Antonio, who has provoked Jupiter's (Shylock's) wrath; but, equally, he might be read as Proteus, who enables the love between Peleus (Bassanio) and Thetis (Portia). Such analogies quickly break down, however, because Shylock is not in love with Portia and Peleus does not save Prometheus. Instead, Portia rescues Antonio with her cleverness in court.[42] The masque's immediate plot does not connect to the larger dramatic narrative, but relates to it only in a general sense, with regard to Bassanio's liberal approach to money. As Antonio observes:

> With such an Air of true Magnificence,
> My noble minded Brother treats his Friends:
> As hardly has been known to *Italy*
> Since *Pompey* and *Lucullus* entertain'd:
> To frame thy Fortunes ample as thy Mind,
> New Worlds shou'd be created.[43]

The lack of substantial relationship between masque and play meant that it could be easily excised. Comparing Gildon's adaptation with Granville's shows how embedded masques could be used to great effect, and how in less skilful hands it could fall flat. The embedded masques of *Measure for Measure* enrich the story, revealing Angelo's corrupted nature. Listening to *Dido* does not provoke sympathy; instead, the tragic tale of love piques Angelo's desire for Isabella. In *The Jew of Venice*, the masque is an easily detached entertainment, for it fails to illuminate dramatic action or character.

The Restoration *Macbeth* and *The Tempest* in the eighteenth and nineteenth centuries

This cluster of Shakespearean adaptations at Lincoln's Inn Fields differs from Davenant's Duke's Company adaptations: Whereas Shakespeare was not mentioned as the source of Davenant's *Law Against Lovers* and in Dryden's prologue to *The Tempest* the adaptation emerged from Shakespeare's 'dust', later Shakespeare adapters were more concerned with their relationship with the 'original' text. Gildon states in his dedication to Nicholas Battersby that his version of *Measure for Measure* is 'much more *Shakespears* than Mine', a rhetorical move that centres Shakespeare.[44] Both Granville and Burnaby use marks to differentiate their lines from Shakespeare's and in his prologue Granville anxiously excuses his textual tinkering, claiming that 'Undertakings of this kind are justify'd by the Examples of those Great Men who have employ'd their Endeavours the same Way'. Granville goes on to cite Davenant and Dryden's work on *The Tempest* as an inspiration for his adaptation, but as we've seen, their approach in 1667 was far less reverential than Granville's in 1701.[45]

The increasing value placed upon Shakespeare's 'original' text, however much it was abbreviated in performance, did not diminish the theatrical appeal of Restoration versions of *Macbeth* and *The Tempest*, which held the stage into the era of David Garrick and beyond. Why were these two plays so enduringly popular with audiences? Perhaps it has something to do with the vitality of the interpolated music in each play, a vitality that was strong enough to withstand the cult of Bardolatry that insisted on performing an unadorned Shakespearean text.

Davenant's *Macbeth* continued to hold the stage until 1744, when David Garrick restored Shakespeare's text, while retaining some of Davenant's lines, including Macbeth's dying words, 'Farewell, vain world and what's most vain in it.

158 SIR WILLIAM DAVENANT AND THE DUKE'S COMPANY

Ambition!' By contrast, Leveridge's music for the witches (which of course used words by Davenant and Middleton) was performed well into the nineteenth century, although his score was sometimes misattributed to Locke or Purcell, both more illustrious composers.[46] Commentary on the witches' scenes written in the eighteenth and nineteenth centuries allows us to understand how those scenes were interpreted and received in successive historical moments. In the pages of *The Spectator* (1711), Joseph Addison recalled the (for him) uncomfortable experience of watching a performance of *Macbeth* while seated near a spectator who was overly fond of the witches:

> Some Years ago I was at the Tragedy of *Macbeth*, and unfortunately placed myself under a Woman of Quality that is since Dead. . . . A little before the rising of the Curtain, she broke out into a loud Soliloquy, *When will the dear Witches enter?* And immediately upon their first Appearance, asked a Lady that sat three Boxes from her, on her Right-hand, if those Witches were not charming Creatures.[47]

Obviously, the 'Woman of Quality' was delighted, not frightened by the witches, a reaction encouraged by Leveridge's jaunty sounding music and the travesty performance of Hecate. In 1773, a critic in the *St. James Chronicle* complained that 'comic actors are permitted to turn a solemn incantation into a ridiculous farce for the entertainment of the upper gallery'.[48] Half a century later, the actress Fanny Kemble remarked that '[w]e have three jolly-faced fellows, whom we are accustomed to laugh at . . . in every farce . . . with a due proportion of petticoats . . . jocose red faces, peaked hats, and broomsticks'.[49] Clearly, the menace of the witches had been entirely eradicated in favour of comedic diversion.

Surviving theatrical scores and arrangements likewise confirm that Leveridge's score was used in *Macbeth* productions – again, with Shakespeare's text, not Davenant's – well into the nineteenth century.[50] Leveridge's score even made its way into North American productions of Shakespeare's Scottish tragedy. An

DAVENANT'S LEGACY   159

1870 article in the Boston-based magazine *Every Saturday* discusses this longstanding performance tradition and calls for reform:

> When Mr. Charles Kean came to revive 'Macbeth,' [1853] after the ornate and elaborate fashion which distinguished his productions of Shakespeare at the Princess's Theatre, he was faithful to the old music, to the singing witches, soloists, and chorus, and Locke or Leveridge enjoyed his own again ... The interpolated words of the songs are in many instances the merest nonsense, and the tunes, if of a catching and popular kind, still are seriously interruptive of the due progress of the events of the play. It may reasonably be held now that the composer's 'improvements' have become exhausted by the prolonged duration of his tenure, and that he may forthwith be ejected from his occupancy.[51]

The reviewer in *Every Saturday* might object to Leveridge's (and Middleton and Davenant's) 'nonsense', but it seems to have been impossible to perform *Macbeth* without the 'old music'. It had become tradition. But the review also hints at the purge that was to come; after centuries of use, Leveridge's score *would* 'be ejected' from the stage by the turn of the twentieth century.

Elements of Shadwell's operatic version of the Davenant-Dryden adaptation of *The Tempest* similarly survived through its interpolated masques, which remained popular with theatre audiences decade after decade. The most frequently performed setting was the previously discussed early eighteenth-century score, likely composed by John Weldon. This music was later printed by Harrison and Company in 1786, a testament to its ongoing popularity, although it was misattributed to Purcell.[52]

Although the parts of the 'Harrison' score continued to hold the stage into the nineteenth century, versions of songs from the 1674 *Tempest* were reset by subsequent composers and used in radically different dramatic contexts. For instance, in 1756 Garrick mounted an ill-fated 'operatic' version of *The Tempest*

160 SIR WILLIAM DAVENANT AND THE DUKE'S COMPANY

that included a new setting by J.C. Smith, one of Handel's pupils. His opera begins with Ariel singing 'Arise ye subterranean winds', a song performed by a Devil in the 1674 *Tempest*. In 1789 John Kemble also mounted a version of *The Tempest* that combined the 'Harrison' score with newly composed music. The singer and composer Michael Kelly, who played Ferdinand, wrote new music for the production, but also reported that it included 'the whole of the delightful music by Purcell [*sic*]' which was 'well got up by Mr. Linley; the accompaniments by himself'.[53] In his *Reminiscences*, William Macready recalls a similar production that combined old and new *Tempest* music. In 1821 he acted Prospero in 'a *mélange* that was called Shakespeare's "Tempest," with songs interpolated by Reynolds, among the mutilations and barbarous ingraftings of Dryden and Davenport [*sic*]'.[54] According to the surviving playbill, this included 'The Original Musick by *Purcell* [*sic*]' alongside additional music by 'Haydn, Mozart, Dr. Arne' and many others.[55]

After Macready became manager of Covent Garden in 1838, he jettisoned the 1674 *Tempest* text in favour of Shakespeare's original. But notably he retained some of 'Purcell's' music – it proved too appealing to eliminate entirely.[56] Macready's compromise – restore Shakespeare's text, but keep Restoration-style music and spectacle – proved a winning formula, and *The Tempest* was performed in this manner at Sadler's Wells and elsewhere throughout the nineteenth century. The 'Harrison' score also made its way to America: an 1897 review in *The New York Times* mentions music by Arne and Purcell [*sic*] as well as '[Wilhelm] Taubert's "Tempest" music composed for the Munich Court Theatre ... and presumably those tunes composed for the play in 1610–11 by R. Johnson'. Given this description, the sound of this revival must have been truly eclectic, with nineteenth-century musical romanticism coexisting alongside the Italianate 'Harrison' score and Johnson's Jacobean songs.[57]

These anecdotes about eighteenth- and nineteenth-century performances of *Macbeth* and *The Tempest* demonstrate the

DAVENANT'S LEGACY

lasting audience appeal of the Restoration approach to Shakespearean performance. Even after Shakespeare's text was restored, the Leveridge and 'Harrison' scores persisted. This approach is unheard of today in mainstream productions – it would be the equivalent of staging Shakespeare with a score originally composed for Charles Kean or Henry Irving. And yet the juxtaposition of Restoration-era music with Shakespeare's text proved a winning formula and persisted in performances of these two plays well into the nineteenth century.

Davenant's approach to Shakespeare adaptation – one that drew upon contemporary music, visual splendour, and rewritten texts – clearly had a substantial and powerful theatrical afterlife and continues to shape performance to this day. Productions that update Shakespeare's language to speak to a contemporary audience, for instance *O* (2001), which adapts *Othello* to an American high school; *10 Things I Hate About You*, a rom-com version of *The Taming of the Shrew* (1999); or 'Play On', the Oregon Shakespeare Festival's project that translated Shakespeare's early modern texts into modern English, are indebted to Davenant and the Duke's Company, whether they know it or not. We can also see traces of this aesthetic in productions that employ cutting-edge technology, such as the Intel co-sponsored *Tempest* at the RSC (2016). The virtual reality Ariel avatar produces a similar sense of wonder in the audience as the changeable scenery at Lincoln's Inn Fields, the machines at Dorset Garden. Baz Luhrmann's frenetic *William Shakespeare's Romeo + Juliet* with MTV-style editing and a popular music compilation soundtrack also incorporates a similar set of intermedial strategies as seen at the Duke's Company, as up-to-date music combines with a distinctive visual vocabulary to produce meaning. Restoration Shakespeare has also had a lasting effect in the opera house. Jeremy Sams's pastiche opera, *The Enchanted Island*, performed at the Metropolitan Opera (2011), drew liberally upon the 1674 version of *The Tempest* for inspiration, combining it in true Restoration fashion with elements drawn from *A Midsummer Night's Dream*.

162 SIR WILLIAM DAVENANT AND THE DUKE'S COMPANY

We hope this book has put to rest any presumption that Restoration adaptations of Shakespeare are lesser or inferior versions of Shakespeare. As we have argued throughout, Restoration Shakespeare is a historical performance genre in its own right, possessing its own aesthetic aims and its own hermeneutic agency. To understand Restoration Shakespeare as anything else is to misunderstand it entirely. Perhaps the best way to appreciate the distinctiveness of Restoration Shakespeare is by studying the theatrical and musical innovations introduced by Davenant and the Duke's Company. We can come to see that those innovations are still part of our theatrical consciousness, still part of the artistic vocabulary used by directors, designers and actors to create performances today. One way or another, Davenant and the Duke's Company are still with us.

NOTES

Chapter 1

1   The final parenthetical is struck through in Aubrey's manuscript; the quotation is taken from John Aubrey, *Brief Lives with An Apparatus for the Lives of the English Mathematical Writers*, vol. 1, ed. Kate Bennett (Oxford: Oxford University Press, 2015), 140.

2   Ibid.

3   Mary Edmond, 'Davenant [D'Avenant], Sir William (1606–1668), poet, playwright, and theatre manager', *ODNB* (accessed 7 October 2019). On Davenant's parentage, early life, and connection to Shakespeare, see also Edmond, *Rare Sir William Davenant* (New York: St. Martin's Press, 1987), 1–26.

4   Edmond, *Rare Sir William Davenant*, 24.

5   Ibid., 39.

6   He had married his first wife, also named Mary, shortly upon his arrival in London. On Davenant's wives, see Edmond, 'Davenant [D'Avenant], Sir William', *ODNB*.

7   Edmond, *Rare Sir William Davenant*, 54.

8   Paula R. Backscheider, *Spectacular Politics: Theatrical Power and Mass Culture in Early Modern England* (Baltimore, MD: Johns Hopkins University Press, 1993), 1–31.

9   On the collaborative nature of the masque and the importance of spectacle, see Stephen Orgel and Roy Strong, *Inigo Jones: The Theatre of the Stuart Court*, vol. 1 (Berkeley: University of California Press, 1973), 1–14.

10 [William Davenant], *Luminalia, or the Festivall of Light* (London, 1637[8]), A[1r].

11 On Lanier's engagement with recitative and Italianate styles more generally, see Ian Spink, 'Lanier family [Laniere, Laneare,

164 NOTES

Laneer, Lanyer, Lenear etc.]', *GMO* (accessed 31 January 2020); on Lanier and *Luminalia*, see Michael Wilson, *Nicholas Lanier: Master of the King's Musick* (London: Routledge, 1994), 185.

12 [Davenant], *Luminalia*, 20–1.

13 There is debate over whether he was officially appointed, although his contemporaries believed him to be the poet laureate; Edmond, *Rare Sir William Davenant*, 73–4.

14 Robert Read wrote to his cousin, Thomas Windebank, 'They say it was very good, but I believe the disorder was never so great at any', *Calendar of State Papers, Domestic Series, of the Reign of Charles I. 1639–40*, vol. 15 (London: Longman & Co., 1877), 365.

15 [William Davenant], *Salmacida Spolia* (London, 1639[40]), D1[v].

16 Martin Butler, 'Politics and the Masque: *Salmacida Spolia*', in *Literature and the English Civil War*, ed. Thomas Healy and Jonathan Sawday (Cambridge: Cambridge University Press, 1990), 70.

17 Davenant's patent is reprinted in Thomas Rymer, *Foedera* 3rd edn, vol. 20 (London, 1744), 377–8. See also John Freehafer, 'Brome, Suckling, and Davenant's Theater Project of 1639', *Texas Studies in Literature and Language* 10, no. 3 (1968): 367–83.

18 Edmond, *Rare Sir William Davenant*, 75–6.

19 Edmond, *Rare Sir William Davenant*, 91; Edmond, 'Davenant [D'Avenant], Sir William', *ODNB* (accessed 14 February 2020).

20 Edmond, *Rare Sir William Davenant*, 93–6.

21 Edmond, *Rare Sir William Davenant*, 97; Edmond, 'Davenant [D'Avenant], Sir William', *ODNB* (accessed 16 February 2020).

22 Edmond, *Rare Sir William Davenant*, 103–20; Edmond, 'Davenant [D'Avenant], Sir William', *ODNB* (accessed 16 February 2020).

23 [Davenant], *A Proposition for Advancement of Moralitie, By a new way of Entertainment of the People* (London, 1654[3]), 2.

24 Ibid., 13–15.

25 *Cupid and Death* was performed again in 1659 in a revised version. The music exists only in Matthew Locke's short score,

NOTES

165

copied for the 1659 production. It remains unclear how much revision took place between 1653 and 1659, if Locke was involved in the 1653 version, or if Gibbons composed the score on his own. Curtis Price, 'Cupid and Death', *GMO* (accessed 21 February 2020).

26 J[ames] S[hirley], *Cupid and Death* (London, 1653), [19], A2[r].

27 On this entertainment, see Edmond, *Rare Sir William Davenant*, 122–3 and Andrew R. Walkling, *Masque and Opera in England, 1656–1688* (Abingdon: Routledge, 2017), 151–2.

28 *A Proposition for Advancement of Moralitie*, 14–15.

29 *The First Days Entertainment at Rutland-House, By Declamations and Musick: After the manner of the Ancients* (London, 1655[6]), 3–40.

30 *The Siege of Rhodes Made a Representation by the Art of Prospective in Scenes, and the Story Sung in Recitative Musick* (London, 1656). On the work's combination of music and scenic effect, see Walkling, *Masque and Opera*, 164–75. Dawn Lewcock reproduces Webb's designs in *Sir William Davenant, the Court Masque, and the English Seventeenth-Century Scenic Stage, c1605–1700* (Amherst, NY: Cambria Press, 2008), 96–102.

31 James Winn analyses Davenant's libretto and discusses its impact on heroic drama and later English opera in 'Heroic Song: A Proposal for a Revised History of English Theater and Opera, 1656–1711', *Eighteenth-Century Studies* 30, no. 2 (1996/1997): 113–37. As Andrew Pinnock and Bruce Wood note, while Davenant discusses his approach to recitative, he does not explain his poetic strategy for the more 'tuneful' or 'dance-patterned end of the song spectrum'; 'The Mangled Chime: The Accidental Death of the Opera Libretto in Civil War England', *Early Music* 36, no. 2 (2008): 272.

32 Niall Allsopp describes Davenant's careful political positioning during the 1650s in chapter 5 of *Poetry and Sovereignty in the English Revolution* (Oxford: Oxford University Press, 2020).

33 Quoted in Janet Clare, 'The Production and Reception of Davenant's "Cruelty of the Spaniards in Peru"', *The Modern Language Review* 89, no. 4 (1994): 834.

34 Clare, 'The Production and Reception', 835.

NOTES

35 [William Davenant], *The Cruelty of the Spaniards in Peru. Exprest by Instrumentall and Vocall Musick, and by Art of Perspective in Scenes, &c.* (London, 1658), 26.

36 Clare, 'The Production and Reception', 836.

37 Edmond, *Rare Sir William Davenant*, 130; Stephen Watkins, 'The Protectorate Playhouse: William Davenant's Cockpit in the 1650s', *Shakespeare Bulletin* 37, no. 1 (2019): 98.

38 We cannot be more precise about the nature of the singing because the music for *The Cruelty of the Spaniards* does not survive.

39 [William Davenant], *The History of Sr Francis Drake. Exprest by Instrumentall and Vocall Musick, and by Art of Perspective in Scenes, &c.* (London, 1659), 1.

40 John Evelyn saw a performance, which he described as being 'after the *Italian* way in *Recitative Music & Sceanes*', *The Diary of John Evelyn*, ed. E.S. De Beer, vol. 3, Kalendarium, 1650–1672 (Oxford: Clarendon Press, 1955), 229. John Aubrey also indicates that it had recitative, although his memory is sometimes faulty (Edmond, *Rare Sir William Davenant*, 134–5). The musical components of the entertainment cannot be determined with absolute certainty as Matthew Locke's 'Symerons Dance' is the only piece that survives. It is no. 279 in John Playford's *Courtly Masquing Ayres* (1662).

41 William Davenant, *The Play-House to be Lett,* in *The Works of Sr William Davenant K^t*, vol. 2 (London, 1673), 72.

42 Winn describes the 'ironic' framing of these older musical works in *The Playhouse to Be Let*, and their influence on post-Restoration operatic forms in 'Heroic Song', 121ff.

43 [Davenant], *The Cruelty of the Spaniards in Peru*, 19.

44 [Davenant], *The Cruelty of the Spaniards*, 18.

45 John Dryden, *The Indian Emperour; or The Conquest of Mexico by the Spaniards*, in *The Works of John Dryden*, ed. H.T. Swedenberg, Jr., Earl Miner, and Vinton A. Dearing, vol. 9 (Berkeley: University of California Press, 1966), 84.

46 On simian dancers, see Michael Burden, 'Dancing Monkeys at Dorset Garden (Henry Purcell's Opera "The Fairy Queen")', *Theatre Notebook* 57, no. 3 (2003): 119–35.

47 Winn, 'Heroic Song', 114.

NOTES

167

Chapter 2

1 On theatrical activity in London in 1660, see Leslie J. Hotson, *The Commonwealth and Restoration Stage* (Cambridge, MA: Harvard University Press, 1928), 198ff.

2 John Downes, *Roscius Anglicanus, or an Historical Review of the Stage* (London, 1708), 18. The production had an all-male cast and likely little or no movable scenery.

3 Sir Henry Herbert to William Beeston, a license for Salisbury Court Playhouse, [June] 1660, Lbl Add. MS 19256 f. 100. See also David Thomas and Arnold Hare, ed. *Restoration and Georgian England, 1660-1788* (Cambridge: Cambridge University Press, 1989), 8.

4 Michael Mohun and the actors at the Red Bull to Sir Henry Herbert, August 14, 1660, Lna CP 40/2751/Mem. 317. See also Hotson, *Commonwealth and Restoration Stage*, 202.

5 See G.E. Bentley's discussion of acting companies on the eve of the Civil War in the first volume of his *The Jacobean and Caroline Stage* (Oxford: Oxford University Press, 1941).

6 Davenant penned the text for *Salmacida Spolia* (1640), the last Stuart court masque performed before the outbreak of the English Civil War. Inigo Jones designed the scenery, costumes, and stage effects. Unusually, both Charles I, playing Philogenes ('lover of the people'), and the pregnant Queen Henrietta Maria performed in it. The queen and her Ladies-in-waiting had earlier performed in Davenant's *The Temple of Love* (1634) and *Luminalia* (1638).

7 Davenant's patent is reprinted in Rymer, *Foedera* 3rd edn, vol. 20, 377–8. See also Freehafer, 'Brome, Suckling, and Davenant's Theater Project of 1639', 367–83.

8 See Bentley, *Jacobean and Caroline Stage*, 6: 305–9. Richard Brome satirized Davenant's ambition in *The Court Beggar* – first performed at the Cockpit in 1640 – by claiming that the proposed theatre would be built not on Fleet Street, but upon barges spanning the Fleet River: '[B]uylding a new Theatre or Play-house / Upon the Thames on Barges or flat boats' (1.1.276–9).

9 Davenant, *A Proposition for Advancement of Moralitie*, 14.

168 NOTES

10 *Calendar of State Papers, Domestic*, Entry Book v, 158; transcribed in Hotson, *Commonwealth and Restoration Stage*, 400.

11 Lna SP29/81. See transcription in Edward A. Langhans, 'The Theatre', in *The Cambridge Companion to English Restoration Theatre*, ed. Deborah Payne Fiske (Cambridge: Cambridge University Press, 2000), 1–18; citation at 1.

12 Lbl Add Ms 19256 f. 47. See transcription in Thomas and Hare, *Restoration and Georgian England*, 11–12, and N.W. Bawcutt, ed. *The Control and Censorship of Caroline Drama: The Records of Sir Henry Herbert, Master of the Revels 1623–73* (Oxford: Oxford University Press, 1996), 226–8.

13 Lbl Add. MS 19256 f. 47. See transcription in Thomas and Hare, *Restoration and Georgian England*, 12.

14 Sir Henry Herbert, petition to Charles II, August 4, 1660, Lbl Add. MS 19256 f. 48. See transcription in Thomas and Hare, *Restoration and Georgian England*, 9–10.

15 In January 1634, Charles I overruled Herbert's attempt to censor a production of Davenant's *The Wits* at the Blackfriars.

16 Sir Geoffrey Palmer, note to Charles II, Lna SP 29/10 n. 108. See transcription in Thomas and Hare, *Restoration and Georgian England*, 11, and Hotson, *Commonwealth and Restoration Stage*, 200.

17 Petition of actors from the Cockpit (Phoenix) in Drury Lane to Charles II, 13 October 1660, Lbl Add. MS 19256, f. 71 See transcript in Thomas and Hare, *Restoration and Georgian England*, 13–14, and Hotson, *Commonwealth and Restoration Stage*, 204.

18 Beeston apparently tried to stage plays without a license, judging from arrest warrants issued in his name in August 1663 and September 1664 (Hotson, *Commonwealth and Restoration Stage*, 213). And yet Downes, in *Roscius Anglicanus*, lists Beeston among those who acted with the King's Company after the 1663 opening of their theatre in Bridges Street (2). Rhodes, whose actors at the Cockpit became the Duke's Company in November 1660, was granted a license for a 'strolling' company (i.e., one that performed in the provinces outside London) in January 1664 (Hotson, *Commonwealth and Restoration Stage*, 216).

NOTES 169

19 Petition of the actors at the Cockpit (Phoenix) to Charles II, 13 October 1660, Lbl Add. MS 19256, f. 71. See transcription in Thomas and Hare, *Restoration and Georgian England*, 13–14.

20 William Davenant, petition to Charles II, June 1660, quoted in Hotson, *Commonwealth and Restoration Stage*, 211.

21 Agreement between Thomas Killigrew and Sir Henry Herbert, 4 June 1662, Lbl Add. MS 19256, f. 66. See transcription in Thomas and Hare, *Restoration and Georgian England*, 15–16. Killigrew agreed to pay Sir Henry forty shillings for every new play that was performed from 11 October 1660 to 4 June 1662 and twenty shillings for every old play performed in the same period.

22 This probably occurred in July 1662, a month after Killigrew's agreement, when the Lord Chamberlain summoned Sir Henry and Sir William to appear before him.

23 When Killigrew died in 1678 the office passed to his son Charles.

24 Quoted in Hotson, *Commonwealth and Restoration Stage*, 211.

25 In April 1662, Killigrew and Davenant convinced Charles II to award them individual patents to supersede the original joint patent. But this was no more than recognition in law of what had become a fact of theatrical life: two different – and rival – companies were staging plays in London. The division of the patents reinforced the consequentially distinctive trajectories that each company would follow. This patent also enshrined in law what had already become common practice: 'all the women's parts . . . may be performed by women'. Charles II, patent awarded to Thomas Killigrew, 25 April 1662, Lna C/66/3013. See transcription in Thomas and Hare, *Restoration and Georgian England*, 16–18.

26 For a sympathetic reappraisal of Killigrew's management of the King's Company, see David Roberts, 'Thomas Killigrew, Theatre Manager', in *Thomas Killigrew and the Seventeenth-Century English Stage: New Perspectives*, ed. Philip Major (London: Routledge, 2013), 63–91. See also Riki Miyoshi, 'Thomas Killigrew's Early Managerial Career: Carolean Stage Rivalry in London, 1663–1668', *RECTR* 27, no. 2 (2017): 13–33. Roberts and Miyoshi challenge the negative characterization of Killigrew offered by Leslie Hotson, Robert D. Hume, and Judith Milhous.

170 NOTES

27 The earliest known performance at Gibbon's Tennis Court was Killigrew's *Claricilla* in 1653.

28 Lna LC 5/137, reprinted in Allardyce Nicoll, *A History of English Drama: Vol. 1. Restoration Theatre* (Cambridge: Cambridge University Press, 1952), 352.

29 Lna LC 5/137, p. 343. The non-Shakespearean plays were John Webster's *The Duchess of Malfi* and Sir John Denham's *The Sophy*. In 1668 the Duke's Company added *Timon of Athens*, *Troilus and Cressida* and the *Henry VI* trilogy to its repertoire.

30 In the first season at Vere Street, 1660–1, the only Shakespeare plays performed by the King's Company were *Henry IV, Part 1*, *The Merry Wives of Windsor* and *Othello*. See William Van Lennep, E.L. Avery, and A.H. Scouten, ed. *The London Stage*, 1: 19–33.

31 A lawsuit that Sir Henry Herbert filed against Thomas Betterton for unpaid licensing fees refers to performances staged by the Duke's Company beginning on 5 November 1660. See Hotson, *Commonwealth and Restoration Stage*, 208.

32 Articles of agreement between Sir William Davenant and the actors at the Cockpit in Drury Lane, 5 November 1660, Lbl Add. MS Charter 9295. See also the transcription in Thomas and Hare, *Restoration and Georgian England*, 33–6.

33 The choice by both patentees to adapt tennis courts into theatres was doubtless inspired by the example of the Théâtre du Marais in Paris, which had been converted from the Jeu de Paume tennis court in the 1630s.

34 In 1695, Elizabeth Barry, Anne Bracegirdle, and Elinor Leigh were among those who left Christopher Rich's tyrannical management of the United Company at Drury Lane to set up their own breakaway company at the theatre in Lincoln's Inn Fields, where the Duke's Company had once performed. Mary Davenant, who inherited the patent after her husband's death in 1668, was not herself an actress in the Duke's Company, but she was the first woman to manage an English theatre company, although the extent of her financial or artistic governance remains uncertain.

35 Katherine Philips to Lady Temple, 24 January 1664, manuscript in the Harvard Theatre Collection; see *The London Stage*

NOTES

171

1: 74. *Pompey the Great* is the English translation (by various hands) of Pierre Corneille's tragedy *La Mort de Pompée* (1642).

36 Lisa A. Freeman, 'Jeremy Collier and the Politics of Theatrical Representation', in *Players, Playwrights, Playhouses: Investigating Performance, 1660–1800*, ed. Michael Cordner and Peter Holland (New York: Palgrave, Macmillan 2007), 135–51; citation at 140.

37 Charles II and the Duke of York lent their coronation robes to the Duke's Company for their 1664 staging of Orrery's *The History of Henry the Fifth*.

38 Lna LC 5/137, 323; see also Thomas and Hare, *Restoration and Georgian England*, 14.

39 See the list of accounts for the Cockpit in Court in Eleanore Boswell, *The Restoration Court Stage (1660–1702)* (Cambridge, MA: Harvard University Press, 1932), 239–41.

40 Because renovations to the Cockpit had only begun a week or so earlier, the theatre must have felt quite bare to its first Restoration audience.

41 Sir John Denham, *The Prologue to his Majesty At the first Play presented at the Cock-pit in Whitehall. . . .* (London, 1660), quoted in Hotson, *Commonwealth and Restoration Stage*, 208–9. Davenant's prologue to *Ignoramus, or the Academical Lawyer*, performed at Whitehall in November 1662, was addressed to Charles II and alluded to James I, his grandfather, having seen the same play.

42 Sir William Davenant, '*Poem to the King's Most Sacred Majesty*', *The Shorter Poems, and Songs from the Plays and Masques*, ed. A.M. Gibbs (Oxford: Clarendon Press, 1972), 371. See Hotson, *Commonwealth and Restoration Stage*, 218–19, and Watkins, 'The Protectorate Playhouse', 89–109.

43 In 1664, the failed playwright Richard Flecknoe contrasted, with some exaggeration, the 'plain and simple' theatres of former times, having 'no other scenes nor decorations of the stage', with the modern playhouses of the King's Company and the Duke's Company, whose 'costs and ornament are arrived to the height of magnificence'. Flecknoe, *A Short Discourse of the English Stage* (London, 1664), G7r.

Chapter 3

1 John Orrell, *The Theatres of Inigo Jones and John Webb* (Cambridge: Cambridge University Press, 1985), 72–4.

2 Andrew R. Walkling describes the scenic capabilities at the Cockpit in Drury Lane in *Masque and Opera*, 163–4.

3 Burden, 'Where Did Purcell Keep His Theatre Band?' *Early Music* 37, no. 3 (2009): 434.

4 *Pepys*, 7 November 1667, vol. 8, 521.

5 *Pepys*, 12 May 1669, vol. 9, 552–3. Burden describes the placement of the musicians in Lincoln's Inn Fields in 'Where Did Purcell Keep His Theatre Band?' 432.

6 On the revised *Siege of Rhodes*, see Walkling, *Masque and Opera*, 175–82. On Pepys and his conflation of actress with role, see Walkling, *Masque and Opera*, 177.

7 Colley Cibber, *An Apology for the Life of Mr. Colley Cibber*, 2nd edn (London, 1740), [241].

8 See James Winn's 'Heroic Song', 121.

9 Langhans, 'The Theatre', 2.

10 Ibid.

11 *Pepys*, 20 November 1660, vol. 1, 297. As J.L. Styan notes, this is an odd comment about 'so makeshift a theatre'; but Pepys did not yet have much experience with playgoing and so he may have been easily impressed, *Restoration Comedy in Performance* (Cambridge: Cambridge University Press, 1986), 19.

12 Powell, *Restoration Theatre Production* (London: Routledge & Kegan Paul, 1984), 41.

13 On the Hall Theatre's equipment and dimensions, see Lewcock, *Sir William Davenant*, 121–4.

14 Killigrew's Bridges Street Theatre probably had similar dimensions also; Tim Keenan *Restoration Staging, 1660–74* (London: Routledge, 2017), 76.

15 Dawn Lewcock argues that the Hall Theatre and the theatre at Lincoln's Inn Fields were fitted out in the same fashion; *Sir William Davenant*, 124. Tim Keenan elaborates upon her argument in chapter 3 of *Restoration Staging*.

NOTES

16 Keenan, *Restoration Staging*, 78–82.

17 *Pepys*, vol. 2, 161.

18 Keenan, *Restoration Staging*, 84–93.

19 *Pepys*, vol. 2, 132.

20 The play was first printed in *The Works of Sr William Davenant K^t* (London, 1673). It is likely that the folio text represents the way it was played at Lincoln's Inn Fields, as there is no record of a performance after 1671, when the Duke's Company moved to a new theatre at Dorset Garden.

21 Davenant, 'The Law Against Lovers', 275, printed in the *The Works of Sr William Davenant, K^t* (London, 1673).

22 Barbara A. Murray, *Restoration Shakespeare: Viewing the Voice* (Madison, NJ: Fairleigh Dickinson University Press, 2001), 40–1.

23 *Pepys*, 19 April 1667, vol. 8, 171.

24 [William Davenant], *The Rivals. A Comedy* (London, 1668); Downes, *Roscius Anglicanus*, 23–4.

25 [William Davenant and John Dryden], *The Tempest, or the Enchanted Island* (London, 1670), 15–16.

26 On the use of machines at Killigrew's theatre, see Walkling, *Masque and Opera*, 60–70.

27 Andrew R. Walkling, *English Dramatick Opera, 1661–1706* (London: Routledge, 2019), 90.

28 Lewcock, *Sir William Davenant*, 149–50.

29 Davenant, *A Discourse Upon Gondibert: An Heroick Poem* (Paris, 1650), 8.

30 Walkling, *English Dramatick Opera*, 54–60.

31 Keenan, *Restoration Staging*, 173.

32 Peter Holland, *The Ornament of Action: Text and Performance in Restoration Comedy* (Cambridge: Cambridge University Press, 1979), 54.

33 Betterton and Harris served as administrators for Davenant's heir, Charles, who did not officially become the head of the company until he reached his majority in 1677.

34 Walkling, *English Dramatick Opera*, 75–6.

174 NOTES

35 Robert D. Hume, 'The Nature of the Dorset Garden Theatre', *Theatre Notebook* 36 (1983): 100; Judith Milhous, 'The Multimedia Spectacular on the Restoration Stage', *British Theatre and the Other Arts, 1660–1800*, ed. Shirley Strum Kenny (Washington, DC: Folger Shakespeare Library, 1984), 42, 63 n.5. The precise date of Betterton's trip cannot be ascertained. Planning for the theatre, whose architect remains unknown, began as early as September 1669. See Walkling, *English Dramatick Opera*, 75–8.

36 Hotson, *The Commonwealth and Restoration Stage*, 232.

37 Brunet, *Voyage d'Angleterre* (1676); quoted in A.M. Nagler, *A Source Book in Theatrical History (Sources of Theatrical History)* (New York: Dover Publications, 1959), 203. Brunet is waxing poetic, referring to the highest tier as 'paradise'.

38 Hume, 'The Nature of the Dorset Garden Theatre', 104.

39 Edward A. Langhans, 'A Conjectural Reconstruction of the Dorset Garden Theatre', *Theatre Survey* 13 (1972): 74–93; John Spring, 'Platforms and Pictures Frames: A Conjectural Reconstruction of the Duke of York's Theatre, Dorset Garden, 1669–1709', *Theatre Notebook* 31 (1977): 6–19; and Robert D. Hume, 'The Dorset Garden Theatre: A Review of Facts and Problems', *Theatre Notebook* 33 (1979): 4–17.

40 Hume, 'The Nature of the Dorset Garden Theatre', 104–7.

41 On the use of the balcony as music space, see Mark A. Radice, 'Theater Architecture at the Time of Purcell and Its Influence on His "Dramatick Operas"', *The Musical Quarterly* 74, no. 1 (1990): 114, and Burden, 'Where Did Purcell Keep His Theatre Band', 434–7.

42 Langhans, 'A Conjectural Reconstruction', figure 1, 82–3 and figure 2, 84–5.

43 Radice, 'Theater Architecture', 119–20.

44 Langhans, 'A Conjectural Reconstruction', 78–9.

45 Hotson, *Commonwealth and Restoration Stage*, 253–5.

46 On the performance date see Judith Milhous and Robert Hume, 'Dating Play Premières from Publication Data', *Harvard Library Bulletin* 22 (1974): 388. Thomas Duffett, *The Empress of Morocco: A Farce* (London, 1674), 30.

NOTES

47 Walkling describes spectacle at Drury Lane in *English Dramatick Opera*, 199–207. A promptbook at the Folger Shakespeare Library (PROMPT T40), *Tyrannick Love: or, the Royal Martyr . . .* (London, 1672), indicates that the special effects in Dryden's play may have been pared back for the production at Drury Lane (Walkling, p. 205).

48 On the intermediality of dramatick opera, see Amanda Eubanks Winkler, 'The Intermedial Dramaturgy of Dramatick Opera: Understanding Genre through Performance', *Restoration: Studies in Literary Culture 1660–1700* 42, no. 2 (2018): 13–38.

49 Christopher Spencer, *Davenant's Macbeth from the Yale Manuscript: An Edition with a Discussion of the Relation of Davenant's Text to Shakespeare's* (New Haven, CT: Yale University Press, 1961), 37. Q1, published by Peter Chetwin, was likely copied from a transcript of Davenant's 'foul papers'. These now-lost 'foul papers' were Davenant's manuscript where he revised Shakespeare's *Macbeth*, crossing through unwanted text and freely making emendations and additions. Q2, published by Andrew Clark, was derived from Q1. Another quarto was issued by William Cademan in 1673; however, this version was almost certainly never staged; it combines the witches' songs penned by Davenant (possibly copied down in the theatre) with Shakespeare's folio text. *Macbeth: a Tragedy. Acted at the Dukes-Theatre* (London, 1673); on this 'bad' quarto, see Spencer, *Davenant's Macbeth*, 8–16. See also his description of Q1 and Q2, 18–24.

50 Spencer has posited that the Yale manuscript might reflect theatrical practice (NHub, Gen. MSS Vol. 548). It may have been copied directly from Davenant's 'foul papers', and seems to have been used to prepare a promptbook because it includes stage directions; Spencer, *Davenant's Macbeth*, 37.

51 Downes, *Roscius Anglicanus*, 71–2.

52 All stage directions are reproduced from Q1, unless otherwise indicated; [William Davenant], *Macbeth, a Tragedy* (London: Peter Chetwin, 1674), 1.

53 [Davenant], *Macbeth*, 3.

54 Ibid., 5.

176 NOTES

55 Ibid., 5–6.

56 Ibid., 40.

57 Ibid., 48–9.

58 Early in *Macbeth*'s performance history, this song had been interpolated from Thomas Middleton's *The Witch*.

59 Spencer, *Davenant's Macbeth*, 121–2.

60 As suggested by Walkling, *English Dramatick Opera*, 88.

61 Lbl Egerton MS 2623, f. 55r. On the prologue, epilogue, and the special effects found in *The Tempest*, see Walkling, *English Dramatick Opera*, 122–38.

62 Downes, *Roscius Anglicanus*, 74.

63 All stage directions are drawn from [Thomas Shadwell], *The Tempest, Or The Enchanted Island* (London, 1674). This stage direction appears on p. 1. Italics reversed.

64 Cary DiPietro notes the alternation between chaos and order in the set design in 'Seeing Places: *The Tempest* and the Baroque Spectacle of the Restoration Theatre', *Shakespeare* 9, no. 2 (2013): 168–86.

65 [Shadwell], *The Tempest*, 5.

66 DiPietro argues that the 1674 quarto might retain staging practices first developed at Lincoln's Inn Fields; 'Seeing Places', 173.

67 [Shadwell], *The Tempest*, 14.

68 For a discussion of these scenes and how the changes were accomplished, see Powell, *Restoration Theatre Production*, 78.

69 [Shadwell], *The Tempest*, 27.

70 Ibid., 29–30.

71 Ibid., 59.

72 Ibid., 30.

73 Ibid., 11.

74 Ibid., 78–9.

75 Ibid., 80.

76 For more on these effects, see Powell, *Restoration Theatre Production*, 82.

NOTES

Chapter 4

1   The second Prince Charles's Men was formed in 1631 after the collapse of the Lord Admiral's Men.

2   If prior experience counted, then Davenant unquestionably had the stronger claim, because he had written plays for the King's Men for over a decade.

3   James Wright, *Historia Histrionica: An Historical Account of the English Stage* (London, 1699), 3.

4   Judith Milhous and Robert D. Hume, 'New Light on English Acting Companies in 1646, 1648, and 1660', *The Review of English Studies* 42, no. 168 (1991): 487–509, citation at 509. As Milhous and Hume document, not a single member of the 1648 'socyety' joined Davenant and the Duke's Company in 1660.

5   Downes carefully explained that his list of plays for 'the Actors . . . under Mr. Thomas Killigrew' derived from Charles Booth, his counterpart in the King's Company. Downes, *Roscius Anglicanus*, A2r–v.

6   Deborah C. Payne, 'Patronage and the Dramatic Marketplace under Charles I and II', *The Yearbook of English Studies* 21 (1991): 137–52; see 142–3.

7   Lna LC 5/137, 343. The warrant is dated 12 December 1660.

8   Lna LC 5/137, 343–4. See also a transcription in Nicoll, *A History of English Drama*, Vol. 1, 314–15.

9   Robert D. Hume, 'Securing a Repertory: Plays on the London Stage 1660–5', in *Poetry and Drama 1570-1700: Essays in Honour of Harold F. Brooks*, ed. Antony Coleman and Antony Hammond (London: Methuen, 1981), 156–72; citation at 157.

10 Lna LC 5/139, 375. See transcription in Nicoll, *A History of English Drama*, Vol. 1, 315.

11 Allardyce Nicoll, 'The Rights of Beeston and D'Avenant in Elizabethan Plays', *The Review of English Studies* 1, no. 1 (1925): 84–91; see 85–6.

12 Lna LC 5/12, 212–13. See transcription in Nicoll, *History of English Drama*, Vol. 1, 315–16.

178 NOTES

13 Both patent companies acted plays not listed in their respective warrants. Gunnar Sorelius, 'The Rights of the Restoration Theatrical Companies in the Older Drama', *Studia Neophilologica* 37, no. 1 (1965): 174–89; see especially 182–3.

14 Initially an opera, *The Siege of Rhodes* was transformed into a play with music for performance in the public theatre. *The London Stage* records thirteen different plays staged by the Duke's Company from the opening of the theatre in Lincoln's Inn Fields to the end of the 1661–2 season. Four of them are Davenant's own (*The Siege of Rhodes, Part 1 and Part 2, The Wits, Love and Honour*), four are by or based on Shakespeare (*Hamlet, The Law Against Lovers, Twelfth Night, Romeo and Juliet*), and the remaining five are by other playwrights, including Philip Massinger's *The Bondman* and Fletcher's *The Mad Lover*. See *The London Stage*, 1: 29–52.

15 Hume, 'Theatre Performance Records in London, 1660–1705', *Review of English Studies* 67 (2016): 468–95; see 468 especially.

16 The main sources for specific theatre performances in London between 1660 and 1705 are: Pepys's diary, the Lord Chamberlain's list of plays attended by the King or Queen (but mostly by Charles II), Sir Henry Herbert's papers, documents from the Lord Chamberlain's office concerning Nell Gwyn's performances at Dorset Garden, and legal records about Penelope Lady Morley that detail her theatre-going from 1696 to 1701. Supplemental information derives from titles pages of printed drama, marginalia and a very small number of playbills. See Hume, 'Theatre Performance Records in London', 468–9.

17 Depledge, *Shakespeare's Rise to Cultural Prominence: Politics, Print and Alterations, 1642-1700* (Cambridge: Cambridge University Press, 2018), 49–51. In the list printed above we have omitted *The Rivals* – Davenant's adaptation of *The Two Noble Kinsmen* – because the original play by Shakespeare and Fletcher does not appear in the First Folio, the basis upon which Davenant's share of Shakespeare's plays was made.

18 Sir Henry Herbert lists 'Revived Play. Mackbethe' in his payment records for November 1663, but there is no evidence confirming that the play was performed at that time. Thus, *The London Stage* lists the first known performance of Davenant's *Macbeth* as 5 November, 1664.

NOTES

179

19 Downes, *Roscius Anglicanus*, 21.

20 Colley Cibber, *An Apology for the Life of Mr. Colley Cibber*, 2nd edn (London, 1740), 84.

21 Downes records that the Duke's Company's first production in June 1661 was Davenant's *The Siege of Rhodes*, whose two parts 'continu'd Acting 12 Days without Interruption with great Applause' (*Roscius Anglicanus*, 21). But given the comparatively small size of the London theatre-going population, long runs for even the most successful productions were not commercially feasible.

22 'Hamlet being Perform'd by Mr. Betterton, Sir William (having seen Mr. Taylor of the Black-Fryars Company Act it . . .) taught Mr. Betterton in every Particle of it'. Downes, *Roscius Anglicanus*, 21.

23 William Shakespeare, *The Tragedy of Hamlet Prince of Denmark. As it is now Acted at his Highness the Duke of York's Theatre* (London, 1676). This quarto was reprinted in 1683, 1695, and 1703.

24 See Hazleton Spencer, '*Hamlet* under the Restoration', *PMLA* 38, no. 4 (1923): 770–91. Spencer, although he was the first to realize that Q6 was Davenant's source text, was no admirer of the adaptation.

25 On different approaches to adapting Shakespeare in the Restoration, see the discussions of individual plays in Murray's *Restoration Shakespeare: Viewing the Voice*.

26 Gerard Langbaine, *An Account of the English Dramatick Poets* (Oxford, 1691), 108.

27 Davenant's *The Law Against Lovers* was printed only in the 1673 *Works*.

28 Downes, *Roscius Anglicanus*, 33.

29 Downes, *Roscius Anglicanus*, 22.

30 Davenant, not a wealthy man, raised the funds needed to convert Lisle's Tennis Court into a theatre by selling some of his shares in the Duke's Company to investors. See Hotson, *Commonwealth and Restoration Stage*, 219–20.

31 *Julius Caesar* is listed among the company's 'Principal Old Stock Plays' while *Titus Andronicus* appears among the 'Old Plays,

180   NOTES

[that] were Acted but now and then' by the King's Company (Downes, *Roscius Anglicanus*, 8–9).

32 See Hume, 'Theatre Performance Records in London', 484; Bawcutt, *Control and Censorship*, 268ff; and Joseph Quincy Adams, ed. *The Dramatic Records of Sir Henry Herbert* (New Haven, CT: Yale University Press, 1917), 116–18.

33 Downes, *Roscius Anglicanus*, 2–9; citation at 8.

34 *The London Stage* 1:20.

35 Eleanore Boswell, *The Restoration Court Stage* (Cambridge, MA: Harvard University Press, 1932), 105. Records from the Lord Chamberlain's office indicate that a company was paid about twenty pounds for each performance at court. Such performances declined significantly beginning with the reign of William and Mary in 1689.

36 See Boswell's 'A Calendar of Plays Acted at Court', in *Restoration Court Stage*, 278–93. See also James Winn, *Queen Anne: Patroness of Arts* (Oxford: Oxford University Press, 2014) and Walkling, *Masque and Opera*.

37 The other four Shakespeare plays were not performed until the late 1680s, by which time James II had succeeded his brother and the rival patent companies had merged into the United Company.

38 *Pepys*, vol. 8, 521.

39 *Pepys*, 29 October 1666, vol. 9, 347. He attended a performance of the comedy *Love in a Tub*, presented by the Duke's Company.

Chapter 5

1 John Dryden, 'To my Dear Friend Mr. Congreve, on his Comedy, Call'd, the Double Dealer' (1694), in *The Works of John Dryden*, ed. A.B. Chambers, William Frost, and Vincent A. Dearing, vol. 4 (Berkeley: University of California Press, 1974), 432.

2 Davenant, *Kings Most Sacred Majesty*, D3v.

3 Articles of agreement between Davenant and the acting company at the Cockpit in Drury Lane, 5 November 1660, Lbl Add MS Charter 9295; Thomas and Hare, *Restoration and*

NOTES

181

Georgian England, 33–36. Pepys mistakenly referred to Salisbury Court as 'Blackfryars'.

4 'Then the Queene personating the chiefe Heroin[e] . . . is sent downe from Heaven'. William Davenant, *Salmacida Spolia a Masque . . .* (London, 1639), B1v.

5 Mary Davenant, 'Epistle Dedicatory', in *The Works of Sr William Davenant K^t* (London, 1673), n.p.

6 Composed by Alphonso Marsh, Davis's song 'Wake all ye dead' survives in *Select Ayres and Dialogues To Sing to the Theorbo-Lute or Basse-Viol . . . The Second Book* (London, 1669), 60.

7 *Pepys*, 18 August 1660.

8 Petition of actors to Charles II, 13 October 1660, Lbl Add. MS 19256, f. 71; Thomas and Hare, *Restoration and Georgian England*, 13–14.

9 Bawcutt, *Control and Censorship of Caroline Drama*, 238.

10 Mary Davis left the Duke's Company shortly after Davenant's death in 1668.

11 *Pepys*, 18 February 1662.

12 *Pepys*, 16 October 1667, vol. 8, 482. Pepys returned to Lincoln's Inn Fields to see *Macbeth* three weeks later and was again disappointed: 'mighty short of the content we used to have when Baterton acted, who is still sick,' *Pepys*, 6 November 1667, vol. 8, 521.

13 On the unique charisma of celebrity actors, see Joseph Roach, *It* (Ann Arbor: University of Michigan Press, 2007).

14 On the bond between actor and role in Restoration theatre, see Holland, *The Ornament of Action*, 65–66, and Tiffany Stern, *Rehearsal from Shakespeare to Sheridan* (Oxford: Clarendon Press, 2000), 150–2.

15 On Betterton's 'two bodies' – one eternal, one decaying – see Joseph Roach, *Cities of the Dead: Circum-Atlantic Performance* (New York: Columbia University Press, 1996), 73–85.

16 Holland, *Ornament of Action*, 81.

17 See John Astington, *Actors and Acting in Shakespeare's Time: The Art of Stage Playing* (Cambridge: Cambridge University Press, 2010), 76–107 *passim*.

182   NOTES

18 Among Davenant's actors, Thomas Lovell was a boy actor
    in the 1630s and Anthony Turner performed at the Cockpit
    in the 1620s. David Roberts, *Restoration Plays and Players:
    An Introduction* (Cambridge University Press, 2014), 75.

19 *Pepys*, 8 January 1661, vol. 2, 8.

20 Charles Gildon, *The Life of Mr. Thomas Betterton* (London,
    1710), 7.

21 John Ogilby, who poached Davenant's actor, was ordered to
    cease 'draw[ing] away any of the company in future'. See
    W.J. Lawrence, 'Restoration Stage Nurseries,' *Archiv für das
    Studium der Neueren Sprachen und Literaturen* (1914): 301–15;
    citation at 301.

22 *Calendar of State Papers, Charles II, Domestic Series 1663*,
    4:214. See also Robert D. Freeburn, 'Charles II, the Theatre
    Patentees and the Actors' Nursery', *Theatre Notebook* 48, no. 3
    (1994): 148–56.

23 Thomas Edlyne Tomlins, 'The Original Patent for the Nursery of
    Actors and Actresses in the Reign of Charles II', in *The
    Shakespeare Society's Papers*, vol. 3 (London: The Shakespeare
    Society, 1847), 162–9; citation at 166. The Nursery patent is
    also reproduced in Lawrence, 'Restoration Stage Nurseries'.

24 *Pepys*, 2 August 1664, vol. 5, 230.

25 'As it is now Acted at the new Playhouse called the Nursery, in
    Hatton-Garden'. James Shirley, *The Constant Maid* (London,
    1667), title page.

26 *Pepys*, 23 April 1669, vol. 9, 531.

27 Charles II told the petitioners of St Giles that 'Playhouses
    should be pulled down when the [religious] Meeting Houses
    were'. See Hotson, *Commonwealth and Restoration Stage*,
    189–90.

28 [Dryden], *MacFlecknoe, or A Satyr upon the trew-blew
    Protestant poet, T.S.* (London, 1682), ll. 74–8. *MacFlecknoe*
    was published several years after Dryden wrote it.

29 *Pepys*, 24 February 1668, vol. 9, 89–90.

30 *Pepys*, 25 February 1668, vol. 9, 91.

31 Cibber, *Apology*, 148.

NOTES

183

32 One of the few historical studies of rehearsal is Stern's *Rehearsal from Shakespeare to Sheridan*, which includes a section on Restoration theatre.

33 Only one Restoration acting 'part' survives. See Edward A. Langhans, 'A Restoration Actor's Part', *Harvard Library Bulletin* 23 (1975): 180–5.

34 Shakespeare, *Macbeth: A Tragedy* (London: Printed for William Cademan, 1673), title page. For a detailed study of the text, see Christopher Spencer, ed. *Davenant's Macbeth from the Yale Manuscript: An Edition, with a Discussion of the Relation of Davenant's Text to Shakespeare's* (New Haven, CT: Yale University Press, 1961).

35 In Betterton's 560-volume library, the only major Shakespearean work is Rowe's edition, for which the actor had helped to research Shakespeare's life. See Jacob Hooke's *Pinacotheca Bettertonaeana* (London, 1710) or David Roberts's modern edition published in 2013 for the Society for Theatre Research.

36 Barbara Murray, 'Performance and Publication of Shakespeare, 1660–1682,' *Neuphilologische Mitteilungen* 102, no. 4 (2001): 435–49.

37 George Guffey, ed. *After the Tempest* (Los Angeles: William Andrews Clark Memorial Library, 1969), 'Introduction', viii.

38 When productions were revived, little group rehearsal was needed because the actors already knew the staging. See Powell, *Restoration Theatre Production*, 101–2.

39 *Pepys*, 23 January 1667, vol. 8, 27.

40 Keenan, *Restoration Staging*, 62.

41 Gildon, *Life of Betterton*, 37.

42 *Pepys*, 2 February 1669, vol. 9, 436.

43 *Pepys*, 1 March 1662, vol. 3, 39.

44 Gildon, *Life of Betterton*, 15.

45 In attributing comments to Betterton, Gildon relied (sometimes verbatim) on earlier works of rhetoric, including Thomas Wright's *The Passions of the Minde* (1604).

46 [Davenant], *Macbeth*, 28.

47 [Davenant and Dryden], *The Tempest*, 17.

184 NOTES

48 Gildon, *Life of Betterton*, 16.

49 Deborah C. Payne, Performing Restoration Shakespeare Colloquium, Folger Shakespeare Library, 18 August 2018.

50 *Pepys*, 19 April 1667, vol. 8, 171; 7 January 1667, 7.

51 Thomas Wilkes, *A General View of the Stage* (London, 1759), 107.

52 Joseph Haslewood, *The Secret History of the Green-room*, 2 vols (London, 1795), 1: lvi.

53 Wilkes, *General History of the Stage*, 107.

54 Cibber, *Apology*, 84.

55 Downes, *Roscius Anglicanus*, 24; Cibber, *Apology*, 84, 134.

56 Cibber, *Apology*, 84.

57 Joseph Roach, *The Player's Passion: Studies in the Science of Acting* (Ann Arbor: University of Michigan Press, 1993), 15. Roach's landmark book demonstrates how the classical rhetoric of the passions dominated early modern and Restoration acting.

58 For an extended study of Downes, see Richard Schoch, *Writing the History of the British Stage, 1660–1900* (Cambridge: Cambridge University Press, 2016), 138–64.

59 Downes, *Roscius Anglicanus*, 24.

60 Downes, *Roscius Anglicanus*, 21. Shakespeare could not have instructed Taylor in the role of Hamlet because while the playwright was alive the role belonged to Richard Burbage.

61 John Guillory, *Cultural Capital: The Problem of Literary Canon Formation* (University of Chicago Press, 1995).

62 Langbaine, *English Dramatick Poets*, I3v.

Chapter 6

1 *Pepys*, January 7, 1667, vol. 8, 7.

2 For an overview of these textual changes, see Mongi Raddadi, *Davenant's Adaptations of Shakespeare* (Uppsala: Studia Anglistica Upsaliensis, 1979), 49–63.

3 Ibid., 37–8.

4 *Pepys*, 19 April 1667, vol. 8, 171.

NOTES

185

5 Christopher Spencer argues that Shakespeare might have written the first twelve lines; *Davenant's Macbeth from the Yale Manuscript*, 67.

6 All citations are from Q1. [William Davenant], *Macbeth, A Tragedy* (London: Printed for P. Chetwin, 1674), 27.

7 Sources from the 1660s are John Playford, 'A Jigg called Macbeth', in *Musick's Delight on the Cithren* (London, 1666), 65; John Playford, 'The Dance in the Play of *Mackbeth*, no. 11', in *Apollo's Banquet for the Treble Violin* (London: Printed by W. Godbid, 1669); and John Playford, 'A Dance in *Mackbeth*', no. 13, in *Apollo's Banquet*. For Robert Moore's argument about this piece, see his 'The Music to *Macbeth*', *Musical Quarterly* 47 (1961): 26–7. Walkling also speculates that another 'Witches Dance' in *Apollo's Banquet* might belong to *Macbeth*; *English Dramatick Opera*, 86.

8 On the jig and witchcraft, see Amanda Eubanks Winkler, *O Let Us Howle Some Heavy Note: Music for Witches, the Melancholic, and the Mad on the Seventeenth-Century English Stage* (Bloomington: Indiana University Press, 2006), 39–42.

9 [Davenant], *Macbeth*, 27.

10 [Davenant], *Macbeth*, 27–8.

11 [Davenant], *Macbeth*, 28.

12 Stephen Orgel, *The Authentic Shakespeare and Other Problems of the Early Modern Stage* (New York: Routledge, 2002), 166.

13 Christopher Spencer has argued that Davenant's source manuscript was closely related to the First Folio version of Shakespeare's *Macbeth*, although notably the First Folio only cues the song whereas Davenant's Q1 interpolates the full lyrics; *Davenant's Macbeth from the Yale Manuscript*, 55. Orgel argues that it is likely that Davenant took his text directly from the King's Men's performance text of *Macbeth*; *The Authentic Shakespeare*, 166.

14 Amanda Eubanks Winkler, 'Introduction', *Music for Macbeth* (Recent Researches in the Music of the Baroque Era), vol. 133 (Middleton, WI: A-R Editions, Inc.), viii.

15 John Dryden, unpaginated preface in [Dryden and Davenant], *The Tempest*. Italics reversed. Radaddi describes the divergent

186 NOTES

scholarly opinions about how much each author contributed to the collaboration in *Davenant's Adaptations of Shakespeare*, 121.

16 On the textual changes, see Radaddi, *Davenant's Adaptations of Shakespeare*, 127–8.

17 Johnson's setting of 'Full fathom five' survives, but 'Come unto these yellow sands' does not.

18 Claude Fretz, '"Marvelous and surprizing conduct": The "Masque of Devils" and Dramatic Genre in Thomas Shadwell's *The Tempest*', *Restoration: Studies in English Literary Culture, 1660–1700* 43, no. 2 (2019): 4.

19 [Davenant and Dryden], *The Tempest*, 37.

20 On Henry Harris as Ferdinand, see Philip H. Highfill, Kalman A. Burnim, and Edward A. Langhans, *A Biographical Dictionary of Actors, Actresses, Musicians, Dancers, Managers, and Other Stage Personnel in London, 1660–1800*, vol. 7 (Carbondale: Southern Illinois University Press, 1982), 127–8. Amanda Eubanks Winkler argues that Davis took the role of Ariel in 'Sexless Spirits: Gender Ideology and Dryden's Musical Magic', *Musical Quarterly* 93, no. 2 (2010): 297–8, and 'A Thousand Voices: Performing Ariel', in *A Feminist Companion to Shakespeare*, ed. Dympna Callaghan, 2nd edn (Chichester: John Wiley & Sons, 2016), 520–38.

21 On the relationship between actor, role, playwright, and audience, see Holland, *The Ornament of the Action*, 55–98. Harris often served as a foil to Betterton, who took more regal roles; David Roberts, *Thomas Betterton: The Greatest Actor of the Restoration Stage* (Cambridge: Cambridge University Press, 2010), 83–101.

22 For more on boy actors/singers see Linda Phyllis Austern, '"No women are indeed": The Boy Actor as Vocal Seductress in Late Sixteenth- and Early Seventeenth-Century English Drama', in *Embodied Voices: Representing Female Vocality in Western Culture*, ed. Leslie C. Dunn and Nancy A. Jones (Cambridge University Press, 1994), 83–102.

23 *Pepys*, vol. 8, 522.

24 *Pepys*, vol. 9, 134.

25 *Pepys*, vol. 9, 195.

NOTES

187

26 Published in London by John Playford, 1674/5. These songs were also issued as part of Playford's 1675 edition of his serial songbook, *Choice Ayres*. For a modern edition of the music for *The Tempest*, see Michael Tilmouth, ed., *Matthew Locke: Dramatic Music* (Musica Britannica), vol. 51 (London: Stainer and Bell, 1986).

27 [Davenant and Dryden], *The Tempest*, 43.

28 Ibid.

29 [Davenant and Dryden], *The Tempest*, 44.

30 Pelham Humfrey's setting and Pietro Reggio's song 'Arise, ye subterranean winds' survive in Paris's Bibliothéque Nationale, Libri MS Rés F 1090, a manuscript probably associated with domestic, not theatrical use. Reggio's song was also printed in *Songs set by Signior Pietro Reggio* (London, 1680) and also appears in a manuscript copied by Daniel Henstridge, in which Henstridge attempts to capture both the sound of Reggio's Italian-accented English and the ornamentation he used. See Rebecca Herissone, 'Daniel Henstridge and the Aural Transmission of Music in Restoration England', in *Beyond Boundaries: Rethinking Music Circulation in Early Modern England*, ed. Linda Austern, Candace Bailey, and Amanda Eubanks Winkler (Bloomington: Indiana University Press, 2017), 171–4.

31 [Davenant and Dryden], *The Tempest*, 15.

32 Tilmouth, 'Introduction', in *Matthew Locke: Dramatic Music*, xviii.

33 For an overview of the singing forces required in Shadwell's *Tempest*, see Walkling, *Dramatick Opera*, 141–2. The document allowing the Chapel Royal singers to perform at Dorset Garden is in the Records of the Lord Chamberlain's Department, Lna LC 5/15, 3 (16 May 1674).

34 [Shadwell], *The Tempest*, 28.

35 Ibid., 16.

36 Herrisone, 'Daniel Henstridge and the Aural Transmission of Music in Restoration England', 171–4.

37 Michael Burden, 'To Repeat (Or Not to Repeat)? Dance Cues in Restoration English Opera', *Early Music* 35, 3 (2007): 397–418.

188   NOTES

38 Langbaine, *English Dramatick Poets*, Ff2v.

39 F.J. Furnivall, *Some 300 Fresh Allusions to Shakspere from 1594 to 1694 A.D.* (London: The New Shakspere Society, 1886), 242.

40 On the history of Shakespeare burlesque, see Richard Schoch's *Not Shakespeare: Bardolatry and Burlesque in the Nineteenth Century* (Cambridge: Cambridge University Press, 2002).

41 Downes, *Roscius Anglicanus*, 33

42 Thomas Duffett, *Epilogue. Being a new Fancy after the old, and most surprizing way of Macbeth* . . . (London, 1674), 30.

43 [Davenant], *Macbeth*, 44

44 [Davenant], *Macbeth*, 27.

45 Thomas Duffett, Prologue, *The Spanish Rogue. As it was Acted by His Majesties Servants* (London, 1674), 22.

46 Milhous, 'The Multimedia Spectacular', 51.

47 John Dryden, 'Prologue and Epilogue to the University of Oxon (1673)', in *The Works of John Dryden*, ed. Edward Niles Hooker and H.T. Swedenberg, Jr., et al (Berkeley: University of California Press, 1956), vol. 1, 147, 148, lines 8, 15, 21–4. Lapland was the traditional home of witchcraft.

48 Anon., 'Epilogue to The Ordinary', in *A Collection of Poems Written upon several Occasions By several Persons* . . . (London, 1673), 167.

49 George Villiers, *The Rehearsal*, in Robert D. Hume and Harold Love, ed. *Plays, Poems and Miscellaneous Writings Associated with George Villiers, Second Duke of Buckingham*, vol. 1 (Oxford: Oxford University Press, 2007), 417 (2.5).

50 Langbaine, *English Dramatick Poets*, M1r–v.

51 [Shadwell], *The Tempest*, stage direction, p. 1.

52 T[homas] Duffett, *The Mock-Tempest: or The Enchanted Castle. Acted at the Theatre Royal* (London, 1675), 5.

53 Duffett, *The Mock-Tempest*, stage direction, 1.

54 [Shadwell], *The Tempest*, stage direction, 20; Duffett, *The Mock-Tempest*, stage direction, 9. The songs in the Dorset Garden production are likewise parodied. In the burlesque Masque of Devils, the demons sing 'Arise! arise! the Subterranean fiends [*sic*]'.

NOTES

189

55 [Shadwell], *The Tempest*, 37, 38.

56 [Shadwell], *The Tempest*, 59.

57 Duffett, *The Mock-Tempest*, 32–3.

58 Walkling, *English Dramatick Opera*, 134. Duffett calls Devoto 'Author Punch' in his 'Epilogue to The Armenian Queen'. Duffett, *New Poems, Songs, Prologues and Epilogues* (London, 1676), 86–7.

59 Duffett, *The Mock-Tempest*, stage directions, 42, 41.

60 The comic libretto derived from Duffett's play is *The songs & masque in the new Tempest* (London, 1675). See Charles Haywood, 'The Songs & Masque in the New Tempest: An Incident in the Battle of the Two Theaters, 1674', *Huntington Library Quarterly* 19, no. 1 (1955): 39–56; transcription of lyrics, 46–56.

61 John Dryden, 'The Art of Poetry. Written in French by the Sieur de Boileau, Made English', lines 81–92 (1683; printed in Chambers, Frost, and Dearing, ed. *Works* vol. 2: 126–7).

62 Montague Summers, Introduction, *The Rehearsal* (Stratford-upon-Avon: The Shakespeare Head Press, 1914), xxi.

Chapter 7

1 Peter Holman and Robert Thompson, 'Purcell Henry (ii)', *GMO* (accessed 29 July 2020).

2 Peter Holman, *Four and Twenty Fiddlers: The Violin at the English Court, 1540–1690* (Oxford: Clarendon Press, 1993), 431–2.

3 Walkling, *English Dramatick Opera*, 267. Roger Savage speculates that up to three people may have executed the adaptation: one person reduced and modified Shakespeare's text; one devised and described the machine effects, and one wrote the libretti for the show's masques. Savage, 'Introduction to *The Fairy-Queen: An Opera*', in *Henry Purcell's Operas: The Complete Texts*, ed. Michael Burden (Oxford: Oxford University Press, 2000), 340. Judging by *Dioclesian*, Betterton was capable of executing the task on his own.

190   NOTES

4   *The Fairy Queen* survives in two quartos printed in 1692 and
    1693. The surviving music score, Lam 3, which is Purcell's
    partial-autograph file copy, does not fully match either quarto and
    lacks music for the song 'When I have often heard young maids
    complaining'. For a lucid explication of the source situation for
    The Fairy Queen, see Rebecca Herissone, *Musical Creativity in
    Restoration England* (Cambridge: Cambridge University Press,
    2013), 135–45, and Bruce Wood and Andrew Pinnock's
    introduction to *The Fairy Queen*, ed. Wood and Pinnock, *The
    Works of Henry Purcell*, vol. 12 (London: Stainer & Bell, 2009).

5   Savage, 'Introduction to *The Fairy-Queen*', 340.

6   Savage discusses the thematic parallels between Shakespeare's
    play and the use of music in *A Midsummer Night's Dream* and
    the interpolated masques in *The Fairy Queen* in 'The
    Shakespeare-Purcell *Fairy Queen*: A Defence and
    Recommendation', *Early Music* 1, no. 4 (1973): 216–17.

7   Walkling, *English Dramatick Opera*, 275.

8   For a transcription of this letter, see Mary Arnold-Forster, *Basset
    Down: An Old Country House* (London: Country Life, [1950]),
    116–17. For the argument regarding the structure of the
    adaptation, see Michael Burden, 'Casting Issues in the Original
    Production of Purcell's Opera "The Fairy-Queen"', *Music &
    Letters* 84, no. 4 (2003): 605. Tiffany Stern has noted that the
    actors rehearsed in the morning while the music and dance
    rehearsals took place in the evening: 'The stage was free after
    performance, and "machines," perhaps already set up for the
    play that had just happened – or set up in advance for the play
    of the next day – could be used for practice, so that evening
    rehearsal could be a combination of a musical and technical
    run-through: ideal for rehearsing operas'. Stern, *Rehearsal from
    Shakespeare to Sheridan*, 166.

9   Michael Burden, 'Aspects of Purcell's Operas', in *Henry Purcell's
    Opera: The Complete Texts*, ed. Michael Burden (Oxford:
    Oxford University Press, 2000), 9.

10 Judith Milhous believes that this machine effect happened.
    See 'The Multimedia Spectacular', 59.

11 *The Fairy-Queen* (London, 1693), 40. Italics reversed.

12 Walkling, *English Dramatick Opera*, 277–8.

NOTES 191

13 Narcissus Luttrell documents the cost in *A Brief Historical Relation of State Affairs from September 1678 to April 1714* (Oxford: Oxford University Press, 1857), vol. 2, 435. Booth's letter to her mother gives the cost as £2,000; Arnold-Forster, *Basset Down*, 116–17.

14 Downes, *Roscius Anglicanus*, 89. Judith Milhous believes that it may have broken even. Milhous, 'Opera Finances in London, 1674–1738', *Journal of the American Musicological Society*, 37, no. 3 (1984): 569–70. As Milhous observes, the Duke's Company (and later the United Company) only staged one operatic extravaganza per year, so that the profits from plays might subsidize the high cost of producing opera.

15 Direct court subsidy for opera ceased in the late 1670s, but many theatre instrumentalists in the 1680s and 90s were moonlighting court musicians, seeking extra cash. See Andrew Pinnock and Bruce Wood, 'Come Ye Sons of Art – Again: Court Cross-Subsidy for Purcell's Opera Orchestra, 1690–1695', *Early Music* 37, no. 3 (2009): 445–66. The manuscript Lam 3 was lost for many years; in 1701 the theatre company had offered a reward for its return, without success. It turned up again in 1901 when John Shedlock, a lecturer at the Royal Academy of Music, discovered the score in the Academy's library; on Shedlock's discovery, see Bruce Wood and Andrew Pinnock, '*The Fairy Queen*: A Fresh Look at the Issues', *Early Music* 21, no. 1 (1993): 45.

16 On Betterton's role in this tumultuous period of theatre history, see Judith Milhous, 'Betterton, Thomas', *ODNB* (accessed 10 August 2020) and Milhous, *Thomas Betterton and the Management of Lincoln's Inn Fields, 1695–1708* (Carbondale: Southern Illinois Press, 1979), 51–68.

17 Milhous, *Thomas Betterton*, 69.

18 Eric Walter White, 'New Light on "Dido and Aeneas"', in *Henry Purcell, 1659–1695*, ed. Imogen Holst (London: Oxford University Press, 1959), 23–4.

19 Milhous, *Thomas Betterton*, 71.

20 Milhous, *Thomas Betterton*, 70–1.

21 A theatrical file copy in Eccles's hand exists for *Macbeth* with two layers of annotations giving the singers' names (Lbl Add.

MS 12219). An annotation in the earlier layer indicates that one of the witches was played by 'Mrs. Willis'. Her appearance in the production suggests that Eccles's *Macbeth* was not first performed at Lincoln's Inn Fields because she remained with Rich's company until 1697. Highfill, Burnim, and Langhans, 'Willis, Mrs. Richard, Elizabeth', in *Biographical Dictionary*, 155–8. Furthermore, in 1695 Henry Herringman and Richard Bentley reprinted Davenant's *Macbeth* with a title page reading: 'As it is now Acted at the Theatre Royal'. If the company at Lincoln's Inn Fields were performing it, surely they would have advertised it as such.

22 Highfill, Burnim, and Langhans, 'Cook, Mr.', in *Biographical Dictionary*, vol. 3, 442–3 and 'Short, Daniel', vol. 13, 368–9.

23 For more on Purcell and *The Tempest*, see Curtis A. Price, *Henry Purcell and the London Stage* (Cambridge: Cambridge University Press, 1984), 203–5.

24 Weldon's setting may have been first performed there around 1712. Margaret Laurie, 'Did Purcell Set "The Tempest"?' *Proceedings of the Royal Musical Association* 90 (1963–1964): 51–2, and Irena Cholij, 'Music in Eighteenth-Century London Shakespeare Productions', Ph.D. dissertation (King's College, University of London, 1996), 72–3.

25 The score was first published in 1786 by Harrison and Company but also exists in a manuscript copy from *c.* 1724 (Lbl Add. MS 37027). On the dating of this score, based on watermark evidence, see Price, *Henry Purcell*, 204.

26 Cibber, *An Apology*, 131.

27 'To feague it away' means to 'to work at full stretch' (*Oxford English Dictionary*). *A Comparison Between the Two Stages* (London, 1702), 42. The authorship of this work has sometimes been attributed to Charles Gildon.

28 *A Comparison Between the Two Stages*, 44.

29 Robert Hume has argued that modern theatre historians have overestimated the practical impact of Collier's treatise; on the Collier controversy, see Robert D. Hume, 'Jeremy Collier and the Future of the London Theatre in 1698', *Studies in Philology* 96, no. 4 (1999): 480–511.

NOTES

193

30 On this performance, see Bryan White, 'A Letter From Aleppo: Dating the Chelsea School Performance of *Dido and Aeneas*', *Early Music* 37, no. 3 (2009): 417–28.

31 For a full consideration of these interpolations, see Eric Walter White, 'New Light on "Dido and Aeneas"', 14–34.

32 As Cholij notes, following Davenant he also sets the play in Turin and includes the character of Balthazar as well as several minor episodes involving Claudio and Isabella and Angelo and Isabella; 'Music in Eighteenth-Century London Shakespeare Productions', 35. For a full comparison of the Davenant and Gildon versions, see Caitlin McHugh, 'Late Seventeenth-Century Alterations to *Measure for Measure*', *Restoration: Studies in English Literary Culture, 1660–1700*, 35, no. 2 (2011): 37–56.

33 Aside from 'Take, o take these lips away', sung in Act 4, Scene 2 by Mariana's maid, and John Eccles's act tunes, the rest of the music is from *Dido*.

34 [Charles Gildon], *Measure for Measure or Beauty The Best Advocate* (London, 1700), 2–3.

35 [Gildon], *Measure for Measure*, 7.

36 In Act 2 Angelo observes: 'And when, my Dido [Isabella], I've Possess'd thy Charms, / I then will throw thee from my glutted Arms, / And think no more on all thy soothing Harms'. [Gildon], *Measure for Measure*, 16.

37 [Gildon], *Measure for Measure*, 28.

38 Ibid., 2.

39 Two mythological masques with surviving music are *The Loves of Mars and Venus* (words: Motteux; music: Eccles/Finger), performed in Ravenscroft's *The Anatomist* (1696), and *Acis and Galatea* (words: Motteux; music: Eccles), which was interpolated into a revised version of Fletcher's *Mad Lover* (1700). Eccles's settings of *Hercules* (1697), *Ixion* (1697), and *Peleus and Thetis* (1701) have been lost. See Roger Fiske, *English Theatre Music in the Eighteenth Century*, 2nd edn. (Oxford: Oxford University Press, 1986), 13.

40 Burnaby, *Love Betray'd; or, the Agreeable Disappointment* (London, 1703), unpaginated preface. Songs by John Eccles and act tunes by William Corbett survive for the production, as do two settings of 'Love in her Bosom end my Care'

194 NOTES

by John Weldon and William Corbett, one of which may have been used in place of the closing masque. On the music in the production, see Kathryn Lowerre, *Music and Musicians on the London Stage* (Farnham: Ashgate, 2009), 312–13.

41 Cholij, 'Music in Eighteenth-Century Shakespeare Productions', 41. A separate libretto for the masque was printed for use in the theatre in 1701 and the text was apparently set by Eccles; Lowerre, *Music and Musicians*, 277. As Lowerre notes, the text of *Peleus and Thetis* continued to be printed all subsequent editions, but in Granville's 1732 collected works the masque text appears with his poems, not as part of the playtext.

42 Lowerre tries to draw allegorical analogies between masque characters and those in the drama (Prometheus as Antonio, Peleus as Bassanio, Thetis as Portia, Jupiter as Shylock), but these parallels are not as sharply or explicitly made in Granville's text as they were in Gildon's; *Music and Musicians*, 277.

43 [Granville], *The Jew of Venice* (London, 1701), 19.

44 [Gildon], *Measure for Measure*, [A3r–v].

45 [Granville], *The Jew of Venice*, unpaginated 'Advertisement to the Reader'.

46 Cholij, 'Music in Eighteenth-Century Shakespeare Productions', 140–1. For a broader consideration of the treatment of musical witchcraft in the eighteenth century, see Eubanks Winkler, *O Let Us Howle Some Heavy Note*, 167–9.

47 *Spectator*, no. 45 (Saturday, 21 April 1711).

48 Quoted in Marvin Rosenberg, *The Masks of Macbeth* (Berkeley: University of California Press, 1978), 8.

49 Rosenberg, *Masks of Macbeth*, 9.

50 On these the later arrangements of Leveridge's score see Eubanks Winkler, *Music for Macbeth*, 99–101.

51 'The Music of Macbeth', *Every Saturday: A Journal of Choice Reading* 1, no. 17 (23 April 1870): 263.

52 See Laurie, 'Did Purcell Set "The Tempest"?' 43–57.

53 Michael Kelly, *Reminiscences of Michael Kelly, of the King's Theatre, and Theatre Royal Drury Lane*, vol. 1 (London: Henry Colburn, 1826), 318. Kemble's version was printed in 1789 as *The Tempest; or, the Enchanted Island. Written by Shakspeare*

NOTES   195

[*sic*]; *With Additions From Dryden: As Compiled by J.P. Kemble* (London, 1789).

54 William Macready, *Macready's Reminiscences, and Selections from His Diaries and Letters*, ed. Sir Frederick Pollock (New York: Macmillan and Co., 1875), 171.

55 Playbill from the Theatre Royal, Covent Garden, Tuesday 15 May 1821. *Nineteenth-Century Collections Online*, https://link.gale.com/apps/doc/AKROHC565334329/NCCO?u=nysl_ce_syr&sid=NCCO&xid=9d4bbfdb (accessed 28 August 2020).

56 According to a contemporary review, this production apparently included music by 'Purcell [*sic*], Arne, Linley, and Corelli', *Theatrical Intelligence: The Monthly Magazine* 26, no. 155 (November 1838): 558. On the restoration of the 'original' Shakespeare by Macready, see Richard Schoch, 'Introduction', *Macready, Booth, Terry, Irving: Great Shakespeareans*, vol. 6, ed. Richard Schoch (London: Continuum, 2011), 15.

57 '"The Tempest" at Daly's: A Beautiful Pageant, with Delicate and Attractive Divertissements and Sweet Music', *New York Times* (7 April, 1897): 6–7.

BIBLIOGRAPHY

Allsopp, Niall. *Poetry and Sovereignty in the English Revolution*. Oxford: Oxford University Press, 2020.

Anon. *A Comparison Between the Two Stages*. London, 1702.

Anon. 'Epilogue to The Ordinary'. *A Collection of Poems Written upon several Occasions By several Persons*. London, 1673.

Adams, Joseph Quincy, ed. *The Dramatic Records of Sir Henry Herbert*. New Haven, CT: Yale University Press, 1917.

Arnold-Forster, Mary. *Basset Down: An Old Country House*. London: Country Life, [1950].

Astington, John. *Actors and Acting in Shakespeare's Time: The Art of Stage Playing*. Cambridge: Cambridge University Press, 2010.

Aubrey, John. *Brief Lives with An Apparatus for the Lives of the English Mathematical Writers*. Vol. 1, ed. Kate Bennett. Oxford: Oxford University Press, 2015.

Austern, Linda Phyllis. '"No women are indeed": The Boy Actor as Vocal Seductress in Late Sixteenth- and Early Seventeenth-Century English Drama'. In *Embodied Voices: Representing Female Vocality in Western Culture*, ed. Leslie C. Dunn and Nancy A. Jones, 83–102. Cambridge: Cambridge University Press, 1994.

Backscheider, Paula R. *Spectacular Politics: Theatrical Power and Mass Culture in Early Modern England*. Baltimore, MD: Johns Hopkins University Press, 1993.

Bawcutt, N.W., ed. *The Control and Censorship of Caroline Drama: The Records of Sir Henry Herbert, Master of the Revels 1623–73*. Oxford: Oxford University Press, 1996.

Bentley, G.E. *The Jacobean and Caroline Stage*. 7 vols. Oxford: Oxford University Press, 1941–68.

Boswell, Eleanore. *The Restoration Court Stage (1660–1702)*. Cambridge, MA: Harvard University Press, 1932.

Burden, Michael. 'Casting Issues in the Original Production of Purcell's Opera "The Fairy-Queen"'. *Music & Letters* 84, no. 4 (2003): 596–607.

BIBLIOGRAPHY

Burden, Michael. 'Dancing Monkeys at Dorset Garden (Henry Purcell's Opera "The Fairy Queen")'. *Theatre Notebook* 57, no. 3 (2003): 119–35.

Burden, Michael. 'To Repeat (Or Not to Repeat)? Dance Cues in Restoration English Opera'. *Early Music* 35, no. 3 (2007): 397–418.

Burden, Michael. 'Where Did Purcell Keep His Theatre Band?' *Early Music* 37, no. 3 (2009): 429–43.

Burden, Michael, ed. *Henry Purcell's Operas: The Complete Texts*. Oxford: Oxford University Press, 2000.

Burnaby, William. *Love Betray'd; or, the Agreeable Disappointment*. London, 1703.

Butler, Martin. 'Politics and the Masque: *Salmacida Spolia*'. In *Literature and the English Civil War*, ed. Thomas Healy and Jonathan Sawday, 59–74. Cambridge: Cambridge University Press, 1990.

Calendar of State Papers, Domestic Series, of the Reign of Charles I. 1639–40. Vol. 15. London: Longman & Co., 1877.

Chambers, A.B., William Frost, and Vincent A. Dearing, eds. *The Works of John Dryden*. Vol. 4. Berkeley: University of California Press, 1974.

Cholij, Irena. 'Music in Eighteenth-Century London Shakespeare Productions'. Ph.D. dissertation. King's College, University of London, 1996.

Cibber, Colley. *An Apology for the Life of Mr. Colley Cibber*, 2nd edn. London: Printed by John Watts for the Author, 1740.

Clare, Janet. 'The Production and Reception of Davenant's "Cruelty of the Spaniards in Peru"'. *The Modern Language Review* 89, no. 4 (1994): 832–41.

Cordner, Michael and Peter Holland, eds. *Players, Playwrights, Playhouses: Investigating Performance, 1660–1800*. Basingstoke: Palgrave Macmillan, 2007.

[Davenant, William]. *The Cruelty of the Spaniards in Peru. Exprest by Instrumentall and Vocall Musick, and by Art of Perspective in Scenes, &c.* London, 1658.

[Davenant, William]. *A Discourse Upon Gondibert: An Heroick Poem*. Paris, 1650.

[Davenant, William]. *The First Days Entertainment at Rutland-House, By Declamations and Musick: After the manner of the Ancients*. London, 1655[6].

BIBLIOGRAPHY 199

[Davenant, William]. *The History of Sr Francis Drake. Exprest by Instrumentall and Vocall Musick, and by Art of Perspective in Scenes, &c.* London, 1659.

[Davenant, William]. *Luminalia, or the Festivall of Light.* London, 1637[8].

[Davenant, William]. *Macbeth, A Tragedy. With all the Alterations, Amendments, Additions, and New Songs.* London: Printed for P. Chetwin, 1674.

[Davenant, William]. *Macbeth: a Tragedy. Acted at the Dukes-Theatre.* London: Printed for William Cademan, 1673.

[Davenant, William]. *Poem to the King's Most Sacred Majesty. . .* London: Printed for Henry Herringman, 1663.

[Davenant, William]. *A Proposition for Advancement of Moralitie, By a new way of Entertainment of the People.* London, 1653.

[Davenant, William]. *The Rivals. A Comedy.* London, 1668.

[Davenant, William]. *Salmacida Spolia a Masque. . .* London, 1639 [40].

Davenant, William. *The Shorter Poems, and Songs from the Plays and Masques,* ed. A.M. Gibbs. Oxford: Clarendon Press, 1972.

[Davenant, William]. *The Siege of Rhodes Made a Representation by the Art of Prospective in Scenes, and the Story Sung in Recitative Musick.* London, 1656.

[Davenant, William]. *The Works of Sr William Davenant, K^t.* London, 1673.

[Davenant, William, and John Dryden]. *The Tempest, or the Enchanted Island. A Comedy. . .* London, 1670.

Denham, John. *The Prologue to his Majesty At the first Play presented at the Cock-pit in Whitehall. . .* London: Printed for G. Bedell and T. Collins, 1660.

Depledge, Emma. *Shakespeare's Rise to Cultural Prominence: Politics, Print and Alterations, 1642–1700.* Cambridge: Cambridge University Press, 2018.

DiPietro, Cary. 'Seeing Places: *The Tempest* and the Baroque Spectacle of the Restoration Theatre'. *Shakespeare* 9, no. 2 (2013): 168–86.

Downes, John. *Roscius Anglicanus, or an Historical Review of the Stage.* London, 1708.

[Dryden, John]. *MacFlecknoe, or A Satyr upon the trew-blew Protestant poet, T.S.* London, 1682.

BIBLIOGRAPHY

Dryden, John. *Troilus and Cressida: or, Truth Found too Late.* London, 1679.

Duffett, Thomas. *The Empress of Morocco Epilogue. Being a new Fancy after the old, and most surprizing way of Macbeth. . .* London, 1674.

Duffett, Thomas. *The Empress of Morocco: A Farce.* London, 1674.

Duffett, Thomas. *The Mock-Tempest: or The Enchanted Castle. Acted at the Theatre Royal.* London, 1675.

Duffett, Thomas. *New Poems, Songs, Prologues and Epilogues.* London, 1676.

Duffett, Thomas. *The Spanish Rogue. As it was Acted by His Majesties Servants.* London, 1674.

Edmond, Mary. *Rare Sir William Davenant.* New York: St. Martin's Press, 1987.

Eubanks Winkler, Amanda. 'The Intermedial Dramaturgy of Dramatick Opera: Understanding Genre through Performance'. *Restoration: Studies in English Literary Culture 1660–1700* 42, no. 2 (2018): 13–38.

Eubanks Winkler, Amanda. *O Let Us Howle Some Heavy Note: Music for Witches, the Melancholic, and the Mad on the Seventeenth-Century English Stage.* Bloomington: Indiana University Press, 2006.

Eubanks Winkler, Amanda. 'Sexless Spirits: Gender Ideology and Dryden's Musical Magic'. *Musical Quarterly* 93, no. 2 (2010): 297–328.

Eubanks Winkler, Amanda. 'A Thousand Voices: Performing Ariel'. In *A Feminist Companion to Shakespeare*, ed. Dympna Callaghan, 2nd edn, 520–38. Chichester: John Wiley, 2016.

Eubanks Winkler, Amanda, ed. *Music for Macbeth.* (Recent Researches in the Music of the Baroque Era). Vol. 133. Middleton, WI: A-R Editions, 2004.

Evelyn, John. *The Diary of John Evelyn.* ed. E.S. De Beer. Vol. 3, Kalendarium, 1650–1672. Oxford: Clarendon Press, 1955.

The Fairy-Queen. London, 1693.

Fiske, Roger. *English Theatre Music in the Eighteenth Century*, 2nd edn. Oxford: Oxford University Press, 1986.

Flecknoe, Richard. *A Short Discourse of the English Stage.* London: R. Wood for the Author, 1664.

Freeburn, Robert D. 'Charles II, the Theatre Patentees and the Actors' Nursery'. *Theatre Notebook* 48, no. 3 (1994): 148–56.

BIBLIOGRAPHY

Freehafer, John. 'Brome, Suckling, and Davenant's Theater Project of 1639'. *Texas Studies in Literature and Language* 10, no. 3 (1968): 367–83.

Freeman, Lisa A. 'Jeremy Collier and the Politics of Theatrical Representation'. In *Players, Playwrights, Playhouses: Investigating Performance, 1660–1800*, ed. Michael Cordner and Peter Holland, 135–51. (New York: Palgrave Macmillan, 2007).

Fretz, Claude. '"Marvelous and surprizing conduct": The 'Masque of Devils' and Dramatic Genre in Thomas Shadwell's *The Tempest'*. *Restoration: Studies in English Literary Culture, 1660–1700* 43, no. 2 (2019): 3–28.

Furnivall, F.J. *Some 300 Fresh Allusions to Shakspere from 1594 to 1694 A.D.* London: The New Shakspere Society, 1886.

Gildon, Charles. *The Life of Mr. Thomas Betterton.* London, 1710.

Gildon, Charles. *Measure for Measure, or Beauty The Best Advocate.* London, 1700.

[Granville, George]. *The Jew of Venice.* London, 1701.

Guffey, George, ed. *After the Tempest.* Los Angeles: William Andrews Clark Memorial Library, 1969.

Guillory, John. *Cultural Capital: The Problem of Literary Canon Formation.* Chicago: University of Chicago Press, 1995.

Haslewood, Joseph. *The Secret History of the Green-room.* 2 vols. London, 1795.

Haywood, Charles. 'The Songs & Masque in the New Tempest: An Incident in the Battle of the Two Theaters, 1674'. *Huntington Library Quarterly* 19, no. 1 (1955): 39–56.

Herissone, Rebecca. 'Daniel Henstridge and the Aural Transmission of Music in Restoration England'. In *Beyond Boundaries: Rethinking Music Circulation in Early Modern England*, ed. Linda Austern, Candace Bailey, and Amanda Eubanks Winkler, 165–86. Bloomington: Indiana University Press, 2017.

Herissone, Rebecca. *Musical Creativity in Restoration England.* Cambridge: Cambridge University Press, 2013.

Highfill, Philip H., Kalman A. Burnim, and Edward A. Langhans, *A Biographical Dictionary of Actors, Actresses, Musicians, Dancers, Managers, and Other Stage Personnel in London, 1660–1800*, Vol. 7. Carbondale: Southern Illinois University Press, 1982.

Holland, Peter. *The Ornament of Action: Text and Performance in Restoration Comedy.* Cambridge: Cambridge University Press, 1979.

BIBLIOGRAPHY

Holman, Peter. *Four and Twenty Fiddlers: The Violin at the English Court, 1540–1690*. Oxford: Clarendon Press, 1993.

Hooke, Jacob. *Pinacotheca Bettertonaeana*. London, 1710.

Hooker, Edward Niles, H.T. Swedenberg, Jr., *et al. The Works of John Dryden*. Vol. 1. Berkeley: University of California Press, 1956.

Hotson, Leslie J. *The Commonwealth and Restoration Stage*. Cambridge, MA: Harvard University Press, 1962.

Hume, Robert D. 'The Dorset Garden Theatre: A Review of Facts and Problems'. *Theatre Notebook* 33 (1979): 4–17.

Hume, Robert D. 'Jeremy Collier and the Future of the London Theatre in 1698'. *Studies in Philology* 96, no. 4 (1999): 480–511.

Hume, Robert D. 'The Nature of the Dorset Garden Theatre'. *Theatre Notebook* 36 (1983): 99–109.

Hume, Robert D. 'Securing a Repertory: Plays on the London Stage 1660-5'. In *Poetry and Drama 1570–1700: Essays in Honour of Harold F. Brooks*, ed. Antony Coleman and Antony Hammond, 156–72. London: Methuen, 1981.

Hume, Robert D. 'Theatre Performance Records in London, 1660-1705'. *Review of English Studies* 67 (2016): 468–95.

Hume, Robert D., and Harold Love, eds. *Plays, Poems and Miscellaneous Writings Associated with George Villiers, Second Duke of Buckingham*. Vol. 1. Oxford University Press, 2007.

Keenan, Tim. *Restoration Staging, 1660–74*. London: Routledge, 2017.

Kelly, Michael. *Reminiscences of Michael Kelly, of the King's Theatre, and Theatre Royal Drury Lane*. Vol. 1. London: Henry Colburn, 1826.

Kemble, J.P. *The Tempest; or, the Enchanted Island. Written by Shakspeare [sic]; With Additions From Dryden*. London, 1789.

Langbaine, Gerard. *An Account of the English Dramatick Poets*. Oxford, 1691.

Langhans, Edward A. 'A Conjectural Reconstruction of the Dorset Garden Theatre'. *Theatre Survey* 13 (1972): 74–93

Langhans, Edward A. 'A Restoration Actor's Part'. *Harvard Library Bulletin* 23 (1975): 180–5.

Langhans, Edward A. 'The Theatre'. In *The Cambridge Companion to Restoration Theatre*, ed. Deborah Payne Fisk, 1–18. Cambridge: Cambridge University Press, 2000.

BIBLIOGRAPHY 203

Laurie, Margaret. 'Did Purcell Set "The Tempest"?' *Proceedings of the Royal Musical Association* 90 (1963–1964): 43–57.

Lawrence, W.J. 'Restoration Stage Nurseries'. *Archiv für das Studium der Neueren Sprachen und Literaturen* (1914): 301–15.

Lewcock, Dawn. *Sir William Davenant, the Court Masque, and the English Seventeenth-Century Scenic Stage, c1605–1700*. Amherst, NY: Cambria Press, 2008.

Lowerre, Kathryn. *Music and Musicians on the London Stage*. Farnham: Ashgate, 2009.

Luttrell, Narcissus. *A Brief Historical Relation of State Affairs from September 1678 to April 1714*. Vol. 2. Oxford: Oxford University Press, 1857.

Macready, William. *Macready's Reminiscences, and Selections from His Diaries and Letters*, ed. Sir Frederick Pollock. New York: Macmillan, 1875.

Major, Philip, ed. *Thomas Killigrew and the Seventeenth-Century English Stage: New Perspectives*. London: Routledge, 2013.

McHugh, Caitlin. 'Late Seventeenth-Century Alterations to *Measure for Measure*'. *Restoration: Studies in English Literary Culture, 1660–1700* 35, no. 2 (2011): 37–56

Milhous, Judith. 'The Multimedia Spectacular on the Restoration Stage'. In *British Theatre and the Other Arts, 1660–1800*, ed. Shirley Strum Kenny, 41–65. Washington, DC: Folger Shakespeare Library, 1984.

Milhous, Judith. 'Opera Finances in London, 1674–1738'. *Journal of the American Musicological Society* 37, no. 3 (1984): 567–92.

Milhous, Judith. *Thomas Betterton and the Management of Lincoln's Inn Fields, 1695–1708*. Carbondale: Southern Illinois Press, 1979.

Milhous, Judith and Robert Hume. 'Dating Play Premières from Publication Data'. *Harvard Library Bulletin* 22 (1974): 374–405.

Milhous, Judith and Robert Hume. 'New Light on English Acting Companies in 1646, 1648, and 1660'. *The Review of English Studies* 42, no. 168 (1991): 487–509.

Miyoshi, Riki. 'Thomas Killigrew's Early Managerial Career: Carolean Stage Rivalry in London, 1663–1668'. *RECTR* 27, no. 2 (2017): 13–33.

Moore, Robert. 'The Music to *Macbeth*'. *Musical Quarterly* 47 (1961): 26–7.

BIBLIOGRAPHY

Murray, Barbara A. 'Performance and Publication of Shakespeare, 1660-1682'. *Neuphilologische Mitteilungen* 102, no. 4 (2001): 435–49.

Murray, Barbara A. *Restoration Shakespeare: Viewing the Voice.* Madison, NJ: Fairleigh Dickinson University Press, 2001.

Nagler, A.M. *A Source Book in Theatrical History (Sources of Theatrical History).* New York: Dover Publications, 1959.

Nicoll, Allardyce. *A History of English Drama.* Vol. 1. Cambridge: Cambridge University Press, 1952.

Nicoll, Allardyce. 'The Rights of Beeston and D'Avenant in Elizabethan Plays'. *The Review of English Studies* 1, no. 1 (1925), 84–91.

Orgel, Stephen. *The Authentic Shakespeare and Other Problems of the Early Modern Stage.* New York: Routledge, 2002.

Orgel, Stephen and Roy Strong. *Inigo Jones: The Theatre of the Stuart Court.* Vol. 1. Berkeley: University of California Press, 1973.

Orrell, John. *The Theatres of Inigo Jones and John Webb.* Cambridge: Cambridge University Press, 1985.

Payne, Deborah. 'Patronage and the Dramatic Marketplace under Charles I and II'. *The Yearbook of English Studies* 21 (1991): 137–52.

Payne Fiske, Deborah, ed. *The Cambridge Companion to English Restoration Theatre.* Cambridge: Cambridge University Press, 2000.

Pepys, Samuel. *The Diary of Samuel Pepys*, ed. Robert Latham and William Matthews. 9 vols. Berkeley: University of California Press, 1970–1983.

Pinnock, Andrew and Bruce Wood. 'Come Ye Sons of Art—Again: Court Cross-Subsidy for Purcell's Opera Orchestra, 1690–1695'. *Early Music* 37, no. 3 (2009): 445–66.

Pinnock, Andrew and Bruce Wood. 'The Mangled Chime: The Accidental Death of the Opera Libretto in Civil War England'. *Early Music* 36, no. 2 (2008): 265–87.

Playford, John. *Courtly Masquing Musick's Delight on the Cithren.* London: Printed by W. G[odbid], 1666.

Playford, John. *Apollo's Banquet for the Treble Violin.* London: Printed by W. Godbid, 1669.

Playford, John. *Courtly Masquing Ayres: Containing almanes, ayres, corants, sarabands, morisco's, jiggs, &c. or two parts treble and basse for viols or violins.* London: Printed by W. Godbid, 1662.

BIBLIOGRAPHY

Powell, Jocelyn. *Restoration Theatre Production*. London: Routledge and Kegan Paul, 1984.

Price, Curtis A. *Henry Purcell and the London Stage*. Cambridge: Cambridge University Press, 1984.

Purcell, Henry. *The Fairy Queen*, ed. Bruce Wood and Andrew Pinnock. *The Works of Henry Purcell*. Vol. 12. London: Stainer & Bell, 2009.

Raddadi, Mongi. *Davenant's Adaptations of Shakespeare*. Uppsala, Sweden: Studia Anglistica Upsaliensia, 1979.

Radice, Mark A. 'Theater Architecture at the Time of Purcell and Its Influence on His "Dramatick Operas"'. *The Musical Quarterly* 74, no. 1 (1990): 98–130.

Roach, Joseph. *Cities of the Dead: Circum-Atlantic Performance*. New York: Columbia University Press, 1996.

Roach, Joseph. *It*. Ann Arbor: University of Michigan Press, 2007.

Roach, Joseph. *The Player's Passion: Studies in the Science of Acting*. Ann Arbor: University of Michigan Press, 1993.

Roberts, David. *Restoration Plays and Players: An Introduction*. Cambridge: Cambridge University Press, 2014.

Roberts, David. *Thomas Betterton: The Greatest Actor of the Restoration Stage*. Cambridge: Cambridge University Press, 2010.

Roberts, David. 'Thomas Killigrew, Theatre Manager'. In *Thomas Killigrew and the Seventeenth-Century English Stage: New Perspectives*, ed. Philip Major, 63–91. London: Routledge, 2013.

Rosenberg, Marvin. *The Masks of Macbeth*. Berkeley: University of California Press, 1978.

Rymer, Thomas. *Foedera*, 3rd edn. London, 1744.

Savage, Roger. 'Introduction to *The Fairy-Queen: An Opera*'. In *Henry Purcell's Operas: The Complete Texts*, ed. Michael Burden 339–44. Oxford: Oxford University Press, 2000.

Savage, Roger. 'The Shakespeare-Purcell *Fairy Queen:* A Defence and Recommendation'. *Early Music* 1, no. 4 (1973): 201–21.

Schoch, Richard. *Not Shakespeare: Bardolatry and Burlesque in the Nineteenth Century*. Cambridge: Cambridge University Press, 2002.

Schoch, Richard. *Writing the History of the British Stage, 1660-1900*. Cambridge: Cambridge University Press, 2016.

Schoch, Richard, ed. *Macready, Booth, Terry, Irving: Great Shakespeareans*. Vol. 6. London: Continuum, 2011.

206 BIBLIOGRAPHY

Select Ayres and Dialogues To Sing to the Theorbo-Lute or Basse-Viol . . . The Second Book. London, 1669.

[Shadwell, Thomas]. *The Tempest, or The Enchanted Island: A comedy as it is now acted at His Highness the Duke of York's Theatre.* London, 1674.

Shakespeare, William. *Macbeth: A Tragedy.* London: Printed for William Cademan, 1673.

Shakespeare, William. *The Tragedy of Hamlet Prince of Denmark. As it is now Acted at his Highness the Duke of York's Theatre.* London, 1676.

Shirley, James. *The Constant Maid.* London, 1667.

S[hirley], J[ames]. *Cupid and Death.* London, 1653.

Sorelius, Gunnar. 'The Rights of the Restoration Theatrical Companies in the Older Drama'. *Studia Neophilologica* 37, no. 1 (1965): 174–89.

Spencer, Christopher, ed. *Davenant's Macbeth from the Yale Manuscript: An Edition, with a Discussion of the Relation of Davenant's Text to Shakespeare's.* New Haven, CT: Yale University Press, 1961.

Spencer, Hazleton. '*Hamlet* under the Restoration'. *PMLA* 38, no. 4 (December 1923): 770–91.

Spring, John. 'Platforms and Pictures Frames: A Conjectural Reconstruction of the Duke of York's Theatre, Dorset Garden, 1669–1709'. *Theatre Notebook* 31 (1977): 6–19.

Stern, Tiffany. *Rehearsal from Shakespeare to Sheridan.* Oxford: Clarendon Press, 2000.

Styan, J.L. *Restoration Comedy in Performance.* Cambridge: Cambridge University Press, 1986.

Summers, Montague, ed. *The Rehearsal.* Stratford-upon-Avon: The Shakespeare Head Press, 1914.

Swedenberg, Jr., H.T., Earl Miner, and Vinton A. Dearing, eds. *The Works of John Dryden.* Vol. 9. Berkeley: University of California Press, 1966.

Thomas, David and Arnold Hare, eds. *Restoration and Georgian England, 1660-1788.* Cambridge: Cambridge University Press, 1989.

Tilmouth, Michael, ed. *Matthew Locke: Dramatic Music* (Musica Britannica). Vol. 51. London: Stainer and Bell, 1986.

Tomlins, Thomas Edlyne. 'The Original Patent for the Nursery of Actors and Actresses in the Reign of Charles II'. In *The*

BIBLIOGRAPHY

Shakespeare Society's Papers, 162–9. Vol. 3. London: The Shakespeare Society, 1847.

Van Lennep, William, E.L. Avery, and A.H. Scouten, eds. *The London Stage, 1660–1800: A Calendar of Plays, Entertainments & Afterpieces*. Part 1. Carbondale: Southern Illinois University Press, 1960.

Walkling, Andrew R. *English Dramatick Opera, 1661–1706*. London: Routledge, 2019.

Walkling, Andrew R. *Masque and Opera in England, 1656–1688*. Abingdon: Routledge, 2017.

Watkins, Stephen. 'The Protectorate Playhouse: William Davenant's Cockpit in the 1650s'. *Shakespeare Bulletin* 37, no. 1 (2019): 89–109.

White, Bryan. 'A Letter From Aleppo: Dating the Chelsea School Performance of *Dido and Aeneas*'. *Early Music* 37, no. 3 (2009): 417–28.

White, Eric Walter. 'New Light on "Dido and Aeneas"'. In *Henry Purcell, 1659–1695*, ed. Imogen Holst, 14–34. London: Oxford University Press, 1959.

Wilkes, Thomas. *A General View of the Stage*. London: Printed for J. Coote, 1759.

Wilson, Michael. *Nicholas Lanier: Master of the King's Musick*. London: Routledge, 1994.

Winn, James. 'Heroic Song: A Proposal for a Revised History of English Theater and Opera, 1656–1711.' *Eighteenth-Century Studies* 30, no. 2 (1996/1997): 113–37.

Winn, James. *Queen Anne: Patroness of Arts*. Oxford: Oxford University Press, 2014.

Wood, Bruce and Andrew Pinnock. '*The Fairy Queen*: A Fresh Look at the Issues'. *Early Music* 21, no. 1 (1993): 45–62.

Wright, James. *Historia Histrionica: An Historical Account of the English Stage*. London, 1699.

Wright, Thomas. *The passions of the minde in generall. Corrected, enlarged, and with sundry new discourses augmented*. London: Printed by Valentine Simmes [and Adam Islip], 1604.

INDEX

Page numbers in **bold** refer to figures.

A Proposition for Advancement of Moralitie (Davenant) 13–14, 26
acting 96–7
acting companies 16, 42, 67
acting company, Davenant's 97–104
  actors 98
  actresses 98–101
  as legal and commercial entities 37–9
  management 100
acting conventions 21–2
acting style 114–18
actor training 96–7, 104–6
  nursery system 106–8
actors
  defections 106
  guidance 113
  line of business 103–4
  retaining 102
  and roles 100–4
actresses 98–101
  lodgings 105–6
  training 104–5
Addison, Joseph 158
aerial effects 65
Albemarle, George Monck, Duke of 41
Albovine (Davenant) 7

Ariels Songs in the Play call'd the Tempest, The 127, **128**
Aubrey, John 3
audience 9, 48
  courtiers 40

Banister, John 126, 127, **128**, 129, 130
Bardolatry 95, 97
Barry, Elizabeth 113, 149, 170n34
Beeston, William 17, 22, 23, 28, 30, 31, 37, 168n18
Beeston's Boys 67, 68, 71
Betterton, Thomas 36–7, 55, 56, 60, 66, 80, 96–7, 97, 100, 109, 130, 148–9
  acting style 115, 116, 117–18
  career 102
  character work 111–12
  Fairy Queen attribution 145
  guidance 113
  as Hamlet 77, **78**, 102–3
  later adaptions 153
  physique 102–3
  roles 101, 102, 104
  on secondary role actors 110
  training earnings 105

INDEX

Bowman, John 153
Bracegirdle, Anne 149, 153, 170n34
Bridges Street Theatre 36, 51, 54, 133
Burden, Michael 47, 146
burlesques
    Macbeth 133–6
    The Tempest 133, 136–42
Butler, Martin 12
Butler, Samuel 5

Cademan, Thomas 7–8
Cambyses (Settle) 55
Caroline court masque 9–12, 14, 25–6, 167n6
casting 2
Channell, Luke 14
Chapel Royal singers 130–1
character work 111–12
Charles I, King 12, 13, 26
Charles II, King 1, 23, 29
    court theatre 39–44, 90–3
    grants royal patents 24–7, 169n25
    restoration 21
Cibber, Colley 48, 108, 115, 152
civic virtues 13–14
Civil War, English 12–13, 26, 40
Clare, John 16–17
classical theatre 95
Cockpit, Drury Lane 17, 22, 24, 28, 30–1, 46
Cockpit-in-Court, Palace of Whitehall 40–1, 43, 90, 92
Coleman, Catherine 47
Coleman, Charles 15
Collier, John 153

Cooke, Henry 15
court culture 9–12
court masques 9–12, 14, 25–6, 167n6
court theatre 39–44
    Shakespeare 90–3
Cromwell, Oliver 16–17, 17
Cromwell, Richard 17
Cruel Brother, The (Davenant) 7
Cruelty of the Spaniards in Peru, The (Davenant) 16–17, 17–18, 18–19
cultural capital 95
Cupid and Death (Shirley) 14

dance 2, 18–19
dancers 11
Davenant, Alexander 148–9
Davenant, Lady Henrietta Maria (née du Tremblay) 8, 107
Davenant, Jane 6
Davenant, John 6
Davenant, Thomas 148–9
Davenant, Sir William 8
    actor training 104–8
    aesthetic 59–60, 66
    approach to Shakespeare 36–7
    arrival in London 6
    canon-forming 118
    and the Caroline court masque 9–12, 25–6, 167n6
    conversion to Catholicism 13
    diplomacy skill 11
    earliest Shakespeare revivals 51–4

INDEX

early life 6–8
education 6
exile 13
family background 6
financial management 39
first production 96
foul papers 175n49
foundational principle 35–6
granted Royal Patent 19, 23, 24, 25–7, 169n25
impact 3
imprisonment 13
influence 2
innovations 35
knighted 13
legacy 143–62
marries Henrietta Maria 8
military career 12–13
operatic experiments 10–11, 12–19
opposition 27–33
performance rights 70–2, 87
performance selection 79–80
performers 35
playwriting career 7, 8
poem to Charles II 42–4
as Poet Laureate 11
political critique 12
rehearsals 108–14
relationship with actors 100
repertoire 67–78
Shakespeare adaptations 2, 5–6, 35–6, 40, 51–4, 80–6, **82**, **84**, 96, 101–2, 109–10, 112, 114, **122**, 124–33, **128**, **132**, 146–7, 161, 175n49
Shakespeare repertoire 73–8
Shakespeare's son rumour 5
syphilis 7

theatre 35–6
vision 15, 33, 33–4, 36
wives 7–8
Davenport, Hester 48, 99–100, 101
Davis, Mary 101, 126–7, 129
Denham, Sir John 41
Depledge, Emma 74–5
Devoto, Anthony 139
Dido and Aeneas (Purcell) 153–5
diplomacy 11
Dolle, William 56–7, **57**
Dorset Garden Theatre 55–9, **57**, 60, 91, 110, 133, 136
   cost 56
   dimensions 57
   layout 56–8
   music room 57–8
   operatic Shakespeare 59–66, **63**
   stage technologies 58
   visual splendour 58
Downes, John 53, 61, 62, 69, 77, 80, 83, 87, 88–9, 116–18, 134
dramaturgy, scenic 55
Dryden, John 18, 53, 71, 96, 107, 124–6, 129, 135–6, 141
Duffett, Thomas 133–42
Duke's Company, the 2, 32, 34, 69
   actor training 104–8
   actors 35
   actresses 98–9
   aesthetic 59–60
   canon-forming 118
   court theatre 91, 92

212 INDEX

earliest Shakespeare revivals
51–4
early productions 36–7
ensemble 98–102
first production 96
management 100
patent to form granted 19,
169n25
performance calendar 74–89,
113
performance rights 36, 70–2
pursuit of novelty 139
rehearsals 108–14
Shakespeare repertoire 73–8
shareholding arrangements
38–9
theatre 35–6, 37, 39, 46–8,
56–9, 57, 133

Eccles, John 149, 150–1, 153
Empress of Morocco, The
(Settle) 56–7, 57
Epicoene (Jonson) 41–2
Exclusion Crisis 81, 143

Fairy Queen, The 144–8, 149,
190n4
Fiorilli, Tiberio 139
First Bishops' War 12
First Days Entertainment at
Rutland-House, The
(Davenant) 15, 16
First Folio 1, 72, 73, 86, 89
Fletcher, John 1, 7, 37, 88
forestage 47–8
France 42–3, 56
Fretz, Claude 126

Garrick, David 97, 114, 159–60
Generall, The (Orrery) 40

Gibbons, Christopher 14
Gildon, Charles 111, 113, 153,
153–5, 157
Gondibert (Davenant) 54–5
Goodman, Cardell 134
Granville, George 155–6, 157
Greville, Fulke, Lord Brooke 7
Guillory, John 118

Hall Theatre, Palace of
Whitehall 49–50, 90,
92–3
Hamlet (Shakespeare) **78**,
117–18
August 1661 performance
36–7, 50, 51, 55, 80
adaption 80–2, **82**, 83, 84,
85
court theatre 91, 93
lasting popularity 77–8
performance calendar 75, 77
special effects 55
harlequinade performances 139
Harris, Henry 37–8, 55, 115,
115, 148
roles 101, 103, 126–7
Harrison and Company 159–60
Hart, Charles 34
Haslewood, John 114
Hecate 124, 134–5, 151
Henrietta Maria, Queen 9, 12,
13
Henry VIII (Shakespeare) 83,
104, 115, **115**, 116–17,
136
Henstridge, Daniel 132
Herbert, Sir Henry 23–4, 28–33,
74, 88–9
Herissone, Rebecca 132
His Majesty's Comedians 30–1

INDEX

historiographical aim 3
History of Sir Francis Drake,
The (Davenant) 16, 17–18
Holland, George 55
Holland, Peter 103
Hough, Daniel 6
Howard, James 83
Howard, Robert 18
Hudson, George 15
Hume, Robert D. 56, 57, 68–9
Humfrey, Pelham 130

Indian Emperour, The (Dryden)
18, 19
Indian Queen, The (Dryden) 18
intermedial approach 18
Interregnum 23

James II, King 40, 144
Jew of Venice, The (Granville)
155–6
Johnson, Robert 124, 126
Jolly, George 106–7
Jones, Inigo 9, 10, 25–6, 40–1,
90
Jonson, Ben 9, 11, 37, 41–2,
72, 88, 90, 152
Julius Caesar (Shakespeare)
91, 93

Keenan, Tim 50, 55, 110
Kelly, Michael 160
Kemble, Fanny 158
Kemble, John 160
Kew, Nathaniel 134
Killigrew, Charles 149
Killigrew, Thomas
actor training 105, 107
court position 40
falling fortunes 51

financial management 39
granted Royal Patent 23, 24,
25, 26–7, 169n25
opposition 27–33
performance rights 68–72,
87–8
relationship with actors
100
side-lines Shakespeare
88–9
theatre 46, 54
King Arthur (Dryden) 60
King Lear (Shakespeare) 83,
91, 93
King's Company, the
actor training 105
advantage 34
burlesques 133–42
court theatre 41–2, 90
falling fortunes 51
parodies 89
performance calendar 74,
113
performance rights 34, 35,
68–72, 87–8
repertoire 86
side-lines Shakespeare 88–9
strategy of ridicule 59
struggle to compete 58–9
theatre 34, 36, 46, 48–9, 51,
54, 58–9, 133–4
King's Men, the 7, 8, 9, 19, 23,
25, 67, 68, 69, 71–2
Knepp, Elizabeth 111

Lacy, John 68, 89
Langbaine, Gerard 81, 118
Langhans, Edward A. 57, 58
Lanier, Nicholas 10
Laurie, Margaret 151

214 INDEX

Law Against Lovers, The
(Davenant) 51, 51–4,
52, 66, 81, 82–3, 85,
101, 110
Lawes, Henry 15
Leigh, Elinor 170n34
Leveridge, Richard 121,
150–1, 158–9
Lewcock, Dawn 54
licenses 22–3
Lincoln's Inn Fields 32, 35–6,
37, 39, 40, 43–4, 46, 59,
60, 110, 133, 149–50
dimensions 50
earliest Shakespeare revivals
51–4
inaugural production 47–8
later adaptions 152–6
movable scenery 49–51
opening performances 74
stage 50
Locke, Matthew 14, 16, 47, 64,
120, 121, **122**, 144
London, theatrical landscape
21–4
Long, Jane 101, 103
Lord Chamberlain 36, 70–1, 74
Lord Chamberlain's office 22–3
Louis XIV, King of France 43
Love and Honour (Davenant) 9
Lowin, John 116–17
Luhrmann, Baz 161
Lully, Jean-Baptiste 43
Luminalia (Davenant) 10–11

Macbeth (Shakespeare) 40,
51–2, 52, 55
Act 1, Scene 3 61
Act 2, Scene 5 121–3
Act 3, Scene 5 61

Act 3, Scene 8 61–2, 123–4
adaption 81, 83, **84**, 85,
101–2, 109, 112, 114,
119, 119–24, **122**,
175n49
burlesques 133–6
character changes 120
court theatre 91, 92–3
Eccles's 150–1
lasting popularity 78
later productions 157–9,
160–1
machine effects 61
manuscript 60
music 120–4, 150–1, 158–9
operatic 60–2
performance calendar 76
plot changes 120
political critique 12
roles 120
textual changes 119–20
trap effects 61
witches' scenes 121–4, 158
machine effects 55, 56, 61, 65
Macklin, Charles 114
Macready, William 160
Master of the Revels 22–4, 28,
29, 30, 31, 32
Measure for Measure
(Shakespeare) 40,
154–5, 157
Middleton, Thomas 8, 124
Milhous, Judith 68–9, 135, 149
Mock-Tempest, The (Duffet)
133, 137–42
Mohun, Michael 22, 24, 28, 30,
31, 34, 68
Molière 43
Moore, Robert 121
moral instruction 26

INDEX

215

morale representations 16
Much Ado About Nothing
   (Shakespeare) 51
multisensory experience 65–6
Murray, Barbara 109
music 2, 10–11, 153
   Macbeth 120–4, 150–1,
      158–9
   The Tempest 126–33, **128**,
      132, 151, 159
musical interludes 55

nursery system 106–8

operatic experiments 10–11,
   12–19
operatic Shakespeare 59–66, **63**,
   159–60
Orrery, Earl of 40
Othello (Shakespeare) 91, 93

Palmer, Sir Geoffrey 29
patent duopoly, 33–9,
   169n25
patronage 9
Payne, Deborah C. 69, 113
Pepys, Samuel 47, 48, 49, 50,
   51, 52, 60, 74, 92, 97,
   101, 102, 107, 108, 109,
   110, 114, 119, 127
performance calendar 74–8,
   113
   1660–1 86
   1661–2 75, 87
   1662–3 75, 87
   1663–4 75–6, 87
   1664–5 87
   1665–6,76, 87
   1666–7 87
   1667–8 87

documentary record 74
   interpretation 79–89
performance perspective 3
performance rights 34–6,
   68–72, 87–8
performance selection 79–80
performance style 18
performance tradition 116–18
Pericles (Shakespeare) 22
plague 76, 87
Platonic Lovers, The (Davenant)
   9
Playhouse to Be Let, The
   (Davenant) 18, 47
playwrights 40
political commentaries 81
Popish Plot 81, 143
Porter, Endymion 7
Powell, Jocelyn 49
Priest, Josias 145
Prince Charles's Men 67
public morals 26
Purcell, Henry 150–1, 153–5,
   160

Queen Henrietta Maria's Men
   22, 67, 68, 71

Raddadi, Mongi 125
recitative 14
Red Bull, the 24, 28, 30, 34, 46
Reggio, Pietro 130, 132, **132**,
   187n30
rehearsal 2, 108–14
repertoire 67–78
   court theatre 90–3
   Duke's Company
      Shakespeare 73–8
   licensing scheme 68
   stock drama 68–72

216 INDEX

Rhodes, John 22, 23–4, 28, 30, 31
Rich, Christopher 148–9
Richards, John 106
Richmond, Frances Howard, Duchess of 6
Rinaldo (Handel) 19
Rivals, The (Davenant) 51–2, 53, 66
Roach, Joseph 116
Rochester, John Wilmot, Earl of 40
roles 100–4, 108
Romeo and Juliet (Shakespeare) 83
Rowley, William 8

St. Germain-en-Laye 13
Salisbury Court Theatre 22, 23, 24, 28, 37, 40, 98
Salmacida Spolia (Davenant) 9, 11, 49, 167n6
Saunderson, Mary 36–7, 48, 97, 99–100
    acting style 115
    roles 101, 103
    training ability 105
scene changes 46
scenery 2, 33
    movable 46, 48–51
    use of 55
Settle, Elkanah 55, 56–7, 57, 145
Shadwell, Thomas 130, 137
Shakespeare, William
    Davenant adaptions 2, 5–6, 35–6, 40, 51–4, 80–6, **82**, 96, 101–2, 109–10, 112, 114, **122**, 124–33, **128**, **132**, 146–7, 161, 175n49
    last play written 96

lasting audience appeal 161
legacy 6
performance rights 69–72
plays rewritten 2
popularity 1–2
Restoration versions 3
shareholding arrangements 37–8
Shirley, James 14, 71
Siege of Rhodes, The (Davenant) 15–16, 46, 47–8, 60, 104, 178n14
singers 47
Skipwith, Sir Thomas 148–9
Smith, William 148–9
Somerset, Robert Carr, Earl of 7
sovereignty, themes of 40
special effects 55
Spring, John 57
stage directions 110
stage technologies 55, 58
stagehands 46, 50–1
Steele, Richard 103
stock drama
    domination 77
    performance rights 68–72
Summers, Montague 141
Sylvester, Edward 6

Tempest, The (Shakespeare) 40, 47, 52, 53
    1695 production 151
    Act 1, Scene 2 64, 65
    Act 2, Scene 3 64–5
    Act 4, Scene 2 65
    Act 5 Masque of Neptune 65
    adaption 81, 83, 85, 109–10, 112, 124–33, **128**, **132**, 146–7

INDEX

217

aerial effects 65
burlesques 133, 136–42
collaboration 124–6
court theatre 92
Curtain Tune 64
epilogue 62
Garrick operatic production
    159–60
Harrison score 159–60
lasting popularity 78
later productions 157,
    159–61
machine effects 65
Masque of Devils 126,
    130–2, 147
music 126–33, **128**, **132**,
    151, 159
operatic 62–6, **63**
performance calendar 76
political critique 12
roles 103
Shadwell revision 130, 137
special effects 55
stage directions 62–4, **63**
structural changes 125
textual changes 125
trap effects 64–5, 131
Temple of Love, The (Davenant)
    9
theatre
    move indoors 2
    restoration of 1
theatre companies, licenses 22–3
Theatre Regulation Act 1843,
    26
Theatre Royal, Drury Lane
    58–9
theatres 45–51
    drop in attendance 143–4
    movable scenery 46, 48–51

reopening (1660) 21–4, 26
transitional 45–8
see also individual theatres
theatrical landscape 21–4
Thurloe, John 16
trap effects 61, 64–5
Twelfth Night (Shakespeare)
    36–7, 83

Underhill, Cave 103
Unfortunate Lovers, The
    (Davenant) 70–1
United Company, the 77, 108,
    144–8, 148–9, 170n34
United States of America
    158–9
Urswick, John 6

Vere Street Theatre 34, 49, 51
Villiers, George 40, 136
visual effects 2

Walking, Andrew 54, 145, 146,
    147
Webb, John 15, 40–1, 46,
    49
Weldon, John 151, 159
Whitehall, Palace of
    Cockpit-in-Court 40–1, 43,
    90, 92
    Hall Theatre 90, 92–3
Wilkes, Thomas 114
William III, King 144, 146,
    149
*William Shakespeare's Romeo +
    Juliet* (film) 161
Wits, The (Davenant) 8
women's roles, women play 2,
    15, 33, 35, 48, 98–101
Wood, Anthony 13

www.ingramcontent.com/pod-product-compliance
Lightning Source LLC
LaVergne TN
LVHW022051200625
814311LV00003B/7